Lacan and the English Language

THE SEA HORSE IMPRINT

Paola Mieli, *Publisher & Director*
Mark Stafford, *Editor*
Martin Winn, *Editorial Support*

This book is published under the aegis and with the financial assistance of Après-Coup Psychoanalytic Association (New York). We also gratefully acknowledge the contributions of the ERIAC Research Centre (Rouen), and of the PROCBENTHAM Bentham Center of the École de droit de Sciences Po (Paris).

Jean-Pierre Cléro

Lacan and the English Language

Translated by Jacques Houis

Agincourt Press
New York, 2020

Originally published as:
Lacan et la langue anglaise
Éditions érès, 33, avenue Marcel-Dassault, Paris, France 2017
All rights reserved
English language rights the author

ISBN: 978-1-946328-27-4

Copyedited
Zachary Slanger

Design and typesetting
Danilo Montanari

Cover design
Danilo Montanari

Agincourt Press
P.O. Box 1039
Cooper Station
New York, NY 10003
www.agincourtpress.org

The publisher welcomes enquiries from copyright-holders he has been unable to contact

To Michael Quinn,
and to my friends at the Centre Bentham:
Anne, Benjamin, Christian, Claire, Emmanuelle, Guillaume, and Malik.

Editorial Note

All quotations of Lacan are original translations by the translator.

TABLE OF CONTENTS

INTRODUCTION
LACAN AND ENGLISH *LALANGUE*[1]

"Not that I am entirely ignorant of English." (Jacques Lacan)[2]

"For who doubts that a Frenchman and a German are able to have the same thoughts and arguments concerning the same things, although they nevertheless use entirely different words? And does this philosopher [Hobbes] not condemn himself when he speaks of conventions we have established by whim regarding the meaning of words? For, if he accepts that something is signified by utterances, why doesn't he want our discourse and our reasoning to be about the thing signified rather than about words alone."[3]

Woven out of intimacy with the language, subservient to its perfidious evasiveness for the francophone who can read English, but

---

[1] We ask some of our readers to patiently await Lacan's explanation, who, at a certain point in his work, speaks of *lalangue*, even of *lalanglaise* instead of *la langue* and *la langue anglaise*. It might appear to be a slip of the tongue, which Lacan, wanting to speak about Lalande, author of the famous *Vocabulaire technique et critique de la philosophie*, in print since 1926, turned into a joke, as he was wont to do. In fact, this is not the case; the documents Dominique Simonney and Erik Porge sent me concerning this question are unequivocal: while there may have been a slip of the tongue on Lacan's part (he wanted to talk about the *Vocabulaire de la psychanalyse* and spoke about the *Vocabulaire de la philosophie* instead), *lalangue* is in no way its product or its effect. The incident, November 4, 1971, involving François Lebovitz, is one of a misunderstanding on the part of our—now departed—philosopher friend, who, probably disconcerted by the novelty of the word *lalangue*, writes on the board, in front of the *Seminar* members, *Lalande* instead of *lalangue*, as a single word, the way *ledit*, *ladite*, or *lesdits* are written, as Lacan wanted it in any case, he who related *lalangue* to *lallation* in his 1975 Geneva lecture. So, the one expected to write the word in front of everyone seems, at that moment, at least, more or less consciously or more or less voluntarily, to have refused. Asked by Lacan to correct the *d* to *gu*, F. Lebovitz does so immediately. The initial reticence, which is neither a slip of the tongue on Lacan's part, nor a parapraxis on F. Lebovitz's, is obviously highly meaningful: who hasn't felt it upon discovering the word.

[2] J. Lacan, *The Seminar of Jacques Lacan Book XXIII: The Sinthome*, ed. J.-A. Miller, trans. A. Price (Medford, MA: Polity, 2016), seminar of January 20, 1976.

[3] R. Descartes, *Réponse à l'objection quatrième des Troisièmes objections faites par un célèbre philosophe anglais*, in *Oeuvres* (Bruges: La Pléiade, 1953), 405–406.

who experiences much more difficulty speaking it, tinged with fascination but also with bitterness, since English will ultimately—so it appears at least—be discredited because judged unsuited to analysis, Lacan's relationship with the English language is both omnipresent in his work and ambiguous.

Omnipresent, because it is rare to read three or four pages of the *Seminar* or the *Écrits* without encountering an English author—be it a poet, painter, psychoanalyst, philosopher, scientist, logician—or to find pages that are not strewn with English terms so encrusted in the text that they cannot be removed in favor of a French equivalent—be it a word chosen for its meaning or an idiom presented for its syntax. As surprising as it is to say, English is as present as German in Lacan's texts, and this was for me a recent discovery. A victim, like most of our contemporaries, of an illusion of perspective, I failed for a long time to question both the supremacy, in the *Seminar*, in the *Écrits* and *Autres écrits*, of those sometimes called the "great authors" of German idealism and the predominance of Freudian concepts in German, whether or not they were revisited or entirely reconfigured by Lacanian research and the changes it ushered in. This is an error that needs to be corrected. Lacan's allusions to English culture and, more widely, to Anglo-Saxon culture in general, are anything but minor. Through the English language, through English authors read in English, through the designation of concepts in English, Lacan expresses fundamental positions of his doctrine and his itinerary; he does not hesitate to press on those he emits and, especially on those he emitted at one time or another, in German. The years of Lacanian writing and discourse were also, for French intellectuals, those of a period of cultural Germanophilia, strangely exacerbated by the war; Kant, Hegel, Marx, Husserl, Heidegger, and a few other authors constituted the language in which pre-war, wartime, and postwar thinkers expressed themselves. Attitudes such as the ignorance of these authors, being unable to or neglecting to cite them, lacking enough German to read them in the original, likely amounted to irremediable deficiencies, or incongruities, whims of principle, absolutely irresponsible biases. No more than others did Lacan escape what functioned as a massive prejudice, since these German authors, translated into French (with a few German words left in parentheses or in the margins), did little more than serve the interests of a culture that was in no way Germanic, but which sought the kind of alterity, of strangeness, of exoticism that it needed in order to take itself seriously. Thus, anything that came from England or the United States, whether minted recently or dating from previous centuries, took on the appearance, from the outset, of a minor product, of which the refutation, or pre-refutation, could be found in some page of Kant, Hegel, or Heidegger. The intellectual did not need to justify what he took, or imagined taking, from German authors because this recourse was absolutely expected, whereas it was necessary to justify even any provisional borrowing from Anglo-Saxon culture. It must be admitted that Lacan contributed to this Germanization of his expression, gladly presenting or displaying his friendship with Heidegger and famous Hegelians such as Hyppolite and Kojève, even though jest can never be totally excluded from his circle of friends or his words. Moreover, when he publishes the *Écrits*, he accompanies them with a table of German expressions he excerpts from Freud and that he used over the course of his text; he doesn't bother composing the equivalent of such an index for English, inevitably allowing one to think that this language's contribution to his thinking is, if not minor, at least secondary compared to the "first" philosophical language.[4] We could add to these reasons that Lacan is not above often accompanying his use of English with "kind words" for the English people, their history, or the American people, which, without denoting a frank antipathy, at least cast certain nuances or shadows over the sympathy he grants them.

However, in this universe, Freud stood out as an exception, since, though a German author drawing his linguistic resources from the German language, he nonetheless knew English, well enough not only to write lectures in the language, but also to speak it spontaneously, without neglecting its slang. But, above all, from the beginning, psychoanalysis was not a narrowly Germanophone movement. Seeking universality and a worldwide notoriety, it worked, and expressed itself in English very early, during Freud's own lifetime. The major psycho-

---

[4] More serious, H. Kreutzen, in his precious reference index of Lacan's *Seminar* that goes from 1952 to 1980, makes a succinct list of German terms (see *Jacques Lacan, Séminaire 1952 à 1980: Index référentiel*, 3ème édition augmentée (Paris: Economica, Anthropos, 2009), 13–14), without going to the trouble of justifying why he does not do the same for other languages, in particular for English, but also for Greek, Latin, and Hebrew. Starting with the first edition of this work, it was possible to spot this attitude, dangerous through the Germanic preference that it intimates and distills in good conscience.

analytic journals are in English; though not without issues of its own, the *Standard Edition* of Freud's complete works is an English edition. Psychoanalysis is thus not typically a German production, and this long before it encountered problems—we won't enter into the polemics related to them—with Nazism. Starting with the period between the wars, any Francophone person who wanted to become a researcher or discoverer in psychoanalysis had to be able to read German and English. Freud himself designated a certain number of his concepts directly in English. As for the indices that identify them, if they are read in a spirit of impartiality, they clearly show that the notions expressed in English easily match the notions expressed in German, and that the number of occurrences of English authors cited is substantially greater than that of references to German authors. As we shall soon see, the problem is not only quantitative; for it would be too easy to reply that it is not the mass of citations that constitutes the true weight on the scales of a text, but the distribution along its arms.

In addition to the preceding, it should also be noted that Lacan's friends were not limited to adepts of the Germanophonic cult, and that a certain number of them or of contemporaries to whom he felt deeply connected through a reciprocal intellectual recognition, like Lévi-Strauss and Foucault, were focused just as much and perhaps even more so on happenings across the English Channel and the Atlantic Ocean than in Germany, as much to learn from as to make a name for themselves. Between those who remained deeply continental and those who took off, Lacan, as a μεταξύ'man in a state of perpetual balance lost and regained day to day, as an at once tragic and burlesque funambulist, thought of himself as a man of mountain passes, dwelling on the narrow ridge that separates inside and outside, without our knowing precisely where.

Perhaps he could have followed in the footsteps of the two friends we mentioned and with whom he shares a certain number of methodological options that can rapidly be termed *structuralist*: after all, he was perfectly able to give a lecture in English, once it was revised and "anglicized" by an Anglophone;[5] but the rootedness, worthy

---

[5] This is what all Francophones do when they publish in an Anglophone journal. Bruce Fink reports that Anthony Wilden, then a student at John Hopkins, helped Lacan write the lecture he gave at John Hopkins University in 1966, titled "Of Structure as an Inmixing of Otherness Prerequisite to Any Subject Whatever," published in 1970 in *The Structuralist*

of a Rabelais[6] or of another untranslatable author, of his research and his findings in the French language decided otherwise. Lévi-Strauss and Foucault express themselves equally in French and English without any loss to what is being expressed; this is not Lacan's case. What he says in French he does not necessarily know how to say in English, even when what he has to say in English, he says apparently directly, without translation, although sporadically; his way of speaking and writing is so idiomatic that, despite Lacan's international reputation, there is no rush to translate his works into English and there are not many candidates capable of making this transformation: besides his competence in psychoanalytic theory, the translator would have to be perfectly bilingual.[7]

From this perspective, it is strange to read his Baltimore Lecture in which he spends too much time saying that he cannot express his ideas in English—*jouissance*, *objet a*, etc.—instead of frankly going forth and doing what is, in fact, difficult to do for a French person who wasn't born speaking English. Lacan only writes in English by rebelling against the language, by asking it to conform to the semantic and syntactic demands of French, without seeking to exploit its own idiomatic resources, which he does not hesitate to point out elsewhere. Lacan

---

Controversy (Baltimore, MD: Johns Hopkins UP, 1979), 186–201. Wilden also translated "The Function and Field of Speech and Language in Psychoanalysis" in *The Language of the Self* (Baltimore, MD: Johns Hopkins UP, 1975). A second student, named Jan Miel, translated "L'instance de la lettre dans l'inconscient" as "The Instance of the Letter in the Unconscious" in *Yale French Studies* 36/37 (1966): 112–147 (see *Écrits* (Paris: Éditions du Seuil, 1966), 236, and the excellent notes of the English version of the *Écrits*, 784–785).

[6] Lacan recognized this proximity with Rabelais, not only of language but also of research. One can read, in "Fonction et champ de la parole et du langage en psychanalyse" (*Écrits*, *op. cit.*, 278–279): "It's the word's virtue that perpetuates the movement of the Great Debt, the economy of which, in a famous metaphor, Rabelais extends to the stars. And we shall not be surprised that the chapter where he presents us, with the macaronic inversion of family names, an anticipation of ethnographic discoveries, shows him to contain the quintessential divination of the human mystery we are attempting to elucidate here."

[7] One shouldn't think that Lacan was systematically disappointed by the English translations of his texts. He sometimes even says that he is satisfied, although his writing in French, thanks to its highly idiomatic nature, scarcely simplifies the translator's task. In the *Écrits*, for instance, he speaks of "two of the most improbable repercussions of [his] teaching" that he was able to "receive from two University students in the U.S.A" in the shape of "the careful (and successful) translation that two of [his] articles merited (including the current one)"—to whit, "The Function and Field of Speech and Language in Psychoanalysis" (*op. cit.*, 236).

does not speak English; he comments on himself in English, as if the true root of his "doctrine" and the locus of his inventions could only be the French language. From this point of view again, there are two very meaningful incidents in his life, which return us to what I previously called the ambiguities of Lacan's relationship with the English language.

One of them is well known, too well known not to have become a kind of chestnut. It comes from the stormy history of the worldwide psychoanalytic movement after Freud's death. It is well known that, at the end of June 1963, facing a room filled with IPA (International Psychoanalytical Association) dignitaries whom he thought he could convince that his doctrine and technique were well founded, Lacan, improvising with difficulty in English, found himself unable (you can't make this up!) to come up with the English for the word "*reste*." While no one in the audience came to his aid with some equivalent like *remainder* or *remnant*, he chose to leave the podium, mortified, it seems, at not having been able to explain a major concept of his theory. Imagine—which isn't difficult when you have yourself been the victim of a similar incident, although on a lesser stage—the consternation, the humiliation but also the extraordinary analytical experience of not being able to express, in a language you thought you knew because you can read it and believe you are able to write it, what you would have no problem saying in your native tongue. The experience of a prodigious, abyssal, narcissistically unbearable loss, especially in front of a large audience, is all the more cruel in that it represents a decisive impotence that cannot be repaired, neither in the moment, nor via a longer temporal detour, for hours would need to be spent over the course of years.

This incident left deep marks, since, as eager as they are to explain what Lacan means by "*La chose*" or the so untranslatable "*jouissance*," the authors of Lacanian lexicons avoid, certainly more involuntarily than intentionally, identifying and discussing "*reste*." An odd omission, because the word "*reste*," while bearing a strong Lacanian imprint, is no more Lacan's invention than *remainder* is, nor would the latter be a new word in the English language if it were chosen to translate "*reste*." The incident probably says a lot about Lacan's lack of fluency in English; but it also shows that Lacan's way of talking, his installation, so to speak, within the French language or, rather, within his own language, which includes, like *Finnegans Wake*, a mixture of words and syntax that, belonging not only to French, discourages translation and disconcerts the desire to translate. Who should translate *Finnegans Wake*?[8] Isn't *Ulysses* already a challenge? When a language becomes too specific to an author, superficially identified as "French" as it may be, it requires being read as such by all, English speakers and German speakers alike, for even the English speakers and German speakers probably get more out of it by reading it as it was written or by listening to it how it was said, than through a so-called translation that would radically disguise it. The same thing is not said in one language and another, and even when it might be possible to transmit in one language what was found in another, it must be mentioned that the transmission does not occur without a remainder, clearly, and that the birth of a concept always happens preferably in a language, inasmuch as a language is identifiable, or at a singular crossroads of languages. The reader of the *Seminar* realizes this on the basis of solid evidence: when a concept is extracted from Lacan's readings, which happens in almost every one of his lessons, it is retained with the word, the particular group of words, or the singular expression used to state it. It is as though the context, in which the concept was found and produced, were reflected in the word directly picked from the language, whether or not this pick is accompanied by an attempt at translation.

Beyond the great traditional distinctions that would have us believe there exist languages neatly separated from each other, that can only mix on condition of crystallizing their mixtures, it may be that each researcher or each discoverer has his or her language and that, appearances to the contrary, the problem is not one of knowing whether what he or she says can be said in one language or another, since they already have to contend with their own.

It is too easily seen as self-evident that languages have well defined borders, stabilized, if not stable, words and syntaxes; not only do they have a history that always changes them, but their speakers only partially identify with them, maybe by believing them to be substantially consistent.

Outside of this event during the IPA organizational meeting, cruelly experienced as an individual failure the scope of which extends beyond Lacan's individual psychology, if there is the least meaning in

---

[8] In a certain sense, *Finnegans Wake* is the cipher of a twentieth-century European intellectual's psychic functioning; or, maybe, the ideal of this functioning.

using such terminology, there is a second event, buried in the *Seminar*, less stunning or, at least, it is possible the humiliation—if the error could still give rise to such affect—was easily counter-balanced if not sublimated by a linguistic heroism, this time more conquering, through a masterful slip of the tongue. It is narrated, not without self-satisfaction, by Lacan to the audience of *Seminar XIX*.[9] The context is that of a grant application on the part of a university researcher, which seemed extravagant to Lacan, whose recommendation was being solicited. He relates that, struck by this presumptuousness, he says on the phone to one of his students: *"I was bowled over with admiration."* And he adds, speaking to the audience: "Naturally, you don't know what it means. I didn't know either. *Bowl* is the bowling ball. I am therefore balled.[10] I am akin to an entire set of pins knocked over by a strike. Believe it or not, what I had initially said to the person on the phone, before, thank God, she corrected me, I who did not know the expression, was: *'I'm blowed over,' Je suis soufflé.* But this is not correct, because *to blow*, which indeed means *souffler*, makes *blown*, not *blowed*. So I said *blowed*; isn't that because, without knowing it, I knew that it was *bowled over?*" Lacan's grammatical error is now, this time, sublimated as a slip of the tongue: "This is where we enter into the slip of the tongue, which is to say, into serious things. But at the same time, it shows us that, as Plato had already glimpsed in the *Cratylus*, it isn't so certain the signifier is arbitrary, since, after all, *bowl* and *blow*, it's not for nothing that they are so close, and that is precisely why I missed *bowl* by a hair. I don't know how you would characterize this amusement, but I find it serious." And Lacan's slip is soon sublimated as the invention of an imaginary English: thus, as concerns one of the words that interests us the most, while *lalangue* came from a slip on *Lalande*, which is far from certain, it is much more from the desire to make the expression be as close as possible to the word *lallation* that Lacan presents the origin of his neologism.[11] Among an error, a slip, and a creative intention, there isn't necessarily a solution of continuity: a mistake in a language can, even while being

---

[9] J. Lacan, *The Seminar of Jacques Lacan Book XIX: . . . or Worse*, ed. J.-A. Miller, trans. A. Price (Medford, MA: Polity, 2018), seminar of February 9, 1972.

[10] No doubt an expression like *"je suis tourneboulé"* interferes with this *sortie* in "English."

[11] Geneva lecture on "Le symptôme," October 4, 1975.

accepted as an error, be highly revealing of something that could not be said otherwise.

To the preceding considerations, in which contingency mixed with necessity must be taken into account, but which, nonetheless, demonstrate the weight of the English language in the formation, formulation, and transmission of Lacan's words, it is necessary to add evidence that is far more closely linked to the Lacanian concepts. How could an author who, from one end of his work to the other, hammered away that *the unconscious is structured like a language*, not fail to conceive of the *signifier* in a considerably wider way than the Saussurian acceptation, and to view just as differently the relationship of signifier and signified? How could he have missed asking himself *the question of the relationship of the unconscious*—but also, as a consequence, of all psychic acts—*with a few vernacular languages, including English*? Before providing direct evidence, apagogical evidence is in order. When, in 1947, Lacan signs his article on "English Psychiatry and the War," he is not yet in possession of his beacon thesis on the unconscious and he roughly upbraids those who stress "the specifically English nature of certain traits" to supposedly explain the behavior of groups from which come the individuals treated by Bion and Rickmann. As soon as the famous thesis on the unconscious appears, the tone changes and the "English" character of things is brought, via language, to the forefront. He will say, without ambiguity, in Baltimore, in February 1966, that when he says "'*as a language,' it is not some special language, for example, mathematical language, semiotical language, or cinematographical language. Language is language and there is only one sort of language: concrete language—English or French for instance—that people talk.*"[12] True connoisseur of Bentham, and not only on the more conventional terrain of the Panopticon, the analysis of which he deliberately left to Foucault, Lacan, who well understood the value of the "theory of fictions," was able to read in the *Springs of Action*, when the author draws the table of combinations of pleasures and pains that make up the passions, the interests, and other motivations, that this table would have been very different if it had been conceived in a language other than English. Ultimately,

---

[12] "Of Structure as an Inmixing of an Otherness Prerequisite to Any Subject Whatever," *op. cit.*, 188.

the author of *Springs* asks not so much translators as interpreters and adaptors to create the equivalent of such a table in their respective languages. He knows or appears to know that certain languages—Bentham is thinking of French—will be disqualified from the outset for translation and that they will not allow for a correct version of his text.[13]

If it is necessary to care about psychic movements and acts—whether real, fictive, or supposed—in relation to the language in which they are uttered, it is precisely because they cannot be translated into another language. The situation is not one of a psyche posted somewhere, transcending all languages, to be better expressed by one of them in general, or more modestly, on such and such a point; languages penetrate us and constitute us, according to all kinds of modalities: it is the job of psychology to take inventory and to capture the organization that makes us believe in the very consistency of our psychic acts. "We are spoken,"[14] says Lacan, thus showing the speaking being's (*le parlêtre*) destiny: "The speaker is a spoken one; this is, after all, what I have been saying for some time."[15] Object transcendence, like what takes on the appearance of a meaning, is an illusion. For, just as there isn't anything substantially extant that is resistant to the languages that would attempt to speak of it, there aren't meanings as substantial as the signifiers that seem to undergird them. No doubt signifiers make us forget their particular consistency and resistance and seem to diffuse them on the signifieds and on what seem to be the objects to which they refer. But while the signifiers, in their op-

---

[13] Besides the text of *Springs of Action*, alluded to here, there is a manuscript letter from Bentham to Dumont, dated August 1, 1815, held by the Bibliothèque publique et universitaire de Genève, number MSS/33/111: "Now Geneva is a place where people are found in abundance, who write not only French but Italian and German. I am desired to suggest to you that the translation of this table, with its appendages, and in as many languages as possible, would be a most desirable event. The author is aware that it contains so many extraordinary terms, partly new and partly old, that the fastidiousness of the French language will make it very difficult to shape for it a French dress, but he thinks the Italian might answer better and that the German would answer admirably. I am therefore to request of you to put a copy into the hand of an Italian, and another into that of a German, to see (if you know of any likely to undertake such a task) what they think of the production; and, if you yourself should be too much engaged with more important matters, to make the same proposal to some master of the French tongue."

[14] J. Lacan, *Sinthome, op.cit.*, 162.

[15] J. Lacan, *Le Séminaire livre XVIII: D'un discours qui ne serait pas du semblant*, ed. J.-A. Miller (Paris: Éditions du Seuil, 2006), seminar of March 10, 1971.

positional interplay, gain a very particular existence and reality, the signifieds are unable to enjoy the same modalities; this led a jocular Lacan to say, to his audience, in his lesson of March 10, 1971: "There are people who imagined that with logic, that is to say, with writing manipulation, you could find a means to have what? *New ideas*, [T.N.: in English in the original] new ideas, as if there aren't enough already as it is!" In a certain sense, Pascal had already established this by using an idea of Descartes': a discourse, because it is the same, can seem to refer to the same ideas and the same objects; but such is not the case, and these objects and ideas can be quite different. It's the fact that the same signifiers are used that makes us believe others have the same ideas as us. The effect of the identity of signifiers is to make us believe they proceed identically, which is a simple allegation.[16] The signifieds constitute a far less consistent imaginary than the regulated symbolic system of the signifiers. If no translation is possible from one language to another, it is because the link between signifiers and signifieds is by no means stable, because no correspondence is possible between one language and another, and because the only thing that can be done between languages is to insert, between the signifiers of an initial suite belonging to one of the languages, a second suite that resides in its gaps, not to definitively fill them, nor with an irreproachable regularity, but in such a way as to make a weaving possible, especially as it can be repeated a certain number of times. The snares of one language can engender the snares of another; one can even interpose them, but they are in no way interchangeable. A Lacan text is a weaving that can be roughly identified as deriving from French, but that inserts other threads through words, expressions, and phrases belonging to other languages. It is worth noting that most theorists, starting with Freud, readily undertake translation projects. Lacan does not. While he translates such and such a text in his *Seminar*, as the need arises, he has not

---

[16] Pascal had indeed said, "we think that all men think the same way. But we think so quite gratuitously, because we have no proof. I do see that we apply these words [to move] in the same circumstances, and that every time two men see a body change place, they both express the sight of this same object with the same words, by both saying it moved. And, from this conformity of usage, we draw a powerful conjecture of a conformity of idea. But this is not totally convincing as to the latter conviction, although it's worth wagering on the affirmative, since we know that the same conclusions are often drawn from different suppositions." B. Pascal, *Les Provinciales et Pensées* (Paris: La Pochothèque, 2004), 889–890.

authored any important translation, nor, to my knowledge, attempted one, as if the exercise were not worth the effort. Where he is interested in translations, it is most often in order to attack them or, when that is not the case—as with Jacques Aubert, who had just retranslated *Ulysses*—it's to have a close look at the enterprise's extreme difficulty.

For languages to be mutually translatable, each one would have to be able to transcend itself in a kind of metalanguage, and this metalanguage would have to be the same for the transcendence of each vernacular language. Nothing can guarantee nor will ever guarantee, outside of an irrational belief, that the transcendence of any language by a common metalanguage is anything but a fantasy comparable to that of a painting in perspective, which, although seen from one point of view, would seem to contain an infinity of points of view that would be easy to find given minimal effort. But, while there is no metalanguage, while the diversity of languages is irreducible, while "one can only talk about a language in another language,"[17] the speakers are destined to little more than a hazardous and precarious identification with this language, even all kinds of languages at the same time and in the most varied proportions, on condition, however, that quantitative discourse retain some value (even more or less risky, more or less scabrous refusals to identify). It is expected that everyone identifies with a language or that others identify everyone with one language rather than another, subject to a penalty that is simple, immediate, and cannot be appealed. Languages certainly create unconsciouses; but it is also unconsciouses that create what we think of as languages, separate from one another

This idea is susceptible to many variations for Lacan. The most amazing, at the same time as the most paradigmatic, is the one Lacan discovered thanks to Jacques Aubert, who pointed it out to him in Joyce's *Finnegans Wake*: English can be the supporting grid for what can also be read in French, but with a very different meaning; or, more precisely, its signifiers can serve as a rebus for other signifiers. The identity between languages is simultaneously real, absurd, and derisory, even when it is clearly audible. It is not difficult for a language to slip into the gaps of another and to hide out there; neither is it to

---

[17] Lacan brings it up again in *Le Séminaire livre XXIV: L'insu que sait de l'une-bévue s'aile à mourre*, unpublished seminar, seminar of May 17, 1977.

assign an order to this occupancy and to subject it to the same process through a similar occupancy. This *method of suites or series* that never stop filling up is combined with a *breach method*, which, because it breaks a suite or a series, has to construct another one or depend on another one, as Pascal had shown in his problem of points.[18]

It should be noted that each element of method, be it the filling of suites with other suites or the breaking of suites that make up the symbol's reality, as soon as this break must be remedied, always happens under the sign of a particular sympathetic identification on Lacan's part. Thus, Joyce is tapped for a method that, in mathematics, is that of Pascal, of Leibniz, of Fontenelle, the recourse to Pascal being essential for the conceptualization of the breach or break. As much as the authors quoted by Lacan, as soon as he perceives—or provokes—the slightest crack in the credit previously due them, find themselves wearing, through affected politeness or irony, the title of "Monsieur"[19] and "Madame"—even when they are several centuries distant from him—as much is he unstinting in his sympathy for those to whom he feels indebted. Besides Freud, and along with Pascal and the fictional character Antigone, Joyce is among the latter, and belongs to their extraordinarily restricted circle. The interplay of identifications that constitute languages and the bridges between languages is thus complex, and it passes, for Lacan, through the authors that write them, without it being possible to treat these authors as substantial subjects.

Before making a list of the nodal points that will punctuate the present book, we need to reveal the guiding thread that will tie them together. We have just seen that Lacan says quite indiscriminately, although he well knows the path is not the same in both directions, that a language is the product of plural unconsciouses and that, the unconscious being structured like a language, it is likely that languages in their plurality, even if they don't correspond to the language in question, should not be discounted either in the constitution of the

---

[18] This problem may also be called the division of stakes. In "Lituraterre," Lacan talks about this "break" that only a discourse can produce, with production effect. *Autres écrits* (Paris: Éditions du Seuil, 2001), 18. It is an interruption in the game that triggers the problem of points and it is something like a contested election (or the thought of the possibility of such) that causes Condorcet to slice the results and analyze the rankings stemming from different types of balloting.

[19] Monsieur Newton, Monsieur Kant, Monsieur Darwin, Monsieur Bertrand Russell, Sir Allen Gardiner, Monsieur Aldous Huxley, Monsieur Winnicott.

unconscious or in the possibility of analysis. Now, Lacan displays not only a diversity, but also, in a manner strangely consonant with the old problematics of languages more or less adapted to such and such an activity (the law for some, diplomacy for others, philosophy for this one, mathematics for that one, or who knows what else?), a disparity of languages in the constitution of the unconscious. In the stenotype I have of the *RSI Seminar*, thanks to L'École lacanienne, which put it online,[20] the script of the February 11, 1975, lesson transmits this enigmatic phrase (it is hard to decide whether the faulty syntax is due to the transcription or whether it was present in Lacan's speech): "It is absolutely certain that neither the English, nor, I won't say English psychoanalysts—I only know one who is English,[21] even then he must probably be Scottish! Lalangue, I think it's English lalangue that stands in the way." The first sentence, (or sentence fragment?) is unfinished. It seems like Lacan is on his way to saying, without being able to as clearly as he does for Catholics or the Japanese,[22] that the English are unanalyzable. There wouldn't be many people left to analyze if he had his way![23] Now, it interests us that he is not able to say so simply because the expression is, at least at first sight, strange, if not completely absurd: by what logic does the fact of being an English speaker deprive someone of the status of analysand? What could there be about the English language that is so hostile to its speakers' access to the status of analysand? On the other hand, the second sentence (or half-sentence) is solidly anchored on a position perfectly reiterated a little further on: "I am not the first to have noted this resistance of English lalangue to the unconscious"; just as Japanese "is opposed to the play, the functioning of the unconscious as such." For this book, on principle, we shall put aside Japanese—although care should be taken that it is not for the same reasons that the Japanese language renders the Japanese unana-

---

[20] At the following address: http://www.ecole-lacanienne.net/ (an address, moreover, that has proven exceptionally helpful).

[21] Which one? It might be one of the analysts we cite in Part IV: Glover, perhaps; the others, such as Reik or Winnicott, had been dead for several years. As for Szasz, Lacan is too critical of him for it to have been him.

[22] J. Lacan, *Sinthome, op. cit.*, 126.

[23] Especially since, if the English are unanalyzable as a result of their language, we would have to attribute the same characteristic to North Americans, to Australians, to South Africans, and so on.

lyzable and the English language renders the English[24] unanalyzable—and limit ourselves to Lacan's affirmations about the English language.

Also leaving aside the research of those who supposedly "noted," before Lacan, "the resistance of English lalangue to the unconscious," what makes up the strangeness, the *oddité*, as Lacan would have put it, of the phrase "the English are unanalyzable," if that is what Lacan meant in the aforementioned lesson, is that, even if it is difficult to distinguish the individual from society, it is nevertheless necessary to find and identify (in one way or another) an individual in order to psychoanalyze him or her,[25] even if it means making much more complex and problematic "what" is, or "the one" (T.N.: "ce," "celui," ou "celle"), being psychoanalyzed; but it is stated, at the same time, that the affiliation of an individual with a particular language would make him or her an unanalyzable being.[26] That the notion of *individual* is particularly obscure and indeterminate, that, in order to characterize it, it is necessary to take into account elements as fundamental and constitutive as language, goes without saying; all the more since language is not a simple means for the individual to constitute him or herself and that it is so little intermediary and instrumental that Lacan wanted to stick the word *Langue* to its article, which is not necessarily audible in every prepositional configuration, but is highly visible in writing. The separated article would turn language into an instrument for a subject, which it cannot be, because it is the subject who, it is

---

[24] Indeed, to this argument, "Lituraterre" adds an important analysis that could well have an impact on English: Japanese, like all languages, divides its speakers, but in such a way that "one of its registers [can] content itself with the reference to writing, and the other, to speech" (*op. cit.*, 19). Didn't Rousseau say that English needed to be learned twice and that, at least for a French person, the way English is pronounced has nothing to do with the way it is written? But it isn't exactly the same issue, since English is not learned by an English speaker, whose native language it is, in the same way a French speaker learns it, whose native language it isn't.

[25] Book VII of the *Seminar* insists on this point: "If analysis has a meaning, desire is none other than that which supports the unconscious theme, the specific articulation of what causes us to become rooted in a particular destiny, the latter insistently requiring that the debt be paid, and it [desire] comes back, returns, and always brings us back to a certain groove, to the groove of what is, strictly speaking, our business." J. Lacan, *The Seminar of Jacques Lacan Book VII: The Ethics of Psychoanalysis*, ed. J.-A. Miller, trans. D. Porter (New York: Norton, 1992), seminar of July 6, 1960.

[26] In which case Americans would not escape the characteristic of being unanalyzable.

claimed, exists sporadically between the links in the signifying chain.[27] From this it follows that English *lalangue* becomes, by condensation into a single word without an article, as the glossary *789 néologismes de Jacques Lacan* points out,[28] *lalanglaise*, on April 13, 1976, where he emphasizes the resources of the English language. He writes a preface, himself, to the English version of *Seminar XI*, May 17, 1976; and he doesn't highlight the difficulties of translating his text, nor the particular difficulty that English poses for analysis, except perhaps—and we will return to this more enigmatic than explicit remark—if we take into account the preface's beginning "When l'esp d'un laps [T.N.: untranslatable], that is to say, for I only write in French: the space of a slip, has no more reach of meaning (or interpretation), only then is one sure to be in the unconscious. One knows it, oneself. But it's enough that notice be taken of it for one to leave it."[29] How is it, then, that a year earlier, in *RSI*, this same language was declared resistant to the unconscious? We don't understand either why English is the only language explicitly promoted or demoted, in any case, given this status, since, at least to my knowledge, there is no *lalallemande* or *lafrançaise*, which, after all, with neither more nor less incongruity, could just as well be uttered and which yet appear—for unknown reasons—more conciliatory with the psychoanalytic act and its theoretical expression.

Which, in passing, seems to say two things that are not necessarily either identical or coherent or compatible. The *first* is that English might be, as the analysand's language, a handicap for analysis; but it remains an enigma as to why it would be so more than neighboring languages, from which it may also incidentally greatly differ. I will admit, however, that the thing is possible, since, if lalangue is radically and absolutely structuring, it is clear that a property that, in it, stood opposed to analysis, would necessarily affect the subject and even the individual in his or her totality who seeks an analysis. But *RSI* evokes this less than a *second* trait: the difficulty of explaining psychoanalytical theory in English; as Lacan puts it, "the amount of difficulty involved in translating [in English the works he has authored]." It isn't necessarily the same thing, although the point in common resides in

---

[27] Lacan said it to the Americans in his 1966 Baltimore lecture: "The subject is always a fading thing under the chain of signifiers." "Of Structure as an Inmixing," *op. cit.*, 194.

[28] *789 néologismes de Jacques Lacan* (Paris: EPEL, 2002), 53.

[29] J. Lacan, "Préface à l'édition anglaise du Séminaire XI," *Autres écrits, op. cit.*, 571.

the supposed "resistance of the English language to the unconscious." Now, the more the author has to say about Japanese, the more the difficulties translating Lacan in English do not appear to certify a general resistance of English to the expression of the unconscious. The presence, in the entrails of this language, of jokes, of limericks, of nonsense, so characteristic of English, and which will turn out to be so decisive for interpretation, or rather, for the reinterpretation of analysand Ella Sharpe's dream, does it not seem, as early as book VI of the *Seminar*, to focus our attention on the polar opposite? Indeed, the dream examined in the February–March 1959 sessions seems entirely built on a limerick for which Lacan discovered a similar substitution; as for the analysis of the nonsense, it appears to confer upon the English language a kind of autonomy that renders it independent from the external accidents of experience. The irony of the very things that run counter to Lacan's distrust is that one of the best dictionaries of Lacanian psychoanalysis is written in English by Dylan Evans, under the title *An Introductory Dictionary of Lacanian Psychoanalysis* (1996).[30]

What makes this position—which we cannot fail to view as a contradiction, especially if we are inattentive to the slightest nuance—extremely enigmatic is that Lacan comes to it quite late, after having let the opposite be known for a long time; I mean that English was, as a statutory or statue language, as permeable to psychoanalysis as French or German. When Lacan has a German immigrant to the United States say that he is *happy* but that he isn't *glücklich*, it is not to suggest that one word is worth more than the other, but indeed to signify that one isn't *happy* the way one is *glücklich*, that these are two words that refer to different feelings that no one, not even the immigrant, can superimpose. Thus, *ego* differs from *Ich*. Similarly, filming an English *baby* is not the same as filming a French *bébé*.[31] While they don't completely coincide, the difference between *corpse* and *body* is as serviceable as that between *Körper* and *Leib*. And it's an advantage English has of being able to distinguish the two nouns, *aim* and *goal*, where French only has *but*: *aim* referring to a trajectory, *goal* indicating something attained or missed. No doubt; how could it be otherwise? Lacan makes distinctions in foreign languages from his francophone

[30] For the first edition. There have been others since 1996.
[31] J. Lacan, *The Seminar of Jacques Lacan Book X: Anxiety*, ed. J.-A. Miller, trans. A. Price (Medford, MA: Polity, 2014), seminar of March 27, 1963.

point of view that appropriate foreign words that he integrates into what one is tempted to call "salangue" [T.N.: play on lalangue, meaning his language). But this language, which we just pastiched in Lacanian style, is also in turn illuminated by its confrontation with the English language. Lacan does not seem to deplore that English says *without*[32] (with being outside) rather than *sans*[33] (without anything). It even happens that Lacan uses English to better express the tenor of a German text, and points it out right away.[34] Most of the time, it is without the French equivalent that he adopts Freud's *talking cure*, his *chimney sweeping*, that he abandons the *"pénible élaboration"* in favor of, even surrounded by French words and clauses, *working through*, or that he discusses *acting out* at length, taking care to distinguish it from *"passage à l'acte."* In the former's case, the effects of *acting out* achieve the consistency of the effects designated in German by *Verwerfung* (foreclosure), *Verdrängung* (repression), *Verneinung* (denial). He sometimes, remarkably, invents French words which already have an equivalent in English. Thus, the word *poignance*, unknown to French dictionaries, even though it is easy to understand that the word is a substantive of what is poignant, is easily expressed by the English word *poignancy*,[35] which is the dictionary acceptation in English. He borrows the word *eftsooneries*[36] from a Joyce scholar. He talks about *scanning*,[37] about *splitting*, a word he captures to designate "the fundamental division of the two signifying chains where the subject is constituted," and he thereby acquires a defined term that would have been impossible to designate otherwise.[38]

---

[32] J. Lacan, *The Seminar of Jacques Lacan Book XVII: The Other Side of Psychoanalysis*, ed. J.-A. Miller, trans. R. Grigg (New York: Norton, 2007), seminar of January 21, 1970.

[33] It's somewhat the same type of observation that might lead one to remark that French says *entre*, letting the number three be heard, where English says *between* and German *zwischen*, both accenting *two* or *zwei*, which represents a wholly different approach to the intercalary than French. The Imaginary of concepts, and even their Symbolic, changes radically from one language to the next.

[34] As may be seen in J. Lacan, *Anxiety, op. cit.*, seminar of December 12, 1962.

[35] The word is found in *Écrits, op. cit.*, 235.

[36] J. Lacan, *Sinthome, op. cit.*, seminar of January 20, 1976: "They are things postponed until later, *after soon*. It's always like that in Joyce. Not only are the effects postponed, they are baffling."

[37] And he assigns this term the meaning of "procedure through which research secures its results through the mechanical exploration of the entire extension of its object's field" ("L'instance de la lettre," *Écrits, op. cit.*, 513).

[38] In *L'expérience émotionelle de l'espace*, P. Kaufmann uses the same technique with Greek words. A complicated idea attaches itself to a word foreign to the language, allow-

He chooses the word *fading* to designate the eclipse of the subject.[39] As often as in German, the concept comes to him in English. True, he correctly attacks *instinctual need* to translate *Bedürfniss*, but the denunciation in *Inhibition, symptôme, angoisse* of the translator's clumsiness in the Standard Edition does not extend to a general condemnation of the English language.[40] He finds it amusing the way French Canadian recycles English, as with the word *canner* that Lacan will use to speak of *"jouissance cannée"*: "a *jouissance cannée*, this is what Freud, in the myth of original sin and his murder, is showing us."[41] It is on the borderline between French and English that he talks about *failure* [T.N.: a pun on the French for "tiny crack"] or *daysens* [T.N.: a pun on the French for "decency"]. In the same way, he plays with the word *fixion*, where the *x* and the *ct* are so easily exchanged between French and English.[42] But let's leave behind the inexhaustible constructions of Franglais, which Lacan sometimes treats like Franglair (francglaire)[43]: it is clearly easier for him to be *Anglogen* than *Germanogen*.

---

ing the defined to become established. I devoted an article to this process, entitled "'Dessaisissement,' 'brillance,' et 'catégories d'expression' dans la philosophie de P. Kaufmann" in the special edition of the journal *Noesis* (Nice: université Sophia-Antipolis, 1999) published by the Centre de recherches et d'histoire des idées. The search for the term foreign to the language being used, in order to set the meaning of words, corresponds exactly to Pascal's statement in *Réflexions sur la géomètrie en général* that "definitions are only made to designate the things that are being named, not to show their nature" (Pascal, *Les Provinciales*, *op. cit.*, 116–117.

[39] "I chose this term," he says in his April 15, 1959, lesson, "for all kinds of philological reasons and also because it became very familiar thanks to the use of communication and voice reproduction devices, when the voice disappears or falls away, becomes faint, only to reappear following some variation in the medium itself, in the transmission."

[40] Bentham, of whom Lacan, as we shall see, had detailed knowledge, shared the practice of introducing foreign terms in his own language, and he theorized the procedure in these terms in *Church-of-Englandism and Its Catechism Examined* (London, 1817), 203: "Say *pretium affectionis*: not because for English use Latin is better than English; but because an expression—which, being borrowed from any foreign language, is stuck into the vernacular language—affords a better chance, than can be presented by any correspondent expression taken from the vernacular itself for laying hold of the attention and fixing itself on the memory."

[41] J. Lacan, *Le Séminaire livre XIV: La logique du fantasme*, unpublished seminar, seminar of April 26, 1967.

[42] *Reflection*, says one, whereas the other says, *réflexion*. The relationship is the same between *connexion* and *connection*.

[43] The word is a little strange because, with its reference to bodily excretions, it seems to denigrate the combination of French and English. Yet, in *La logique du fantasme* (*op. cit.*), on March 8, 1967, Lacan clearly said that, despite his taste for the French language,

More serious is the critique of "the ambiguity of roots in English," which "leads to singular avoidances." Thus, the suffix *less* (as in *meaningless*), which is the same as *los* (*sinnlos*) in German, is not systematically accompanied by the possibility of having the same word be preceded by the prefix *Un* (as in *Unsinn*); thus English loses, where this point is concerned, German's finesse.[44] But we have seen French and German, in turn, be lacking in other ways better covered or approached by English, without Lacan being able to say that these languages *resisted the unconscious*, whatever meaning we might want to give the expression. Should the -ing forms so characteristic of English be incriminated, which pass from the adjective to the verb and from the verb to the noun, allowing a kind of permanent flux between grammatical functions otherwise sufficiently differentiated? Lacan had shown, in another register, it is true, in Japanese, that too easy a resolution of contradictions was not an advantage for the expression of the unconscious. Isn't that what fails to happen in English, endowed as it is with the facilities and accommodations of its gerund, which allow speaking the fluctuation of the actual and the potential? Isn't it better to have a language filled with cuts, with impossibilities of saying, and with difficulties repairing breaks to allow passage for the expression of the unconscious? Perhaps? In any case, Lacan does not address this directly. Was it a Sphinx who spoke about English, or is there some rationality to what was said?

The difficulties we encounter seeking a coherent discourse on his part regarding English, at least where this last point is concerned, may have to do with a deeper question: is it so certain that the signifiers from which analysis begins and that it is up to the analyst to select to kick off his or her work are those of some vernacular language or other? That analysis occurs in a vernacular language, sometimes in several, is one thing; that it is in this kind of language that the unconscious expresses itself is another. But we would only be shifting the question, since we would still need to ponder the particular relation

---

"the use of Franglais did not bother him in the slightest." Taking the example of the expression *acting out*, he points out that it is a term of "extraordinary pertinence," all the more as he isn't able to translate it into French.

[44] This needs a little more nuance, however, because, in English, almost the same idea can be expressed by saying *shameless* and *unashamed*, *relentless* and *unrelenting*. But such examples are rare and the circuit from prefix to suffix is not systematic in English the way it is in German.

English maintains with this kind of language in order to become an obstacle for it. Does Lacan invite us to revive the languages quarrel in a new setting? It is certainly no longer a question of detecting or of choosing the most philosophical or the most juridical, but does it make any more sense to seek the most psychoanalytic language, the most suitable for psychoanalysis to flourish in all its forms?

On the verge of being ready to speak of contradiction, one has to be very careful. That there is a culture of *jokes, limericks*, and *nonsense* in the English language certainly does not disqualify it from being a working language of the unconscious, but English continues to be quite particular compared to French and German. Lacan points this out in a note in *Écrits*, when, spotting the equivalent of the French "*mot*" in the German *Witz*, he adds these words, excluding English: "The far greater difficulty of finding this equivalent in English is instructive: *wit*, weighed down by the discussion that goes from Davenant and Hobbes to Pope and Addison, leaving its essential qualities to *humor*, which is something else. *Pun* remains too narrow, however."[45] English does not balance its modalities of wit the way other languages do and, like every language, it has its own ways of doing so. The remark poses the question, but does not shed much light on the matter. This is the kind of difficulty that Lacan asks us to face.

For greater clarity, it is possible to group the three questions that will serve as axes for the whole of our research as follows.

First, the universal problem behind the question—which can seem very particular, if not singular—of Lacan's relationship with the English language is that of knowing what, of the Symbolic or the Imaginary, gives rise to the other. The philosophies have often landed on one side or the other of the two possibilities, without one of them being really decisive when the time came to conclude: is there a rational position on this question to which psychoanalysis might be able to give shape and of which philosophy could take advantage? When addressing this question, philosophy has never been able to overcome the antinomies it produced other than by resolving them in the form of conviction. It is true that Lacan's solution, at which we will see how he arrives, generates another question, which is that of the way *language* should be understood: should we give language the very wide

---

[45] J. Lacan, "L'instance de la lettre," *Écrits, op. cit.*, 508.

meaning the semiologist does, to the extent that the term *language* would include what would once have been called *morals*? Or the narrow sense of the linguist? It is clear that the proposition *The unconscious is structured like a language* differs according to whether *language* is understood in a wide or narrow sense.

Second, and in a more general way, does psychoanalysis enable us to overcome a certain number of antinomies beyond that of the Symbolic and the Imaginary (the intuitive, the affective), the distinction between language and speech, between the collective and the individual? What is it that should allow this discipline to better surmount antinomies than philosophy itself, which can only skeptically encounter them or dogmatically settle them? While German philosophy has often allowed itself to get caught up in this dialectic, is that the case with English philosophers? Don't they have at their disposal a language that allows them to better avoid this trap? But, quite strangely, Lacan—whom we have a hard time envisaging being content with a recourse to experience in order to resolve antinomies—does not fully take advantage of this recourse to the English language.

Henceforth, and *lastly*, there is no escape from a third series of questions: how is it possible for a language that—like English—allows so well for the production of certain concepts or of certain conceptual elements of psychoanalytic theory to be at the same time an obstacle to the productions of the unconscious? Unless Lacan only meant to say that English allowed conceptualization in psychoanalysis with greater difficulty than German, which bore it in its womb, and French, which he knows "by experience"? There is no denying that, when it comes to certain areas at least, English turns out to be an efficient instrument.

We stand ready; after all, the deciphering of enigmas is the very work of the psychoanalyst, and it is with this guiding thread that we intend to lead our investigation. However, since we expect to show the multiplicity and variety of the points of contact of Lacan's work with the English language, this Ariadne's thread will be unspooled in a labyrinth that articulates six regions or juxtaposes six interlacing areas that we had to untangle somewhat.

The first part will be devoted to the use Lacan made of several English (or Anglophone) philosophers: Jeremy Bentham, George Berkeley, Charles Sanders Peirce, Bertrand Russell, Jaako Hintikka, William Hogarth, and Thomas More. Lacan only ever refers to a philosopher because he defended a particular thesis, for example, the theory of fictions (Bentham) or names (Russell).

The second part, very similar to the first because of the themes addressed, deals with research in the fields of logic and linguistics; it is particularly focused on Lacan's remarks about a few authors and his way of using them: Claude Lévi-Strauss (who wrote a certain number of important articles in English), Roman Jakobson, Noam Chomsky, Gottlob Frege (whom Lacan reads in English), George Boole, Willard Van Orman Quine, and Alfred North Whitehead.

The third part deals with the importance of English literature for the construction of Lacan's work. Three big names stand out in particular here: those of James Joyce and a few of his commentators (who allow him to reopen the dossier and increase knowledge of writing and the nature of the signifier), William Shakespeare and a few Shakespeare scholars (around whom will coalesce the figure of the *ghost* and the reflection on the *father* and the *name of the father*), and Edgar Allan Poe, whose "Purloined Letter," a short story whose title, according to Lacan, was less than ably translated by Baudelaire as *La lettre volée* [T.N.: The Stolen Letter] when it should have been *La lettre détournée* [The Diverted Letter], is the subject of a long examination in *Écrits*. However, while the majority of references are clustered around these three names, they are not the only ones to share Lacan's attention; Lacan, thanks to his rich knowledge of English literature, is able to cite, in an original fashion and according to his needs, Lewis Carroll, Jonathan Swift, William Wordsworth, Aldous Huxley, Henry Miller, Walt Whitman, Vladimir Nabokov, William Blake, and several others.

The fourth part is entirely devoted to the readings in English of his psychoanalyst colleagues, who expose their work mainly in this language. In addition to Freud himself, often consulted and cited in English, this list includes Alice and Michael Balint, Melanie Klein, Ernest Jones, Donald W. Winnicott, Havelock H. Ellis, Erich Fromm, William Gillespie, Edward Glover, Hermann Nunberg, Theodor Reik, Phyllis Greenacre, Gregory Bateson, René Spitz, Thomas Szasz, Lucia Tower, Otto Fenichel, William R.D. Fairbairn, and other analysts cited less frequently. Especially during the early seminars, the session plan is almost invariably the same: concerning that year's theme, an article deemed important is presented, then critiqued according to the emerging Lacanian categories.

The fifth part, finally, focuses on the few English scientists whom, while they are neither psychiatrists, nor psychologists, nor psychoanalysts, Lacan draws on in his epistemology and his reflection about methods; this is when the names Darwin, Newton, Harvey, and Von Neumann (for game theory) appear insistently. It is noteworthy that certain authors are read in English simply because these German-speaking writers, like Fenichel and Frege, were translated into English before being translated into French, or, like Popper, became English-language authors during the course of their career, which leads us to believe that Lacan only reads German or only consults it in order to get an exact sense of the concepts used by canonical authors. While speaking English is painful for him, reading seems much easier in this language than in German, which is quite close to the typical circumstance of intellectuals in the decades following the Second World War.

We should add, as a forewarning to the reader and in order to avoid any misunderstanding, that we have not sought to be exhaustive, that we have deliberately neglected sentences that were hardly comprehensible, if not incomprehensible, found in the manuscripts we consulted, when they did not exist in the works published by les éditions du Seuil. The difficulties we encounter reading the typed transcriptions are, most of the time, tied to the oral style of the *Seminar*, and maybe also, occasionally, to bad audio conditions experienced by the transcriber. We haven't sought to improve the style of the sentences, but sometimes we edited coarse or crude elements that did not seem to serve any purpose. We hope this editing did as little harm to Lacan's discourse as Bruce Fink hoped his English translation of *Écrits* would, when he wrote, at the risk of worrying the reader, about editing a certain number of obscurities that existed in the original French version.[46] Doubt cannot fail to be raised when one measures the extent to which obscurity is relative to the person judging it. Finally, we simply set aside reviews of books and articles when they were of no theoretical interest and consisted of no more than attacks, deserved or not, such as that meted out to Havelock Ellis' book.

---

[46] Indeed, the translator's note ends on these words, which are not lacking in ambiguity: "Should the English sometimes strike the reader as obscure, I can only point to the difficulty of the French and indicate that I have already removed as many obscurities as I could at this time." J. Lacan, *Écrits: The First Complete Edition in English*, trans. B. Fink (New York: Norton, 2006), xii.

I

LACAN AND THE ENGLISH PHILOSOPHERS

The English philosophers in whom Lacan was deeply interested are few. The only names of Anglophone philosophers that appear with any regularity, if one accepts distinguishing them from psychoanalysts, psychologists, psychiatrists, and linguists, are those of Bentham, Berkeley, Hintikka, Hogarth, Thomas More, Peirce, Russell, and the philosophers who were engaged in a polemic with the latter surrounding proper names. When he cites Wilkins, for instance, the Anglican bishop of Chester, it is for the extremely narrow borrowing of a word this seventeenth-century author is credited with inventing, *nulliquity* or *nullibiety*, which is found in *An Essay Towards a Real Character and a Philosophical Language* (London: 1668). The author intended it to refer to the fact of being nowhere; Borgès had brought this to Lacan's attention,[1] who may have consulted *Roget's Thesaurus of English Words and Phrases* (1862). But the borrowing is strictly that of a word, radically removed from its context, since he makes it a component of the very notion of *jouissance* that he is elaborating: "the old nullibiety, of which I had restored in earlier times the luster it deserves for having been invented by Bishop Wilkins, and which denotes the quality of what is nowhere, what is it? It's jouissance."[2] Nothing will be found concerning Hobbes, a philosopher who could have been useful to him in several ways,[3] and whom Freud himself cites with pertinence and finesse regarding the question of the feeling of the passage of psychic

---

[1] Lacan says it in a note in "Le séminaire sur 'La Lettre volée,'" *Écrits, op. cit.*, 23.

[2] J. Lacan, *Le Séminaire livre XVI: D'un Autre à l'autre*, ed. J.-A. Miller (Paris: Éditions du Seuil, 2006), seminar of May 21, 1969.

[3] Such as the theory of fictions. Doesn't Hobbes provide one of the rare seventeenth-century definitions of fiction? One can also consider his theory of language, which replaces the Cartesian subject (the cogito expression is just a way of speaking that isn't even valid in every language), his theory of authority, and, more generally, his dynamic conception of the psyche.

life in dreams; nothing in the *Seminar* on Hume,[4] other than an opportunity to stumble over English syntax and misinterpret a Coleridge text;[5] nothing on Locke; nothing on Mill, except on the remarks he made in his *System of Logic* about proper names, the importance of which he saw in the mid-nineteenth century. It is perhaps through these "deficiencies" that we clearly see that while Lacan never mistakes the meaning of a philosophical doctrine, he is not a philosopher. Certainly not in the sense that the University expected at that time and still expects from philosophers that they acquire a knowledge of the authors who chronologically dot the history of concepts. It is understandable therefore that we do not attach much importance to chronological order when dealing with the English philosophers as considered by Lacan.

Lacan thus cuts a wide swath among the authors who might have interested him, even if, going against the University at the time, he does not find the English philosophers unworthy of reading and does not consider them refuted *a priori* because of their legendary

---

[4] He could have cited him for reasons somewhat similar to those that might have incited him to refer to Hobbes. It should be noted, however, that this is in the *Seminar,* because in "Position de l'inconscient" (*Écrits, op. cit.*, 839), there is a stunning little remark about the cause that implies not only having read the author but also a deep comprehension of the text.

[5] If the version we are using to read *Le Séminaire livre* VI (1958–1959), *Le désir et son interprétation*, is trustworthy, the one L'École lacanienne broadcasts via its website, we read, although quite indistinctly, the name Hume in the April 8, 1969 lesson: "As in many other domains, Coleridge is the first to have plumbed the depths of what there is in *Hamlet*—about this first scene [the one with the ghost's appearance] that Hume himself, who was so much against ghosts, believed in that one, that Shakespeare's art managed to make him believe despite his resistance. The force he deployed against ghosts, he says, is similar to that of a Sampson. And here, Sampson is levelled. It is clear that it is because Shakespeare came very close to something that wasn't the ghost, but that was, in effect, this encounter, not with a dead person, but with death itself, which, after all, is the key aspect of this play." It is true that Krutzen's index, in its third edition, confirms this reference. It was very worrisome, though, because it was impossible to know to which exact text of Hume's Lacan alluded; this stopped being a concern as soon as, consulting the Coleridge text, it became obvious that Lacan mistook a conditional for an imperfect, leading to a misinterpretation. Indeed, Coleridge says: "Hume himself could not but have had faith in this Ghost dramatically, let his antighostism have been as strong as Sampson against other ghosts less powerfully raised." S.T. Coleridge, *Shakespeare and the Elizabethan Dramatists* (Edinburgh: J. Grant, 1905), 210. Coleridge does not claim, and with good reason, in this text, that Hume really felt this emotion. Lacan's rendez-vous with Hume was therefore missed twice.

empiricism. Lacan does not seek to take on, vis-à-vis the philosopher authors, the totalizing attitude of a sum of accumulated knowledge based on concepts, articulated in a critical manner. Lacan freely uses the theses he needs; he is not interested in knowing whether the author amended them later, how they were initially discovered, how they are articulated with or nuanced by other theses. His attention is not centered on the author by trying, perhaps because of some in any case absurd project, to be "fair" to his work, that is to say by trying to take into account and "balance" all of its aspects. He's interested in a given concept, in a given argument pertaining to the concept, in a given articulation of concepts; the author's name being no more than the labelling of these very segmented practices that refuse the big picture from the outset, be it that of authors artificially brought together or made up of a single author. Curiously, if the analytic philosophers did not almost unanimously reject it—most of the time without bothering to examine it—his approach could be called *analytical*.

This radicalism, which can be shocking where nuance might be expected, is perfectly understandable in light of Lacan's intentions regarding the philosophers. When Lacan turns to them, he is already in possession of an idea that he will modulate and develop the entire time of the *Seminar* and, more generally, of his research: the fundamental idea of the tripartite nature of The Real, The Symbolic, and The Imaginary. The content and the relations of these notions will evolve over the decades of the *Seminar*, but the structure stays in place: he uses it as a compass in order to orient himself in the work of any author. Lacan quickly identifies in what sector he can expect from an author, segments already worked out, insights on an element of the Real-Symbolic-Imaginary, or on the articulation of two elements, if not on the entire structure. His challenge is to quickly make the necessary adjustments between the philosopher's language and his own montage and to seek to learn of the philosopher or the analyzed work only what he needs for his own research. Lacan translates the author into his own language and only on this condition does he learn from him or her. The author is then usually held to be insufficient and generally disqualified; but he is punctually examined, the result of the examination contributing to the construction of the edifice to which Lacan, as builder, invites his listeners. This device is singularly active and will turn out to be particularly effective for the examination of the English philosophers he assembles.

Our concern is to grasp what is specifically *English* in the manner of conceiving the symbolic, the fictive, in the very way Hume said that certain discoveries were only possible in certain nations,[6] as he put it, although they could then spread to every other. Rather than nations, we would prefer to speak of one of their constitutive elements: languages. Thus, what we shall later call "Hume's law"—although it is never expressed in these terms by the Scottish philosopher—holds that inventions and creations are only possible in certain cultural and, more specifically, linguistic contexts; but also that, once these inventions and these creations are done in one language, they can be transferred into and developed (sometimes more effectively than in the original language) in other languages.

---

[6] There are cultural contexts more propitious than others to the birth of science and technology: "it is impossible for the arts and sciences to arise, at first, among any people unless that people enjoy the blessing of a free government." As for Hume's other observation in this regard, in his essay "Of the Rise and Progress of the Arts and Sciences," it consists of noting "though the only proper Nursery of these noble plants be a free state; yet may they be transplanted into any government. ..." (*Essays and Treatises on Several Subjects Volume I: Essays Moral, Political and Literary* (London: Thoemmes Press, 2002), 119, 128.)

1

JEREMY BENTHAM

What is at stake, reading Bentham, is to know which entity, symbolic or affective (emotive), is the basis for the other. Hume had clearly answered that the passions were the foundation of the symbolic and he had drawn all the ensuing practical conclusions—political, moral, ethical, juridical—but also the theoretical conclusions, for, in his eyes, nothing happens in the realm of ideas, including mathematics, without what he calls "conception," that is to say, a particular mental bond that makes us faithful to the symbols we produce. Now, for Bentham, this theory of affectivity, on the one hand, that of the limitation of intellectual work by conception, on the other, are errors that need to be rectified. Given Lacan's way of using philosophy—by this I mean instrumentalizing it—it is easy to understand that he would be interested in this aspect, which is particularly present in Bentham.

Without claiming to have discovered Bentham's theory of fictions, which he owes to the publication of Ogden's book, introduced to him by Jakobson, Lacan immediately measures Benthamian utilitarianism with this yardstick. He has no interest in and will not show any for the Panopticon, when ten years later Foucault highlights this famous penitentiary system to which French intellectuals of the 1960s tend to reduce the figure of Bentham. If it's worthwhile to read Bentham in the 1950s, it is for what he says about the notion of *fiction* that he is learning to theorize, which is something that was not done by those who, for a very long time—because the notion was not unknown to the Greeks (πλάσμα) and the Latins (the "*fictio*")—used it correctly and even those who, in the seventeenth century, such as Descartes, Hobbes, and Leibniz, had given it the meaning of an epistemic tool. Lacan, who had already stated that "the truth has the structure of fiction" before experiencing the shock of reading it in Bentham,[1]

---

[1] Bentham wrote that "Truth is a fictitious entity.... Truth is a mighty queer sort of

is on the same wavelength with Bentham's efforts to show that truth is a construct and that it only appears to be a kind of revelation or unveiling of the real. "*Fictitious* does not mean illusory or inherently misleading"; fiction is not on the order of error, because the one using it normally knows that it isn't true, that it contains contradictions it can express. If we want to translate *fictitious* into French by *fictif*, it is necessary to point out right away that "it is in the sense," Lacan says, "that I already articulated to you, every truth has the structure of fiction."[2] And Lacan in 1959 gives Bentham's *fiction* and *fictitious* the meaning of *symbolic*: "The fictitious is not in essence what is deceptive, but strictly speaking what we call the symbolic."[3] He will never forget this theme nor its proximity to his own theory of truth. Indeed, ten years later, February 26, 1959, he says:

> take the term *fictions* to mean representing nothing illusory or deceitful, affecting whatever falls under its power, what it contemplates, with nothing of the sort, but covering specifically what I have promoted aphoristically by stressing that truth, inasmuch as its place can only be where speech occurs, that truth in essence—pardon this *in essence*, it's to make myself understood, don't give it the philosophical heft the term carries—truth, let's say, of itself, has the structure of fiction.[4]

It becomes clear what Lacan sees in Bentham's use of the term *fiction*. Certainly, fiction loses the aspect of an equivalent to the imagination it had under Hobbes;[5] it is on the order of language. Bentham

---

personage in the abstract, as sleepery as an eel." *Deontology Together With a Table of the Springs of Action and Article on Utilitarianism* (Oxford: Clarendon Press, 1983), 354.

[2] Lacan draws the conclusions of this position to the point of daring to write, in "Position de l'inconscient," that "psychoanalysts belong to the concept of the unconscious, since they constitute its address" (*Écrits, op. cit.*, 834), which Bruce Fink, his translator, cites as one of those provocative statements the meaning of which he is absolutely uncertain. See *Reading Seminar XI: Lacan's Four Fundamental Concepts of Psychoanalysis*, ed. R. Feldstein, B. Fink, and M. Jaanus (Albany, NY: State University of New York, 1995), xiv.

[3] J. Lacan, *Ethics of Psychoanalysis, op. cit.*, seminar of November 18, 1959.

[4] J. Lacan, *D'un Autre à l'autre, op. cit.*, seminar of February 26, 1969.

[5] *The Elements of Law, Natural and Politic* Part 1, Chapter 3, Section 4. "As when the water, or any liquid thing moved at once by divers movements, receiveth one motion compounded of them all; so also the brain or spirits therein, having been stirred by divers objects, composeth an imagination of divers conceptions that appeared singly to the sense. As for example, the sense sheweth us at one time the figure of a mountain, and at another time the colour of gold; but the imagination afterwards hath them both at once

defines it as such, though not without ambiguity, by opposition to what he understands as *real entity*:

> By this term—fictitious entity—is here meant to be designated one of those sorts of objects which, in every language, must for the purpose of discourse be spoken of as existing—be spoken of in the same manner as those objects which really have existence, and to which existence is seriously meant to be ascribed, are spoken of—objects of the existence of which a serious persuasion is seriously intended to be produced—but without any such design as that of producing any such persuasion as that of their possessing each for itself any separate, or strictly speaking any real existence. Take for instance the word Relation, Situation, Faculty, Power, and the like. Real entities being the objects for the designation of which, in the first place, at the earliest stage of human intercourse, and in virtue of the most urgent necessity, words in the character of names were employed—between the idea of a name and that of the reality of the object to which it was applied, an association being thus formed, from a connection thus intimate sprung a very natural propensity, viz., that of ascribing reality to every object thus designated: in a word, of ascribing reality to the objects designated by words which, upon due examination, would be nothing but so many names of so many fictitious entities.[6]

The fictional is what engenders the imaginary. Thus, what is experienced as a passion or an emotion is an oscillation between pleasure and pain; this articulated play only creates the toughness of what causes the evanescent signified of passion. Bentham reverses the classic view of ethics, of morality, and of politics, which consists of relying on the passions and their supposed regulation by reason or by contrary passions: passion does not hold up on its own, it only gives the illusion of consistency because it is held by the language that structures it. In the language of his own theorization, Lacan says forcefully:

---

in a golden mountain. From the same cause it is, there appear unto us castles in the air, chimeras, and other monsters which are not *in rerum natura*, but have been conceived by the sense in pieces at several times. And this composition is that which we commonly call FICTION of the mind." (ed. F. Tönnies, F. Cass, & Co. (London: Cambridge UP, 1984), 10). However, here again, Lacan missed a confrontation with Hobbes that could have been decisive.

[6] J. Bentham, *De l'ontologie et autres textes sur les fictions* (Paris: Éditions du Seuil, 1997), 87.

Bentham "approaches the question on the level of the signifier."[7] To understand it, you have to go to what structures the play of affect; sentience does not hold up of itself and what we think of as living only holds up because it is supported by signifiers.

On this issue, Lacan also highlights his interest in Alexander's work, when he speaks of the "big article" on the *Logic of Emotions*:

> Just as in Chapman Ishman's recent article, it is necessary to introduce into what we usually consider the affective register, a dialectic. Alexander starts from the well-known logico-symbolic pattern where Freud deduces the various forms of delusion from the various forms of denial—*I love him-I'm not the one who loves him-He's not the one I love-I don't love him-he hates me-he's the one who loves me*—which yields the genesis of several delusions: jealousy, passion, persecution, erotomania, etc. It is therefore in a symbolic structuration, an elevated one since it involves very elaborate grammatical variations, that we grasp the transformations, the very metabolism, that occur in the preconscious order.[8]

Until the end of the *Seminar*, this "Benthamian" position is held by Lacan; it is not that affects are nothing: "The speaking being gives us the opportunity to notice how far the effects of lalangue go in that he presents all kinds of affects that remain enigmatic." But these affects are results: "These affects are what result from the presence of lalangue inasmuch as, knowledge-wise, it articulates things that go much farther than what the speaking being supposes in the way of spoken knowledge."[9] They are not motors, although they might appear to be.

The field opened up by Bentham is one that allows witnessing the interplay of the symbolic and the imaginary; this he does in every which way, in the ethical and political realm as well as the epistemological realm. In the practical realm, we mustn't be content with big words and big ideas from which we claim the ability to derive the entire system of responsibilities or laws; it is necessary, instead, to show what really crafts these big words and big ideas, and replace their preten-

---

[7] J. Lacan, *Ethics of Psychoanalysis, op. cit.*, seminar of May 11, 1960.

[8] J. Lacan, *The Seminar of Jacques Lacan Book I: Freud's Technical Papers*, ed. J.-A. Miller, trans. J. Forrester (New York: Norton, 1991), seminar of June 16, 1954.

[9] J. Lacan, *The Seminar of Jacques Lacan Book XX: Encore: On Feminine Sexuality, the Limits of Love and Knowledge*, ed. J.-A. Miller, trans. B. Fink (New York: Norton, 1998), seminar of June 26, 1973.

sion with the reality of the procedures that allow citizens to effectively be bound together. It isn't enough to demand equality and liberty in order to have them or create them; they need to be installed by laws that make it impossible to have an interest in wanting their opposite, or that authorize the powers enabled to do so, to make decisions, each in its own sphere, that most closely conform to the greatest happiness of the greatest number. As for the realm of theory, it's the whole of *Chrestomathia* that provides the best example, at the beginning of the nineteenth century, of the play of the symbolic through which there is an attempt to seize hold of the real, the methods, the concepts and the words to represent them and, through the images of which, at the same time, we build conceptual momentum and find that it breaks down after a short distance. Bentham shows, with multiple examples, how the metaphorical designations through which concepts are designated, as well as represented, trigger ideas and constitute at the same time the worst obstacles to the constitution and the articulation of concepts. Bachelard, too, spoke of this momentum of the image, but one must add that this take-off falters at the very moment we most need help in order to conceptualize.[10] The image makes a fragment of the concept function according to its own rhythm and conditions, which quickly leads to the latter's drift. In reality, the image is not, of itself, its own principle; the symbolic alone sustains it: such is the reversal relative to Hume, for example, who thought that languages resembled one another because of the same imagination shared by all men, whatever their language. The consequences of this reversal are considerable, and Lacan will register them on the terrain of psychology from the beginning of his teaching, when it comes time for him to distance himself from *Object Psychology*, which desperately tries to find a correspondence between faculties and objects; as if it were necessary to find an object for the emotions, when the answer lies elsewhere, since it is the symbolic that crafts the emotions and accounts for their logic, rather than their supposed reference to objects that are discoverable, on the model of what happens when we know something.[11]

---

[10] On all these questions, and to find the most examples, Bentham's *Chrestomathia* (Andesite Press, 2017) may be consulted.

[11] A. Chapman Ishman's article, published in April 1951 in the *Psycho-Analytic Review*, "highlights the emotion's information, purported to be the last reality we encounter and,

Lacan immediately sees two things: that Bentham's research is far from ridiculous and, drawing the quickest conclusion, that Freud's research rushes into the seesaw motion operated by Benthamian utilitarianism. Let's see the two points: "This figure (Lacan is talking about Bentham) is far from deserving the discredit, if not the ridicule, that a certain philosophical critique may manifest when it comes to his role in the course of the history of ethical progress."[12] We can assume that the criticism of Bentham comes from two sources: from the Kantians, if not from Kant himself, who ignored Bentham;[13] from Bergson and the Bergsonians, who did not ignore him, but attacked him while feigning to criticize the work of twelfth- and twentieth-century psychophysics and psychophysiology.[14] Thus, according to Bergson, the calculation on pleasures and pains is absurd because it supposes a common denominator between affective realities that are not able to have one: what could a present pleasure and a past pleasure have in common, even if I identify with both? What could a pleasure and a pain have in common that I should be able to balance them? What could a pleasure or a pain that I experience have in common with a pleasure or a pain experienced by someone else? A reality value is therefore granted to experienced pleasures and pains, while the symbolic events through which they are confronted and articulated are discredited. Now, as fictional as the symbolic elements are, they must nevertheless be the starting point, rather than from some whiffs wrongly regarded as real, if one wants to understand psychic functioning. The end of *Seminar VII* says it perfectly:

---

strictly speaking, the object of our experience. This concept is a response to the desire to grasp, somewhere, an object that resembles as much as possible the objects of other registers." J. Lacan, *Freud's Technical Papers, op. cit.*, seminar of June 16, 1954.

[12] J. Lacan, *Ethics of Psychoanalysis, op. cit.*, seminar of November 18, 1959.

[13] Kantianism built its moral philosophy against utility; although utility caught up with it because moral law has to concern us and cannot be entirely developed in a sphere radically divorced from all interest—whether characterized as "pure" or not—and of all utility. We shall leave aside this aspect of things, since the English philosophers, particularly those Lacan cites, are not Kantian.

[14] The name Bentham is not found in any works published by Bergson; but it is clear, through the courses taught at Lycée Henri-IV, that utilitarianism is indeed the doctrine targeted by the criticisms that the *Essay on the Immediate Data of Consciousness* apparently only addresses to Weber and Fechner.

Concerning all institutions in what they have of the fictional, in other words of the fundamentally verbal, his research does not consist in reducing to nothing all these multiple, incoherent, contradictory rights, examples of which are provided to him by English jurisprudence, but, on the contrary, from the symbolic artifice of these terms, themselves creators of texts as well, to see what, in all of that, could be used for something, which is to say to be subject to an equitable distribution (*faire justement l'objet du partage*).[15]

In *Seminar XX*, from the years 1972–1973, he again stresses Bentham's thought that considers the symbolic in its most linguistic aspect: "Utilitarianism, where Bentham is concerned, isn't at all what people think.... Utilitarianism doesn't mean anything different from that—the old words, those that are already used, it's what they are used for that we need to think about. Nothing more."[16] Calculation, far from having to be rendered impossible to thought, is the essence of Lacanian desire. It isn't the imaginary that holds the key to the symbolic, but indeed the reverse: hence the change.

Bergson's critique would be well-founded if pleasures and pains existed as transcendent beings and could be added to or subtracted from one another. But something completely different is involved here and, with Bentham as much as with Lacan, it's from the syntax to the element that the consequence matters; the signifier only exists as a signifier in relation to other signifiers, according to multiple functions and combinations; the signified has no inherent consistency: it is only fantasized based on the operations. Who, if not Bergson and for the needs of his own critique, would go fantasize the existence of little pleasures and little pains, adding up to create who knows what surfaces and what chimeric volumes.[17]

Lacan then proceeds to the conclusion we called rapid, but which in reality opens up its own field of research: "It is inside this opposition between fiction and reality that the seesaw movement of the Freudian experience takes place."[18] Psychoanalysis constructs the

---

[15] J. Lacan, *Ethics of Psychoanalysis, op. cit.*, seminar of May 11, 1960.

[16] J. Lacan, *Encore, op. cit.*, seminar of February 13, 1973.

[17] Maybe Leibniz toyed with the idea as one of the possible uses of his infinitesimal calculus. But he admitted not being enough in love with these small quantities to give them an ontological value.

[18] J. Lacan, *Ethics of Psychoanalysis, op. cit.*, seminar of November 18, 1959.

symbolic that underlies the supposedly lived elements. Lacan returns to this point in the same terms ten years later, in the February 26, 1969, lesson: the *Theory of Fictions* "is quite simply the most important thing written from the perspective we call Utilitarian." Lacan's reading was thus the opposite of the one Élie Halévy had devoted, at the beginning of the twentieth century, to the works of Bentham and the Utilitarians. Halévy had dared to write that everything Bentham had written in volume VIII of the Bowring edition should be forgotten; to the contrary, and with good reason, Lacan regarded this volume as the most important aspect of Bentham's thought and the starting point that explained the rest of his work: "One could scarcely do better, considering things from a sociological perspective, which better isolates what is going on in the category of the symbolic, that happens to be precisely the one updated, but in a completely different way, by the Freud event and what followed."[19] The passage occurs with the Freudian "Constructions in Analysis," which no longer require the supposed "reality" of the return to origins and which take note of the fact that the empirical phenomenality of supposed memories is not found where it is thought to be.

Three things remain to be established concerning Bentham. The *first* has to do with Ogden, who was so interested in the theory of fictions that he wrote a collection of Benthamian positions on the question, to which Lacan returned February 17, 1971; the *second* is to show that, as early as the first year of the *Seminar*, Lacan was very close to Benthamian themes, while he did not yet know the theory of fictions; *finally*, his interest in Bentham for the theory of fictions was not only speculative, it was decisive in leading him to conceive a certain number of psychoanalytical actions.

First of all, Lacan did not fail to notice that Richards and Ogden were "the two leaders of a position born in England, completely in keeping with the best traditions of English philosophy, who created, early in the Century the doctrine called 'logico-positivism,' whose major work is titled *The Meaning of Meaning*." Lacan's critical position regarding this "meaning of meaning" corresponds to his distrust of metalanguage and of interpretation. It is dangerous to seek a meaning beyond meaning, because it risks building on sand under the pretext

---

[19] J. Lacan, *D'un Autre à l'autre, op. cit.*, seminar of February 26, 1969.

of extending the foundation and rendering the imaginary redundant instead of building and establishing the symbolic:

> In other words, it suffices that a philosophical text be caught *in flagrante* of nonsense for it to be thereby automatically discounted. It is only too obvious that this is a way of editing things that scarcely allows us to find our way, because if we start from the principle that something lacking meaning cannot be essential to the development of a discourse, we shall quite simply lose track....[20] That this process in some sense forbids any articulation whose meaning cannot be grasped is something that, for example, would lead to not being able to use mathematical discourse, which, according to the most qualified logicians,[21] is characterized by the fact that at such and such a point, we can no longer give it any meaning. This does not stop it from being, precisely, of all discourses, the most rigorously developed. Besides, we find ourselves thereby at a point that is absolutely essential to highlight concerning the function of writing.[22]

Lacan sees the danger, or rather the inanity, of the demand for meaning which can only replicate as "meaning of meaning" and "meaning of meaning of meaning," indefinitely and in vain, if this production of meaning is not a genuine work of constitution of the levels of meaning. Now, these so-called levels of meaning can only seriously exist if the symbols that bear them are modified: the real work of meaning is done on the symbols, which do not necessarily require knowing what they mean in order to work on them. In other words, it isn't the "conception" of symbols that propels them forward, it's their own work which can go—which must go, not through a contingent accompaniment that risks being costly and constraining—all the way to discrediting any imaginary accompaniment. There exists a work of writing on itself, as is best seen in mathematics: the symbol constructs itself; the imaginary follows. Here, we obviously recognize Russell's position, often referenced by Lacan, and one to which we shall return.

---

[20] Pascal had said something comparable in his *Réflexions sur la géométrie en général*: "Every time a proposition is inconceivable, we must suspend judgment and not deny it because of this, but examine its opposite, and if we find it obviously false, we can boldly affirm the first one, as incomprehensible as it may be. Pascal, *Les Provinciales et Pensées et opuscules divers* (Paris: Le Livre de Poche/Classiques Garnier, 2004), 123.

[21] Here, Lacan is obviously thinking of Russell, for example.

[22] J. Lacan, *D'un discours qui ne serait pas du semblant*, seminar of March 17, 1971.

In 1954, while he does not yet speak of Bentham[23] in the same terms he does starting with *Seminar VII*, his theory of the meaning of words is nevertheless very close to Bentham's and Berkeley's; the meaning of a word is the whole of its uses. Indeed, it would be difficult to claim that the meaning of a word is concentrated in a signified understood as a kind of abstract and general idea, since these authors, starting with Locke, who himself had scarcely overcome the contradiction, criticized abstract and general ideas, which they considered pure fantasies, without their own consistency or the existence of objects related to them. Thus it is that "If you want to know the meaning of the word *main* (hand) in the French language, you must catalog its uses, not only when they represent the organ, but also when it figures in the expressions *main-d'oeuvre* (workforce), *mainmise* (stranglehold), *mainmorte* (mortmain), etc. The meaning is given by the sum of its uses."[24] Now, it is not entirely by chance that Lacan chose the example of the hand to talk about the uses of a word. This seeming contingency brings us right back to our starting point. In *Chrestomathia*, the classification of occupations explores entire rafts of techniques, divides them into branches, articulates them, and links them to all sorts of positions and activities of the hand. Thus, what Lacan, in an Anglo-Saxon vein, says about the meaning of words could also be said about the hand, which shapes the articulation of the whole of the techniques, conveying the proof that symbolization is a much more general activity than that of words, even if the language of words in particular records it and is always intertwined with it in one way or another. The strangest thing is that, via different channels, Bentham and Lacan—we saw it à propos of a privileged word—both refer to Bishop Wilkins' book, *An Essay Toward a Real Character and a Philosophical Language*. Lacan extracts a word from it, *nulliquity*; Bentham addresses five pages of the work, from page 243 to page to page 248 of the 1668 version.

Finally, we do not think that the theory of fictions never went beyond being a subject of speculation for Lacan, since we see him in the *Seminar* on transference, for instance, treat transference as a fiction, and its logic as that of fictions. Thus, *Seminar VIII* states:

---

[23] In 1954, in the November 17 lesson, Bentham is still only considered the one who took hedonism as far as possible. This is no longer the direction that will interest Lacan five years later.

[24] J. Lacan, *Freud's Technical Papers, op. cit.*, seminar of June 16, 1954.

We shall have, at the point the transference appears, like, strictly speaking, a source of fiction. In the transference the subject creates, builds something. Consequently, it is not possible, it seems to me, to not integrate right away in the function of transference the term *fiction*. To begin with, what is the nature of this fiction? And if it is a fiction, what is being feigned? And since feigning is involved, for whom?[25]

Important questions relate to fictions with a view to making them operational.

[25] J. Lacan, *The Seminar of Jacques Lacan Book VIII: Transference*, ed. J.-A. Miller, trans. B. Fink (Medford, MA: Polity, 2015), seminar of March 1, 1961.

2
GEORGE BERKELEY

From Berkeley, Lacan seems to expect another recourse and along another axis than Bentham's. No doubt, the primacy of the symbolic is displayed in Berkeley in unexpected ways that confirm the Benthamian contributions we just examined; but using Berkeley's has more to do with the extension of language: with this philosopher we find the idea of a language-based, linguistic foundation for perceptions and affects. Is this to say, as the Aristotelean tradition has held, that languages intimate ways of perceiving and feeling? Or that the percepts function *like* elements of language? It is certainly the type of question the Lacanian itinerary causes to resonate within psychoanalysis.

To understand Lacan's attachment to Berkeley, it is necessary to start from Lacan's protestations at seeing his own idea of the *signifier* assimilated to Saussure's, or to an expanded version of the one that can be found in Saussure's *Cours de linguistique générale*. These protestations are legitimate, not only because, as "Lituraterre" reminds us, the signifier did not need to wait for the Saussurian stamp of approval to have legitimacy in psychoanalysis,[1] but also because Saussure falls into two traps Lacan manages to avoid, thanks to his knowledge of English philosophy and most particularly of Berkeley's philosophy. In *Seminar XX*, during the April 10, 1973, lesson, after having paid a lengthy homage to F. Recanati, who had just spoken, quoting Berkeley, he adds: "It is certain that, had Berkeley not been among my earliest foods, probably many things, including my casual use of linguistic ref-

---

[1] In "Lituraterre" (*Autres écrits, op. cit.*, 15) Lacan reminds his reader, who might have too much of a tendency to understand his concept of *signifier* in a Saussurian manner, that "when [I] turn to the 52nd letter to Fliess, it is to read what Freud might express using the term he forges: WZ, *Wahrnehmungszeichen*, closest to the signifier, at a date when Saussure had yet to reproduce it (from the Stoïc *signans*)." Notice the swipe at the *Cours de linguistique général*, whose invention, regarding the sign, consists of repurposing the Stoic concept by limiting its scope to the language of words. Jakobson will have exactly the same thing to say about Saussure.

erences, would not have been possible."[2] In what way was this early acquaintance with Berkeley able to change Lacan's attitude towards linguistics? Lacan provides few elements, it is true, but what he offers in the *Seminar* is enough for us to begin to answer this question.

We just noted that the Saussurian *signified* did not differ from a *general idea* or an *abstract idea*, which had been widely criticized, for two centuries, in the English tradition and called non-thinkable or non-representable.[3] We have also seen Lacan substitute, for this supposed *general idea*, held to be the equivalent of the *signified*, a body of word usages, which was, besides its Benthamian way of conceiving the meaning of words, the Berkeleyean response to the difficulties left behind by Locke in his *Essay Concerning Human Understanding*, in his huge Book III, dealing with language. If Locke is right in his critique of general ideas, and if words have a meaning, it is contradictory to make meaning consist in these general ideas; instead, it is right to speak of it as a cluster of word usages.[4] Meaning does not consist in ideas that replicate our use of things. And Lacan was quite right to refer to *Alciphron* who, in order to show that the meaning of words does not consist in a reference to some transcendent idea, chooses precisely the example of imaginary numbers, which can be written, which can operate, but which cannot be thought. What idea can we have of $\sqrt{-1}$? And yet, how could the algebraist do without it?[5] There is no

---

[2] J. Lacan, *Encore, op. cit.*, seminar of April 10, 1973.

[3] Locke had said of general ideas that they were "contrivances of the mind, which have a lot of difficulty in them and don't offer themselves as easily as we tend to think. For example, it requires some effort and skill to form the general idea of a triangle (though this isn't one of the most abstract, comprehensive, and difficult), for it must be neither oblique nor rectangle, neither equilateral, equicrural, nor scalenon; but all and none of these at once." (*An Essay Concerning Human Understanding* B.IV, chap. VII, S 9.) Berkeley had picked up the idea, drawing from it all the relevant conclusions.

[4] G. Brykman, who tends to refer more to Wittgenstein than Lacan in order to establish this idea of Berkeley's, wrote two masterly books on the subject: her thesis, *Berkeley, philosophie et apologétique* (Paris: Vrin, 1984), and *Berkeley et le voile des mots* (Paris: Vrin, 1993).

[5] "...[S]igns may imply or suggest the relations of things; which relations, habitudes, or proportions, as they cannot be by us understood without the help of signs, so being thereby expressed and confuted they enable us to act with regard to things: that the true end of speech, reason, science, faith, assent, in all its different degrees, is not merely, or principally, or always the imparting or acquiring of ideas, but rather something of an active, operative nature, tending to a conceived good; which may sometimes be obtained, not only although the ideas marked are not offered to the mind, but even although there

correspondence between signs and ideas, not so much because there are two suites that are ignorant of one another, but rather because one of the suites is no more than a fantasized supposition and cannot happen other than by fiction.[6] And Berkeley does not complain about it. In some sense, there is less danger in accepting an entity like $\sqrt{-1}$ than entities like *square* or *circle* or *1*, because in the latter cases it is possible to harbor the illusion that these terms refer to objects that exist independently of my discourse, whereas $\sqrt{-1}$ does not evoke any object, although its position allows problems to be solved, as Berkeley and Leibniz concur. We are able to see that signs do not represent ideas, but that ideas emanate, for better or worse, from signs and their use.[7] We can also see why psychoanalysis is not oriented toward a manipulation of ideas, but rather toward the interplay of signifiers that, it is supposed or suggested perhaps, underlie the former.[8]

But we must go further. While the play of signifiers is relatively independent of what we call *sense*, it is not in the way Saussure

---

should be no possibility of offering or exhibiting any such idea to the mind: for instance the algebraic mark, which denotes the root of a negative square, hath its use in logistic operations although it be impossible to form an idea of any such quantity. And what is true of algebraic signs, is also true of words or language modern algebra being in fact a more short apposite and artificial sort of language, and it being possible to express by words at length though less conveniently, all the steps of an algebraical process." *Alciphron: Or the Minute Philosopher*, Dialogue 7, No. 14., *The Works of George Berkeley, D.D., Bishop of Cloyne*, Volume 2 (London: George Bell and Sons, 1898), 456. The same basic idea is found a few pages earlier in Dialogue 7, No. 12, of *Alciphron*, when Berkeley concludes that, in terms that Lacan has always upheld, "the science of arithmetic in its rise, operations, rules, and theorems, is altogether conversant about the artificial use of signs, names, and characters."

[6] In Dialogue 7, No. 5, omitted in later editions, Euphranor says: "But every time the word man occurs in reading or conversation, I am not conscious that the particular distinct idea of a man is excited in my mind." (Berkeley, *op. cit.*, 437)

[7] Thus the root $\sqrt{-1}$ seems very badly named, from Lacan's point of view, when the value it represents is called *imaginary*, whereas it is clearly more *symbolic* than *imaginary*: "There is nothing less imaginary than $\sqrt{-1}$, as what followed it showed, since that is where the complex number originated, in other words, one of the most useful and fertile things to be created in mathematics." J. Lacan, *...or Worse, op. cit.*, seminar of June 1, 1972.

[8] While explicitly referring to Bentham, although it is apparent how much this thesis owes to Berkeley, Lacan wondered, May 1, 1977, if "psychoanalysis operates, since from time to time it operates, through what is called 'a suggestion effect'? For the suggestion effect to hold, it supposes that language has a hold on what we call man. It isn't for nothing that, in its time, I manifested a certain preference of a certain book of Bentham's that talks about the utility of fictions. Fictions are oriented toward service, ultimately justifying it." J. Lacan, *L'insu qui sait de l'une-bévue s'aile à mourre, op. cit.*

speaks of *the arbitrary nature of the sign*. The link between signifier and signified is unmotivated, according to Saussure. By expanding the meaning of *signifier*, Berkeley could help Lacan free himself of this idea of *arbitrary* by giving it instead the meaning of an autonomy constructive of signifying possibilities,[9] which owe nothing to the objects of experience to which language appears tied. Now, while Lacan endows the signifier with a much wider acceptation, since any psychic element can play the role of *signifier*, the link, for the sake of convenience and keeping in mind all that has just been said, to what is called the *signified*, is not one of arbitrary exteriority. Revising the classification often made of Berkeley's philosophy, as an idealism, in order to castigate it, Lacan is able to give it a perfectly acceptable meaning, and use it to refine his own conception of the relationship of the real, the symbolic, and the imaginary, which, we should remember, functions as an interpretative grid whenever Lacan is working with an author. The relationship of signifiers in Lacan has no more exteriority in its functioning than ideas do in Berkeley, who contests material reality independently of the sensations we have and that we believe, erroneously, derive from its transcendence. The latter, far from qualifying certain matter, derives from language, which makes us believe, if we are not careful, that its own work (which consists in constituting objects) simply derives from things such as they are, through an inverted or specular mechanism, of which we are almost always the dupes. The "contained" nature of the play of signifiers ought not be interpreted as if it were placed alongside what it signifies and as though exterior to it. *Interior* and *exterior* are separated in no way other than in the manner of a Moebius strip, which leaves the question of knowing which

---

[9] In *Alciphron*, which Lacan admits was one of his favorite readings, Euphranor states: "Upon the whole, it seems the proper objects of sight are light and colours, with their several shades and degrees; all which, being infinitely diversified and combined, do form a language wonderfully adapted to suggest and exhibit to us the distances, figures, situations, dimensions, and various qualities of tangible objects: not by similitude, nor yet by inference of necessary connexion, but by the arbitrary imposition of Providence, just as words suggest the things signified by them." To Alciphron, who, taken aback, asks: "How! Do we not, strictly speaking, perceive by sight such things as trees, houses, men, rivers, and the like?" Euphranor answers: "We do, indeed, perceive or apprehend those things by the faculty of sight. But, will it follow from thence that they are the proper and immediate objects of sight, any more than that all those things are the proper and immediate objects of hearing which are signified by the help of words or sounds?" (Berkeley, *op. cit.*, 289)

is the inside and which is the outside undecidable, and participates thereby in a topology infinitely more real than a geometry that dogmatically claims to make this distinction and leads only to abstractions outside the bounds of the real.

An inside and an outside seem to be self-evident, if we consider the organism, namely an individual who is, indeed, really there. The inside is what is in his bag of skin, the outside is everything else. To think that the idea he has of this outside must also be inside the bag of skin seems to be, at first glimpse, quite modest and self-evident.[10] This is precisely the basis for Bishop Berkeley's argument. Of the outside you only know what is in your head. Consequently, whatever may be involved, it will always be an idea. Whatever you say concerning the world, I will always be able to point out that it comes from your idea of it.

And Lacan seems to outline the project of psychoanalyzing this philosophical idea according to which what seems exterior to us cannot be without also being interior,[11] and to which he had just given the most adequate expression:[12] "It is really quite singular that such an image was able to become, at a moment in history, so prevalent, that a discourse was able to rely on it, that could not effectively be refuted, at least in a certain context, that of an idea made to support the concept of idea. It is in the idea that gives such an advantage to ideas that consists, in the end, the secret node of what is called *idealism.*"[13]

It is clear that the real is not what is external to our ideas, beyond them and transcending them; such a reality is, with Berkeley, as with Leibniz as well, strictly imaginary, and can be legitimized as such, but certainly not as regards the real. No doubt the real is a kind of law that weighs on the relationship of the symbolic and the imaginary, but is not exterior to them, as though magnetizing them from

---

[10] Here we find the thinker of the intermediary, of Greek, of mediation, of the hole, the edge, the mucous membranes, that is Lacan.

[11] Thus does the Moebius strip become the fundamental representation of this key idea of Berkeley's philosophy.

[12] We have only to think of what Schopenhauer said concerning Berkeley, that "madman cloistered in his impregnable bunker," to realize the extent of the damage. To be fair, however, we must remember that work has been done in England and France to allow Berkeley to be known in a more useful way than as the voice of an unbearable idealism. It is not impossible that in France this work was impelled by the Lacanian jolt and awakening.

[13] J. Lacan, *D'un Autre à l'autre, op. cit.*, seminar of April 30, 1969.

the other side of an impassable line. Mathematics, too, which can account for its relations without reference to a transcendent exteriority, is not one to distribute its constituent parts *partes extra partes*, but rather to constitute itself in topology or in some *analysis situs*, which does not require the imaginary of a *res extensa*. Mathematics does not "represent" anything of reality; it accounts for things through an internal movement: this is how they are real or express the real. The analyticians of the eighteenth and nineteenth centuries understood this perfectly.

In essence, Bentham provides the key to this process in his theory of fictions and shows how it extends to politics at the same time as the political danger of this false belief which does not dissipate as long as one does not have the key. Indeed, while language leads us into ontological errors, it is necessary to understand how this is possible: nouns (substantives) easily create, although in a completely illusory manner, the substances that are objects, or something that we take to be objects; now, the actual existences are the qualities that we only gather most of the time in the form of adjectives. Adjectives are, in reality, more fundamental than nouns, but we are not usually aware of this and we act as though the illusory discourse of substances were the most fundamental.[14] The political consequences of this process, so ably detected and condemned by Berkeley, then by Bentham, are evident and are pushed to the limit by the latter. For, in the interplay of *adjectival laws*, which define habilitations so that each may make the decisions appropriate to their sphere, and *substantive laws*, which claim to regulate things themselves rather than tasks, it is always a question of knowing how to allocate the sector of validity and which ones have primacy over the others. It is clear that utilitarianism imposed the idea that it was illusory to believe that *substantive laws* are the key to the others, as if the good, supposedly seen, allowed defin-

---

[14] Bentham makes note of this in his *Universal Grammar*, Chapt. V, in Bowring, VIII, p. 347-348: "An adjective is the name of a quality or relation, accompanied with an intimation of existence of a subject in which it is, to which it belongs, of which it is a or the property. *Celer puer*, a boy in whom is the quality of celerity. The corresponding abstraction-denoting substantive, is the name of the quality unaccompanied by any such intimation of such substantive existence. Though the name of the abstract fictitious entity, the quality, be prior in the order of tradition, to the adjective name, it was not probably in the order of existence. *Bonus* existed before *bonitas*- (as its brevity imports), *humanus* before *humanitas*."

ing tasks for each person from the outside. The primacy of utility implies,[15] to the contrary, that it be adjectively defined, in each act and, even more so, in each rule. Utility puts the stress on human activity rather than on the good or goods, as if they existed of themselves in the manner of transcendent objects. This latter point did not escape Lacan's notice, who spotted it in Bentham, as he pointed to the long historical path that led to it:

> The long historical elaboration of the problem of the Good leads in the end to the question of how goods are created, in that they are organized not on the basis of so-called natural and pre-determined needs, but on that of providing the material for a distribution, relative to which the dialectics of the Good are articulated, to the extent it acquires its effective meaning for Man.[16]

This inversion of the stress and this substitution of the object by the act are not without consequence for the psychoanalytic act itself, as we shall see when we analyze Lacan's critiques of other analysts.

For the time being, we should point out that, even though he had drawn from his reading of Berkeley something that helped advance his own thinking, it took a certain courage for Lacan to so openly manifest his admiration for Berkeley, at a time when, in France at least, English studies had not yet acquired the importance they have over the last few decades.[17] It could be that this importance, still fragile, but that no one could contest from the 1980s onwards, owed, directly or indirectly, a part of its growth to Lacan's *Seminar*, as he showed the ways in which a twentieth-century man could take an interest in it without being ridiculous or appearing to be a dilettante. It is even particularly remarkable that Lacan, in the debate over the interpretation

---

[15] Condemned by the texts against the new infinitesimal calculus (respectively in 1734 for *The Analyst* and in 1735 for *The Defence of Free-Thinking in Mathematics*), utility, nevertheless, does seem to be the legitimate substitute for and the essence of meaning in *Alciphron* (1732).

[16] J. Lacan, *Ethics of Psychoanalysis, op. cit.*, seminar of May 11, 1960.

[17] G. Beauvalon translated *Siris* in 1920; the same year, he edited C. Renouvier's translation of *The Principles of Human Knowledge*. In 1925, he translated the *Dialogues Between Hylas and Philonous*, which Lemaire re-translated the following year. Then came Leroy's translations: *The Analyst* in 1936, a selection of works in 1960, and in the years that followed.

of Berkeley, enters through the door of an audacious reassessment of his anti-materialism: after all, the formula *interior-exterior*, which one might imagine a little hastily represents the distinction between the psychic, on the one hand, and the bodily or the physical, on the other, also applies to the organism itself, of which the epidermis cannot be thought to clearly and decisively separate the interior from the exterior. This division is as enigmatic when it is thought to be in the service of conceiving of matter as when it is used to set the duality of body and soul. While the substantialist formulation cannot be used to establish the dualism of body and soul, which is rejected by Berkeley, it cannot either be used for the sole benefit of the psyche, since what we might be tempted to call *matter* gives rise within itself, at the same time, to the same dualism and its impossibility. This interpretation is fascinating enough to free us from the extravagances of idealism by skillfully showing that the problem raised by Berkeley would apply equally to a materialism. Might matter not have an intimate texture no more metaphorical than the interiority of the spirit? And might not spirit have, with no more of a metaphor than matter, an exteriority?

From Berkeley, Lacan was able to draw the best possible correction of the trivial parlor, dressing room, bedroom image used to illustrate the psyche. It is clear that Berkeley's notion of space, the linguistic aspect of the interplay of ideas in his work, dispensed envisaging the unconscious as something hidden or hiding something as *inside* a room. Nothing is interposed in this way and the unconscious is a certain kind of linguistic functioning the modalities of which need to be studied. Was an English writer needed to free the "first" Freudian topic from its weight of realism? It could be, in any case, that Berkeley's philosophy was only possible in the English language, which, we have pointed out, is the most apt to express events without the counterweight of realism ordinarily required by other languages (French and German, principally).

3
CHARLES SANDERS PEIRCE

In the *Seminar*, Peirce is brought up to address points that appear quite disparate when gathered from the last two decades of Lacan's teaching. The author's theses are instrumentalized with the aim, if not of resolving, at least of putting into perspective the solutions to problems faced by Lacan. Given that, since the beginning, the idea of the theory of fictions interests him, it is understandable that he would pay attention to the direction taken by Pierce's commentary and work on logic, which is that of an elaboration of the theory in question, as it was bequeathed by Bentham, with the notorious insufficiency that comes from not knowing whether the fictitious entity is distinguished from the real entity by a subjective intention or a syntax effect. It's obviously on the side of syntax that Lacan tends to place the theory of fictions, since he identifies it with the functioning of what he calls the symbolic, subjectivity having little function other than imaginary.

When an entity is a fiction, what distinguishes it, in its behavior, from a real entity? As the question has, over the last few decades, greatly advanced in the field of literary theory, regarding the status of literary texts and the statements that constitute them, I would like to take my examples and references from this field in order to highlight the difficulties. I can, reading Joyce's *Ulysses*, ask myself the question of Leopold Bloom's hair color. Leopold Bloom is a fictional character, he has hair, which must have a color, which one? Suppose I say *Leopold Bloom has greying hair*, and that Joyce does not mention this, what is the status of this phrase? Is it true? false? probable? probable within the limits of the descriptive traits delivered or suggested by Joyce? But, since the character Bloom is already an invention, what can be the status of an inference concerning him if the author did not plan to address it?

We should understand that it certainly isn't by opposing *literature*, as a phenomenon of language, to the *real*, thought to be directly experienced, that the *fictional* can be opposed to the *real*. What we call the *real* is, as much as the *fictional*, connected to an act of language, as Berkeley began to show in the most decisive way;[1] similarly, on condition of giving language a wide acceptation, which is to say by transforming into signifiers ideas that allow reference, at least in appearance, to transcendent objects, the greatest part of what we call the *real* is tied to the act of recalling the *past*[2] or to an act of anticipation, which could not be felt in the same way as the present; in one case it no longer leads to the same feel that we had in the present, it doesn't yet lead to it in the other. And we must not seek the slightest evidence that would allow us to verify the identity of the object projected into the past or the future with what it was or what it will be when it is present; such verification is impossible because any criterion that we might use to guarantee the real could not perform this function, neither in the direction of the past nor in the direction of the future. Language envelops and structures what we call the *real* in the same way as what we call *literature*; it could even be that what we call *literature*, bearing down more directly on the capital constituted by words—their organization into clauses, sentences, and texts—gives yet more immediate access, and in a more decanted manner, to the frameworks of the real, since, unconcerned with the real, literature pays no attention to a kind of limitation imposed by sensation and, more generally, by sensibility, which an interest in the real seems to take more into account. Literature fabricates and calculates, via language, deliberately, its sense effects or, if one prefers, its *imaginary* effects, which the *Vorstellungsrepräsentanzen* normally only calculate unconsciously. What the real usually leaves to the artisanal efforts of the divine, through the infinite multiplicity of the possibilities able to lead to a world the reality of which we seem to perceive, literature places in the hands of an author who, by mastering the scales of language, seems to direct what the reader is given to feel. But, if it isn't through the existence of words, clauses, sentences, and texts that literature is distinguished from the real, is it through a particular organization of its elements that the distinction is made possible?

The logic systems addressing this point, over the last few years, have tried to make progress in the research. And it is—whether their

---

[1] *An Essay Toward a New Theory of Vision* (Dublin: Aaron Rhames, 1709), §46.

[2] Bergson shows this excellently in "Essai sur les données immédiates de la conscience," *Oeuvres* (Paris: PUF, 1970), 86.

authors admit to it or not, whether they are even aware of it or not—in Pierce's vein that they were constructed. This is especially clear when, nowadays, John Woods seeks the logic of fictions in the area of three-valued logic.[3] It is, in any case, in this area that Lacan valued reading Peirce in order to refine his own doctrine of the real-symbolic-imaginary structure: "Charles Sanders Peirce built his own logic, and the fact that he stressed relations led him to create a three-part logic. I follow the very same path, with the difference that I call the things involved by their name—symbolic, imaginary, and real, in the right order."[4] The expression "in the right order" risks being somewhat enigmatic for those who are not familiar with Peirce's philosophy: we shall see, through the interplay of orders, that the third term relates the second to the first.[5] Ten years earlier, January 12, 1966, he already saw the need for a three-valued logic, recognizing quite fairly that the logicians knew what they were doing: "A statement is true or false. There are good reasons to presume that this way of handling things is completely inadequate, as, it must be said, modern logicians realized, hence their attempt to establish a multivalent logic." And he picked up on the theme again, January 11, 1977, still associating Pierce's name to his quest for a three part logic: "Peirce was really struck by the fact that language does not, strictly speaking, express relation; and that really is something striking: that language does not allow for a notation like x having a certain type—and not another—of relation to y makes it indispensable that we acquire a three-part logic."

The propositions that use fictions, like those that are used in novels, for example, are neither true nor false like those that are supposed to express reality. What system of relations must be established in order to give meaning and value to these propositions (or to reject them)? What has to be taken into account in the relations to be able to distinguish a statement that contains fictions from one that does not, a fictional statement from one that purports to be real? Is it enough to invoke an author's intention to make such distinctions? It is immediately apparent that this invocation is impossible because one cannot gain access to something like an author's substantial reality, much less

---

[3] J. Woods, *The Logic of Fictions: A Philosophical Sounding of Deviant Logic* (Paris: Mouton, 1974).

[4] J. Lacan, *Sinthome, op. cit.*, seminar of March 16, 1976.

[5] We shall explain this point at the end of the chapter.

his or her intentions. Going forward, we need to turn our attention to what the text itself puts into relation. And it is this difficult path—language does not spontaneously express every type of relation—that seems the surest; for fiction is not what follows the same logic as the real, the only difference being that the speaker or writer makes it up in one case and refers to the real in the other. Fictional texts do not function the same way as texts that express the real.

It can be shown quite easily in two ways. The *first*, by highlighting a paradox in Peirce's logic that did not escape Lacan. In the June 11, 1974, lesson, for example, Lacan wonders about the possibility of recording, in a logic of relations, differences like those that distinguish the passive voice from the active. Oddly, where this point is concerned, the discourse of fiction does not function the same way "real" discourse does. Woods subtly demonstrates this by showing that the very syntax of the literary text often registers the difference between the "real" and the "fictional." Conan Doyle was able to write, with a reasonable degree of confidence that the reader would find it plausible, *Sherlock Holmes had tea with Gladstone*. On the other hand, it would be more difficult for him to make the reader accept, knowing that Gladstone was one of the most famous political leaders in English history, at the very time Conan Doyle situates his narrative, the proposition *Gladstone had tea with Sherlock Holmes*, a proposition that, nevertheless, seems analytically equivalent to the preceding one. Isn't *to have tea with someone* a completely reciprocal relation? In reality, Woods points out that it isn't at all and that, while this shared tea can easily fit the biography of Sherlock Holmes, it is more difficult to accept as an element of Gladstone's biography. It is possible to insert a sequence from Gladstone's life in Sherlock Holmes' life, but much less easily the reverse. It is as though fiction were able to bear and, to a certain extent, suppose the incursion of little pieces of reality, whereas a real biography would be radically polluted and distorted by certain types of fictional elements, even if they are small in number.

Certainly, for fiction to exist as such and to really play its role as fiction, it has to be able to express itself factually, exactly as though the propositions it uses to present itself related a fact, or facts. If I read *Sherlock Holmes lives in London, on Baker street*, I am caught up in the snare of fictional discourse, which is not the case if I read *Arthur Conan Doyle had his Sherlock Holmes character live in London, on Baker street*. This second sentence installs me in the real, or at least installs the first one in fiction, by making it so the reader is not installed in the fiction, but grasps the sentence from a point of view that tells the truth about the fictional world, from which he is distinct, and from which he is expected to be distinguished. For the text to have its effect as fiction, its author must exclude from his propositions the notions of *author, character, insertion of a character in a world*; he must not openly and manifestly install an order that relativizes the laws of the first sentence by making them dependent, through a kind of redirection. This pulling apart can be expressed as follows: the world in which *what* I say, or *what* I write, or *what* I read is true is not the world in which my act of speech, writing, or reading is true. The act of speech, reading, or writing must fade away or be put in parentheses to let only their object exist, only their choke point or reversal, as if the object itself were conveyed through the discourse. What is true in one world is not what is true of another world.[6] If weaving yarns is the art of producing fictions, their products are not true in the same world as the weaving itself.[7] The telling installs its boundary between two worlds; it can take the side of one world by fading, a world it loses as soon as it reveals itself as storytelling. But, despite all these complications, it is apparent that the syntax of a fictional world is far from being entirely superimposable onto that of a world the reality of which author and reader have no doubt.

If the allusion to Peirce allowed us to develop an aspect of the theory of fictions, it is because, without reference to Bentham, it is true, Peirce distinguishes a *firstness*, a *secondness*, a *thirdness* that are not without reminding us of the organizations of the orders of fiction

---

[6] J. Woods, *op. cit.*, 108.

[7] In his previously cited article, "Truth in Fiction," David Lewis expressed this point as a formal proposition: "A sentence of the form 'In the fiction f, Φ' is true iff <if and only if> Φ is true at every world where f is told as known fact rather than fiction." Later, Lewis provides a more refined formulation of this first law when he transforms it into a tensioning of worlds in which the plausible triumphs. This is the same order of logic as the one that led Hume to say that certain miracles are plausible: we can accept some very improbable exceptions to natural laws if it were even more improbable that we were lied to by those reporting them. Indeed, David Lewis arrives at a statement of this kind: "A sentence of the form 'f, Φ' is non-vacuously true iff, whenever w is one of the collective belief worlds of the community of origin of f, then some world where f is told as known fact and Φ is true differs less from the world w, on balance, than does any world where f is told as known fact and Φ is true. It is vacuously true iff there are no possible worlds, where f is told as known fact."

derived from the orders of real entities and the need to go through a higher order of fictions to found an order of fiction of lesser degree.[8]

But there is a second path that could have been connected to the *Tyche*, a concept so central to Lacan's thinking, especially in *Seminar XI*. Lacan missed the connection. Peirce is invoked later, when the *Tyche* (τύχη) is no longer involved, but when the need for a trivalent logic continues to be felt. Trivalent logic allowed Peirce, in conformity with his pragmatism, to confer a status to probability that was not merely "subjective" and to endow chance with a certain reality. Laws are not what exist; and when there is some stability in the universe, it is what is problematic and must be explained as the result of a provisional evolution from a primordial chaos.[9] Only chance exists, and it does not only exist because of a subject who does not know how to interpret the real, a real thought to keep within itself what the subject does not know or does not yet know; it is the real itself that is a game of chances.[10] A logic needed to be created that allowed giving meaning and value to a discourse confirming the fact that no one knows whether a battle will take place tomorrow, without being content to

---

[8] Wishing to illustrate his talk in the third of the eight lectures given by Peirce at Cambridge in 1898, the author uses an example that Bentham could have used to illustrate his theory of fictions: "The people born in the last census-year may be considered as a sample of Americans. That *these* objects should be Americans has no reason except that that was the condition of my taking them into consideration. There is Firstness. Now the Census tells me that about half those people were males. And that this was a necessary result is almost guaranteed by the number of persons included in the sample. There, then, I assume to be Secondness. Hence we infer the *reason* to be that there is some virtue, or occult regularity, operating to make one half of all American births male. There is Thirdness. Thus, Firstness and Secondness following have risen to Thirdness." "Lecture Three: The Logic of Relatives," *Reasoning and the Logic of Things*, ed. K.L. Ketner (Cambridge, MA: Harvard UP, 1992), 148–9. Or rather: "Thirdness is the mode of being of that which is such as it is, in bringing a second and third into relation to each other." Letter to Lady Welby of October 12, 1904, *Semiotics and Significs: The Correspondence Between Charles S. Peirce and Victoria Lady Welby* (Elsah, IL: The Press of Arishe Associates, 2001), 24.

[9] "To suppose universal laws of nature capable of being apprehended by the mind and yet having no reason for their special forms, but standing inexplicable and irrational, is hardly a justifiable position. Uniformities are precisely the sort of facts that need to be accounted for." *The Essential Peirce: Selected Philosophical Writings Volume I 1867–1893*, ed. N. Houser and C. Kloesel (Bloomington, IN: Indiana UP, 1992), 288.

[10] "The party... of which I am a member, holds that uniformities are never absolutely exact, so that the variety of the universe is forever increasing." *Collected Papers of Charles Sanders Peirce Volume VI: Scientific Metaphysics*, ed. C. Hartshorne and P. Weiss (Cambridge, MA: Harvard UP, 1935), 69.

attribute this ignorance to a subject stricken with cognitive incapacity and impotence. Just as, in the theory of errors, the subject does not need to take entire responsibility for the fact that measurements, of the same "object" with the same instruments, always differ: they don't differ in such a way that there is one that is hidden or not yet discovered to be the right one; they differ inherently, as experience itself shows, without the subject needing to bear alone the responsibility or the accusation, as though having to be repentant. Approximation is not a repentance; it is the very being of things.[11] It is unfortunate that Lacan did not relate this aspect of Peirce's logic to what might be called his own "*Tychism*." With Peirce, as with Lacan, the *Tyche* is not a curse of which the real must be cleansed and found innocent, in such a way that the subject, who takes on every ill, needs to bear it like a cross. Peirce could have said, with Lacan, that: "What Aristotle calls the *Tyche* is for us the encounter with the real."[12] The *Tyche* is that real which brings about, without our wanting it and in an encounter that is always bungled, a being able to choose.[13] Nonetheless, in these echoing formulations that seem to unite Peirce and Lacan, we must be aware that, while Lacan clearly states that "no roll of the dice in the signifier will ever abolish chance," it's "for the reason that no chance exists outside of language, and under whatever aspect it is conceived, of automatism and encounter."[14]

Here again, about this use of Peirce that seems to focus on trivalent logic systems, one might ask what to make of the fact that they

---

[11] "The absolute exactitude of the geometrical axioms is exploded; and the corresponding belief in the metaphysical axioms, considering the dependence of metaphysics on geometry, must surely follow it to the tomb of extinct creeds. The first to go must be the proposition that every event in the universe is precisely determined by causes according to inviolable law. We have no reason to think that this is absolutely exact. Experience shows that it is so to a wonderful degree of approximation, and that is all. This degree of approximation will be a value for future scientific investigation to determine; but we have no more reason to think that the error of the ordinary statement is precisely zero, than any one of an infinity of values in that neighborhood. The odds are infinity to one that it is not zero; and we are bound to think of it as a quantity of which zero is only one possible value." *The Essential Peirce: Selected Philosophical Writings Volume I 1867–1893, op. cit.*, 273–4.

[12] J. Lacan, *The Seminar of Jacques Lacan Book XI: The Four Fundamental Concepts of Psychoanalysis*, ed. J.-A. Miller, trans. A. Sheridan (New York: Norton, 1981), seminar of February 5, 1964.

[13] *Ibid.*, seminar of February 26, 1964.

[14] J. Lacan, "La métaphore du sujet," *Écrits, op. cit.*, 892.

were discovered in English, even though, once discovered, they had no difficulty entering other languages. We are left to consider hypotheses here that are based on the following fact: it was the domain of probability that first opened up the possibility of intermediary values between the true and the false; the probable is not a mode of being that can be sanctioned by the true and the false in the same way as other propositions, to the extent that the reasons to believe that an event, or a sequence of events, have a chance of happening may not be affected by truth or falsehood, though the facts appear to support them or challenge them. There is a way of measuring probability that eludes the truth or falsity of things, or events, understood as a conformity or non-conformity; things and events can be measured on the basis of the action anticipated to be performed on them in order to change them. What is measured, then, is the probability of their changing as a consequence of this action; they are only discussed because they are the target of the action. One does not evaluate the chances of being right when believing something the way one evaluates the things themselves. These points, which have been known since the Greeks addressed them—Diodor Kronos' paradox, in this instance—can be generalized by the notion of *fiction*, which, as we have seen, required a three-value logic. The link to the English language, besides the fact that Peirce was Anglophone, is that the study of probability that yielded a trivalent logic comes from a conception of *chance* or of *the probability of being right*, which saw the light of day under Bayes.[15] Bayes wrote his *Essay Towards Solving a Problem in the Doctrine of Chances* in English and would probably not have been able to conceive it in another language, even though, once written, it was able to be formulated—not without difficulty—in other languages, in particular French, according to what might be called "Hume's law."[16]

---

[15] Peirce is not Baysian, however; but he does adhere to the "frequentist" conception (according to which probability is a frequency). He, nonetheless, does not fail to oppose it to the logical, if not psychological, conception (today, we would speak of subjective probability), which he does not misconstrue. See Charles Sanders Peirce, *Reasoning and the Logic of Things*, ed. K.L. Ketner (Cambridge, MA: Harvard UP, 1992), 61–67.

[16] See this work note 6 page 40.

4

BERTRAND RUSSELL AND PROPER NAMES

Before considering the question of proper names, to which Lacan paid particular attention, we need to consider the several positions, inspired by Russell, the author of the *Seminar* took regarding the philosophy of language.

More than anything else, for Lacan, Russell is the one who came up with the idea, envied by Lacan, according to which "mathematical discourse has no meaning" and is such that "one never knows [what one is talking about] or whether what one is saying is true."[1] In a certain sense, where meaning is concerned, Lacan feels that Berkeley had said the same thing in *Alciphron*: there is no need to conceive of what signs mean—this would be mostly impossible anyway—to make them function rigorously. But it may be as regards *truth* that Russell moves away from the classic version; Berkeley had specifically reproached the mathematicians of his time (Newtonians and Leibnizians) for giving short shrift to the truth in favor of utility.[2] This was not without injustice where it concerned Leibniz, who had hierarchized the truths without neglecting to point out that while the "symbolic truths" were of a higher order than Descartes' obvious truths, they were themselves outstripped by the intuitive truths, the logical principles of which Leibniz outlined in his *Meditations on Knowledge, Truth, and Ideas*; but, fair or unfair, such was Berkeley's reading, and this requirement for truth, confused with knowledge, obviously discredited him in Lacan's eyes. Indeed, about Russell, Lacan would later say:

---

[1] J. Lacan, *D'un Autre à l'autre, op. cit.*, seminar of January 8, 1969. In his article, *Recent Work on the Principles of Mathematics*, which he had published in *The International Monthly* (July 1901), Russell wrote that "mathematics may be defined as the subject in which we never know what we are talking about, nor whether what we are saying is true." *The Collective Papers of Bertrand Russell Volume III: Toward the Principles of Mathematics 1900–1902* (New York: Routledge, 1993), 366.

[2] Not without, however, contradicting the gist of his thinking.

If you read at any point in his writings Mr. Bertrand Russell, who, moreover, took care to state it plainly, mathematics specifically deals with statements about which it is impossible to say whether they have a truth, or even whether they signify anything at all. It's all a rather pointed way of saying that the care he took to specifically promote the rigor of the shaping of mathematical deduction is something that, certainly, addresses something other than truth, but in a fashion that is not after all unrelated to the truth, otherwise there would not have been the need to keep it at a distance in such a forceful manner![3]

He says essentially the same thing when, a few months later, he returns to the front where, it seems to him, he is making common cause with Russell:

He is after all the one who expressed something like this, that mathematics is something that is articulated in such a way that you don't even know whether it's true or whether it has a meaning. That doesn't stop it from proving specifically this: that you can't give it just any one, neither in the register of truth nor in the register of meaning, and that it resists to the extent that, to reach that result which I consider a success, the way it establishes that it's real, it's precisely that neither meaning nor truth are dominant, they are secondary, and that there, the position, this secondary positon these two things called *truth* and *meaning* have, different from what they are used to, makes people's head spin somewhat when they go to the trouble of thinking.

It may have been through reading Russell that Lacan dared to separate, to the extent he did, the construction of knowledge from the notion of truth.

On this point, it is clear that he is close to Russell, as long, however, as the intrusion of the real is not stressed, Lacan being alone in considering it at the root of the bifurcation of truth and meaning. He seems to be just as admiring of the event-based (as opposed to substance-based) conception developed by Russell in the empirical sciences. The atom is not a substance, but a series of events. The physicist does not need to presuppose things: the representations that correspond to them—sensations and their memory—suffice to con-

---

[3] J. Lacan, *. . .or Worse, op. cit.*, seminar of December 2, 1971.

stitute physics. Physics does without useless inferences by adopting Berkeleyan positions:

> A way out of this reference to being is attempted, Russell's way out, that of the event, which is something else altogether than the object. The wager is Russell's, whose only event-based reference, to whit that of space-time overlapping, is something we can call an encounter, and henceforth, the true shall be defined as the probability of a certain event, the false as the probability of an impossible event.[4]

Such a position is not simply in agreement with Berkeley, whose immaterialism is well known, and is tied to his critique of substance, a critique that should have, had he been consequent or entirely free of any apologetic considerations, led him to Hume's positions, which condemn with equal vigor the substantiality of the mind and that of material objects. The critique of substance is relatively easy to formulate in the English language, of which the constructions allow an easy passage from verbs to their nominal or adjectival forms, making the treatment of events effortless, whereas a language that grants too much space to substantives, like French, most of the time gets caught up in this kind of passage.[5] In any case, Lacan, who devotes consider-

---

[4] J. Lacan, *Le Séminaire livre XIII: L'objet de la psychanalyse*, unpublished seminar, seminar of January 12, 1966. It is not incidentally that Lacan quotes Peirce in *The Sinthome*. While the word *Sinthome*, in Lacan, condenses a certain number of notions into a single word that he forges in an original way (symptôme [symptom], saint homme [holy man], ceint homme [belted or contained man], etc.), the word implies a process of invention with which Peirce was familiar. In his classification of signs (in *Collected Papers Volume 8*, 334), Peirce distinguishes the *qualisign* (when a sign is of the nature of an appearance) and the *legisign* (when the sign is of the nature of a general type) from the *sinsign* (when it refers to an individual object or event). It is at least curious that, seeking to disqualify the English language in its capacity to express the unconscious, Lacan has recourse specifically to linguistic processes quite similar to those of the great American author, with whose work he was well acquainted. We will go so far as to suggest that the famous *lalangue*, which we have pointed out was not the result of a slip of the tongue on Lacan's part, as it has sometimes been said, may owe something of its form to Peirce.

[5] We have shown elsewhere, in a contribution entitled *Réflexions sur la critique de Kant des paralogismes du point de vue d'une théorie des fictions* (Montréal, 2017), to what extent the English language, as a vehicle for the formulation of thought, greatly defused the dialectical illusions condemned by critical philosophy, to which fall prey much more easily other European languages, such as German (the language of *The Critique of Pure Reason*) and French (a language which may be particularly targeted by the procedures and results of the *Critique's* dialectic part.)

able space in his work to the *encounter (rencontre)* and *tyche (τύχη),* could only acquiesce to the thesis he detects in Russell.[6] Has he read *The Analysis of Matter,* where the primacy Russell grants to events over things is particularly salient? The play on words *l'âme à tiers* (homonym of *la matière!*) that he creates January 11, 1977, justifying Peirce's ternary logic, could not have been more pertinent in accounting for the probabilistic conception of the real encountered there.

This point is much more important than it seems, and it has been judiciously highlighted by P. Kaufmann in his book on *Kurt Lewin,* the first pages of which stress that there isn't a great distance between the methods of psychoanalysis and those of microphysics; for instance, that this distance may be less than with certain methods used by the so-called social sciences (which custom opposes to the natural sciences).

There is nevertheless a point on which Lacan parts company with Russell ; it is the one he finds in *Meaning and Truth,* the very day he recommends it to his audience, now able to consult it in French. No more than he accepts in any domain an absolute primary situation supposedly behind all other situations—be they perceptual, conceptual, or affective—does Lacan accept a supposed language object from which increasingly complex linguistic structures are elaborated, each higher level existing in a metalinguistic relationship with the previous, less complicated, more elementary levels. There is no original experience, since "experience can only be situated from another discourse",[7] but neither is there a first language:

> Mr. Bertrand Russell conceives of language as a superposition, a scaffolding of an indeterminate number of successive metalanguages. Each propositional level being subordinated to the control, to the reprise of the proposition in a superior sequencing, where it is, as first proposition, called into question. I'm being extremely schematic of course about that which you can see illustrated in the work itself.[8]

---

[6] But also in Peirce, who speaks of *tychism.*

[7] J. Lacan, "Lituraterre," *Autres écrits, op. cit.,* 14.

[8] J. Lacan, *Le Séminaire livre XII: Problèmes cruciaux pour la psychanalyse,* unpublished seminar, seminar of December 9, 1964.

Lacan could have learned from reading Peirce that no representation is first; it is only ever the representation of a representation, even at the most basic level. F. Recanati, in his contribution to Lacan's June 21, 1972, *Seminar*, highlights this point through diagrams that seem to come directly from Husserl's *Lessons* on the *Phenomenology of Internal Time-Consciousness*; but, whereas Husserl showed how, from a current perception, a bank of memories is gradually built up, immediate at first, then increasingly mediated, according to a degradation of *Abschattungen*, Peirce, for whom the object can only ever be reached through its *representamen*, holds that:

A *Sign*, or *Representamen*, is a First which stands in such genuine triadic relation to a Second, called its *Object*, as to be capable of determining a Third, called its *Interpretant*, to assume the same triadic relation to its Object in which it stands itself to the same Object. The triadic relation is *genuine*, that is its three members are bound together by it in a way that does not consist in any complexes of dyadic relations. That is the reason the Interpretant, or Third, cannot stand in a mere dyadic relation to the Object, but must stand in such a relation to it as the Representamen itself does. Nor can the triadic relation in which the Third stands be merely similar to that in which the First stands, for this would make the relation of the Third to the First a degenerate[9] Secondness merely. The Third must indeed stand in such a relation, and thus must be capable of determining a Third of its own, but besides that, it must have a second triadic relation in which the Representamen, or rather the relation thereof to its Object, shall be its own (the Third's) Object, and must be capable of determining a Third to this relation. All this must be equally true of the Third's Thirds and so on endlessly....[10]

---

[9] Through this word, a trace of the *Abschattungen* problematic is visible.

[10] Charles Sanders Peirce, *Collected Works Volume II: Elements of Logic* (Cambridge, MA: Harvard UP, 1932), 156. F. Recanati cites this text, without identifying the source, in his "Intervention au Séminaire du Dr. Lacan," *Scilicet* 4: 63. On page 69, he adds, still citing Peirce, but identifying his source on this occasion: "[But] an endless series of representations, each representing the one behind it, may be conceived to have an absolute object at its limit. The meaning of a representation can be nothing but a representation. In fact, it is nothing but the representation itself conceived as stripped of irrelevant clothing. But this clothing never can be completely stripped off; it is only changed for something more diaphanous. So there is an infinite regression here." (*Collected Papers of Charles Sanders Peirce*, ed. by C. Hartshorne & P. Weiss, vol. I, *Principles of Philosophy*, Harvard University Press, Cambridge, 1931, p. 171). "Finally, the interpretant is nothing but another representant to which the torch of truth is handed along; and as representation, it has its inter-

And, after this description, quite skillfully, Lacan considers his thesis apagogically demonstrated, according to which there is no metalanguage. Indeed, the metalinguistic disposition of language as envisaged by Russell supposes something like a language-object that cannot be found anywhere. It must be admitted that a researcher in the theory of fictions would be tempted by this scaffolding, apparently quite close to what is found in Bentham when he distinguishes, from the play of real entities, those of the fictional entities of the first order, of the second order, of the umpteenth order. Now, it is precisely a Russellian reading that could be applied to the theory of fictions that is rejected by Lacan, since he does not accept the absolute beginning supposed by the language-object's ground or floor:

> In order to compose his language made of the scaffolding, of the babel-like edifice of meta-languages one atop the other, Mr. Bertrand Russell [has to suppose] a base, so he invented the language-object. There must be a level, which unfortunately no one is able to grasp, where language is, within itself, pure object. I dare you, in advance, to find a single conjunction of signifiers that can have this function.[11]

At the same time, a relativistic reading of the theory of fictions is implicitly advocated here: real entities are not such absolutely, but only relative to the discourse they convey; in any other discourse, they could be considered fictional entities. That there is no language-object is not without consequences for psychology.

The opposition to Russell is also concentrated on the question of proper names, of which the dialectic is doubly interesting to Lacan: as evidence in his research concerning the name of the father and as a point of resistance to Saussure's positions (who had neglected the question of proper names on principle). The January 13, 1965, lesson stresses the importance of the question which requires a range of ca-

---

pretant again. Lo, another infinite series" (*idem.*). On many occasions, Lacan stresses that "the signifier represents the subject for another signifier" (J. Lacan, *Le Séminaire livre IX: L'identification*, unpublished seminar, seminar of March 21, 1962; J. Lacan, *Anxiety, op. cit.*, seminar of December 12, 1962; J. Lacan, *D'un Autre à l'autre, op. cit.*, seminar of November 13, 1968...).

   [11] J. Lacan, *Problèmes cruciaux, op.cit.* The same argument is developed at the end of the January 13, 1965 session.

pabilities: "About proper names, not only linguists, but also logicians, if not—let's say the word, which is not unmerited in Bertrand Russell's case, *thinkers*—hesitate, slip up, or make a mistake when they face the question of identification, regarding the privileged usage thought to be that of the proper name as designating the best way to indicate the location of the particular as such." As early as *Seminar IX*, December 20, 1961, Lacan had spotted this thesis through which Russell loses his way as far as Lacan is concerned: "Russell defines the proper name, as follows, it's *a word for particular* [T.N.: in English]. A word to designate particular things as such." Now, adds Lacan, "in any description, there are two ways of proceeding." *Either*, it consists of "describing them in terms of their quality, their coordinates, their location, from the mathematician's point of view, if I want to designate them thus. This point, for example, let's say that here, I can tell you: it's to the right of the canvas, at about this height, it's white, and this and that. That's a description, Mr. Russell tells us. It's the ways there are of designating as particular in any description, that's what I'm going to call *proper names*." The proper name is what results from increasingly tight, precise determination, which only designates a being able to be shown or that it was possible to show before this task of determination. Unfortunately, it is possible to say *this* or *that* or *these* or *those* about many things: Russell's analysis is off to a bad start in this area.

    Or, it's the second alternative, the point is named, it is baptized: "It is no less paradoxical that Mr. Russell coldly contemplates the possibility of calling this same point: *John*." Here, Lacan begins to worry: "We need to acknowledge that there is the sign of something maybe going on here that is beyond our experience, because the fact is that it is rare for a geometric point to be called *John*." It is true that this is unconventional, but whether a point is called *John*, *M*, *N*, *O*, or Ω makes no difference. This is where Lacan turns to the linguist, by invoking Gardiner's critique, already well underway, of Russell, who famously came up with another example: "Here is where the linguist becomes alarmed, all the more since, between the two extremes of Russell's definition *word for particular*, there is this entirely paradoxical consequence that, consistent with his own logic, Russell tells us that we have no right to consider *Socrates* a proper name, given that, for a long time, Socrates has not been an individual... as such, he is no longer what Russell calls a word to designate the particular in its particularity."[12]

Socrates has not been a proper name for a long time. There exist, of this proper name, multiple functions other than that of designating a particular individual, since it is possible to use it to designate the typical Greek philosopher, the philosopher who has not written, the philosopher who resists political power, the individual with the syllogisms that conclude he is mortal, etc. But isn't it possible to say as much about any proper name? Are proper names distinguished by the extreme singularity Russell ascribes to them? In all proper names, sometimes directly—as in the name *Smith*—but more often indirectly, and phonetically, common nouns emerge from proper names. Thus, concluding his February 10, 1976, lesson, Lacan plays with his own name to fracture it, before reconstituting it like those Japanese magicians Rousseau mentions, who reassembled, by throwing them into the air, the parts of a body they had just dismembered: "Well," he tells his audience, "you must have some of your claque, and even your *ja-claque*, since, as well, I will add the *han* [T.N.: *phew*], which is the expression of the relief I feel at having completed this journey today. That's how I reduce my proper name to the most common noun."[13] Now that's a lesson signed by an author who vulgarizes or communizes his name!

If we think proper names are sheltered from the dilution common nouns experience, we are mistaken, because when we discover or possess a proper name, we think—even unconsciously—of the anagram or the entwining of the common nouns that comprise it. The resistance of the proper name to its usages in the propositions it enters into is not an exclusive property of this name, but it fulfills at most a function with which it is partially identified for better or worse. The proper name is so not alone in this function that it resists in the same way as certain unfamiliar common nouns borrowed from another language. It is indeed to produce this resistance effect that we use *acting out*, or *talking cure*, or *chimney sweeping* [T.N.: in English in the original]. It would not be less pertinent to say *passage à l'acte, soins par la parole*, or *ramonage*. The words of one's own language irresistibly

---

[12] J. Lacan, *L'identification, op. cit.*, seminar of December 20, 1961.
[13] J. Lacan, *Sinthome, op. cit.*, seminar of February 10, 1976.

submit to an erosion that soon renders them unrecognizable. Pascal already noted, in a different context, that unfamiliarity with and hostility towards an utterance better preserved its meanings, and certainly its signifiers, than sympathy or too great a familiarity, which always end up diluting what, through love, they wish to conserve.[14] What we just said shows that Russell bungled his distinction, which could only be saved by a paltry psychological recourse to intention, that of targeting a singular (or an individual). All the more since, as Lacan points out in *Seminar XII*, we can make proper names plural and speak of the Durands and the Duponts, to signify in some context a class of people, Russells, say, to allude to logicians or logicians of a certain type, or allow all kinds of meanings or allusions that aren't in any way singular. It is also possible to make verbs or adjectives with names, like caricaturists know how to inscribe the face of a politician into the mold of another man, of some other thing, or of some animal.[15]

Shall we go farther with John Stuart Mill, who, in his *A System of Logic*, distinguished the *connotation* from the *denotation* of words? *Denotation* signifies the reference the word appears to make to the

---

[14] Pascal shows, in the fragments of the *Pensées*, that hatred and incomprehension better conserve signifiers and signifieds than sympathy or comprehension, which abandon any belief to dilution. "This people [T.N.: the Jewish people] disappointed by the poor and ignominious coming of the Messiah, became his cruelest enemies, with the result that of all people in the world they can least be suspected of favour toward us, and are the most scrupulous and zealous observers imaginable of the law and the prophets, which they maintain incorrupt. Thus it is that those who rejected and crucified Christ, who was for them a cause of scandal, are the same who hand down the books which bear witness to him and say he will be rejected and a cause of scandal. Thus they showed he was the Messiah by refusing him, and he was proved as much by the righteous Jews who accepted him as by the unrighteous who rejected him, since both were foretold." B. Pascal, *Pensées*, trans. A.J. Krailsheimer (London: Penguin Classics, 1995), 176. Book III of the *Seminar* says, somewhat awkwardly—but the idea is no less remarkable—that "the more it doesn't signify anything [meaning, the less it signifies], the more the signifier is indestructible." It is through the signifier that the sign is preserved; it is through its signified that it breaks up. And so it becomes clear that it is through "this portion of nonsense that is strictly speaking the unconscious" that language and the play of signifiers are preserved. Lacan says in structural terms the same thing Pascal said in affective terms (about hatred and sympathy). Lacan is not content to observe the conservation of signifiers, through the transmitters, thanks to their incomprehensibility; he also adopts the audience's point of view: "The less we understand, the better we listen," he says.

[15] Can't it be said that, toward the end of a term, some president had become Chiraced, Lepened or Mitterandized? Daumier, in his time, had turned Louis-Philippe into a pear.

object or the signified, whereas *connotation* signifies the multiple ways in which words refer to each other, giving language a kind of autonomy relative to the contingent incidents of the empirical milieu in which it bathes. Thus the proper name implies, according to him, a privilege of denotation over connotation, in that it has no meaning.[16] Gardiner departs from Mill's thesis because he recognizes that proper names have a meaning, even Durand has one: "In its use the stress is put not on the meaning, but on the sound, as distinctive."[17] Now, asks Lacan, "is it so true that each time we say a proper name, we are psychologically made aware of this stress being put on the sound as such? It is absolutely not true. I no more think of the sound, Sir Allan Gardiner, when I am talking to you about it, than when I am talking about *verwurzeln* or about anything else."[18]

What changes in a proper name relative to *verwurzeln* when it is communicated in the French language so that it does not diffuse its meaning and seems to gather it within stationary limits, by remaining a German word:

> is that, despite the appearance of small oscillations (here *Köln* is called *Cologne*), the proper name is preserved in its structure, its sound structure no doubt, but this structure is distinguished by the fact that, exactly, this one among all others, we have to respect it and this, by reason of, exactly, the affinity of the proper name with the mark, the direct designation of the signifier as object, and here we are again, apparently brutally stumbling across the *word for particular*.

The proper name resists the change of language; it is even for this reason that common nouns coming from other languages are turned into proper nouns. Thus, just as there is a movement to communize proper nouns, there exists the inverse movement to make a common noun proper in order to give it consistency. The proper and the common, far from being intrinsic properties of certain words, are decidedly functions that do not coincide with the play of individualization and universalization, nor with the play of connotation and denotation. This dialectical work has convinced us: but does Lacanian

---

[16] J. Lacan, *Problèmes cruciaux, op. cit.*, seminar of January 6, 1965.
[17] J. Lacan, *L'identification, op. cit.*, seminar of December 20, 1961.
[18] *Ibid.*

psychoanalysis allow us to go further? "This is where a function is inserted, which is that of the subject, not the subject in the psychological sense, but the subject in the structural sense."[19] The proper name is a function tied to the subject's division, to its impossibility of coinciding with itself, which means that it breaks up into diverse, empirical and transcendental roles, person, author, actor, and several other functions. The proper name masks; it exists only by giving to be or to do something: "The particular is named by a proper name, it is in this sense that he is irreplaceable, which is to say that he can be missing, that he suggests the level of the lack, the level of the hole. Is it as an individual that I am called Jacques Lacan or rather as something that can be lacking? Following which, this name will go toward what? Covering another lack." This is where we find the function of the subject, not as substance but as signifier for another signifier, in a diplomatic representation, as he puts it in *Seminar XII*.[20] Lacan specifies: "The proper noun having a floating function, so to speak, the way it is said that there is a part of the personnel, of language's personnel in this case, that is floating"; this may be when we best understand that Lacan is very close to the Hobbesian themes of *author* and *person*, but he unfortunately wasn't aware of them or he inopportunely neglected them. The proper name is the *ego* (as function) considered, if you wish, to be *you, or he/she*; it is the collective of a considerable number of functions that do not follow the *I* mode but perform more or less the same tasks, seen from different perspectives. The formulation then comes closer to the dangerously phenomenological one of *Being and Nothingness*: the proper name "is made to go fill holes, to give them its obturation, to give them its closure, to give them a false appearance of suture."[21] The name is what remains, more or less provisionally, after death, or simply when we are failing and can no longer fill that in whose place it abides. It suspends above the void. Has Lacan gone so far beyond, on this question at least, a Sartrean concept, that of the full and the empty? We may suspect as much. Only, this dialectic

---

[19] *Ibid.*

[20] Seminar of May 5, 1965. The idea is frequently expressed in similar terms, before the lessons in *L'identification* (December 6, 1961) and *Anxiety* (December 12, 1962), and after this lesson.

[21] *Ibid.*

takes on a more logical cast in Lacan's discourse, where it is nourished by all the diversity found in topology.

Once again, one might wonder what is specifically Anglophone in this kind of research? It is clear that only English authors were consulted for this investigation that Saussure had bypassed as not belonging to his purview or his field. Lacan's attachment to this kind of question is a way of staking out his difference concerning linguistics—at least Saussurian linguistics—as we shall see more clearly in our second part by developing other arguments.

5

SPORADIC, APPROPRIATE, OR INCONGRUOUS REFERENCES
TO SEVERAL PHILOSOPHERS

If we want to be thorough, which isn't very difficult, given the relatively modest number of English or Anglophone philosophers cited by Lacan, we should add to those whom we have just analyzed the rather singular manner our author has of approaching three disparate names—Hintikka, Hogarth, and Thomas More—both because of the different eras in which they became known and the different areas of thought they investigated.

JAAKKO HINTIKKA

Hintikka was the subject of a sustained discussion on February 19, 1974, for having written *Models for Modalities* and *Time and Necessity*. The first work is gratuitously attacked; the second allows Lacan to recognize, somewhat pointlessly, that Hintikka had preceded him in his research on Aristotle's *Organon*. Lacan would have been better off to point out, to the philosophers of his time, that he had addressed a grievance Hintikka perhaps best resolved, or at least began to settle. To overcome their sloth, Lacan had suggested they construct a substitute for transcendental aesthetics, given that the intuitive nature of space and time, affirmed against Leibniz by Kant in this part of *The Critique of Pure Reason*, had become untenable given the developments in mathematics and logic since the nineteenth century. Space and time, or better, spaces and times, are susceptible of logical treatments as relations of very diverse types and dimensions. The famous paradox of symmetrical objects purported to prove the intuitive nature of space and time turned out to be quickly susceptible of a logical treatment. But he had gone further and had proposed, in the same fashion as Hintikka, although apparently both of them were unaware of their similar positions, that the space and time of game theory, of which the formal as well as logical aspects were apparent to both, could advantageously replace the famous "*a priori* forms of sensibility."[1] Without prejudging their results, it is obviously regrettable that these views did not face each other and were not conjugated.

We will soon encounter *The Critique of Pure Reason* again, this time in its "dialectical" part; this is where the confrontation of the English and German, English and French languages, is most instructive. Let's say in the meantime that the transcendental dialectic, which targets the illusion of objectification, could not be as pertinent in English, for example, as in German, and perhaps even more so than in French, the structure of which feeds into the transcendental illusion.

WILLIAM HOGARTH

Hogarth brings up an entirely different issue, this time focused on an important detail connected to his theory of beauty, which Lacan relates to his own conception of writing. We know that Lacan increasingly turned to mathematical expression in order to model the structuring of psychic elements or events. The search for signifiers that constitute a kind of writing would give rise to a particularly resistant engraving. This was, at least, the goal of any of Lacan's lessons. In *Seminar XIX*, during the March 8, 1972, lesson, reflecting on the barred S through which he symbolized the split subject, irremediably fated to being cut away from himself, he allows himself an impression and a suggestion; he finds this S to have "like all writing, a quite lovely form," adding: "whether the S is what Hogarth considers the line of beauty, it isn't completely by chance, it must have a meaning somewhere, and that it is necessary to bar it, surely has one as well."[2] The remark is cryptic and suggests that there exists an essential complicity between beauty and writing, that beauty is never evanescent, since it is inscribed, but also that what is graven, graphed, is always lovely (T.N.: *ravissant*), meaning that it holds one's attention and doesn't let go. What is striking, in the work, is always that it inscribed something that makes us feel that if we weren't seeing it inscribed, now, we would

---

[1] We have made this point and the difficulties of such a position in "'Il faut réécrire L'Esthétique transcendantale': Deux interprétations de Kant par Lacan et Hintikka." in *Kant, les lumières et nous,* A. Labib and J. Ferarri, ed. Maison Arabe du livre. (UR Lumières et modernité, ISSH de Tunis, Société des études kantiennes de langue française.), 2009, 367–389.

[2] J. Lacan, ...*or Worse, op. cit.*, seminar of March 8, 1972.

have thought it impossible for it to ever be thus manifested. That writing is able to bring into existence, to generate something that is neither the copy nor the reflection of anything else inspires admiration.

The play of sinuosity and the ever straight bar, even if it presents obliquely, becomes clearer four years later when Lacan is further involved in his research concerning the topology of knots. The interplay of the bar and the S, when the supple part coils around a rigid part, is nearly the principle of every knot that is not a simple relationship to the rope itself but that aims to grip and secure something: "This is how a knot is written. It already yields an S." He traces a sinuosity enveloping an oblique bar. He immediately points out that any letter, any written element, in its very simplicity, always involves an interlacing. Almost always, the letter doubles back on itself from where it leaves. Its itinerary is that of a takeoff and a sinuous encirclement on returning; to verify this, it is instructive to see what happens at the elementary level of the written letters of the alphabet of the languages that have one. Many letters turn around an axis. Nothing can be set to awaken the mind, if not simply to constitute it, that does not proceed from this back and forth. The holes need to be toured, a path followed on an embankment or an overpass, in order to hold a meaning's imaginary; and when they don't have any holes, the segmented nature of the letters is the equivalent of a back and forth itinerary. It's probably this little excursion of each letter that makes it apt, if it is tied to other letters that do the same thing, to hold onto meaning. To the scales that Pascal used to represent any action of language, we should substitute this activity involving segments, curves that dive underneath and return above, and holes, already present in each elementary letter. The letter is basically a knot. Calligraphy is not all that distant from the art and science of knots. Lacan showed it from the outset with the famous *Purloined Letter*, which never wanders too long without finding its destination; henceforth, he considers the question in detail, in its fractalization. One could add that everything that signifies makes the same gesture; this applies to mathematical figures as well as to the written laws of physics; the odyssey is the figure of signs. Is it by chance that Galileo figured the apparently disparate law of gravity and equivalence of motion by using the example of a ship crossing the Mediterranean, as though making a distant allusion to Ulysses? If not, why bother to specify the location? Any discourse is an odyssey because any graph fundamentally is one as well. The voyage itself is a cipher of letters and numbers because it carries within itself the idea of a return. No one will be surprised that it is in his book on the author of *Ulysses* that Lacan tightens the knots left a little loose in *Seminar XIX*: that the knot is written like an S, "that is something that does have a close relationship with the agency of the letter such as I promote it. And it also gives beauty a credible body. Hogarth, who had often reflected on the question of beauty, thought that it always had something to do with this double inflection." Without allowing that Hogarth's idea was "true," and even while judging it harshly, Lacan nonetheless recognizes the legitimacy of an aesthetic theory that finds beauty in the relationship of the symbol to itself and that finds its reality therein, rather than in some relationship with the subject who enjoys it or derives pleasure from it, or in some referral or link to the real: "But, after all, this [Hogarth's idea, even if materially false] tends to link beauty to something other than the obscene, which is to say the real. Writing alone is beautiful. Why not?"[3] It is not to the extent that it copies anything—which, for instance, might be beautiful—or that it submits to any rule other than the one it establishes itself[4] that a sign is beautiful, but inasmuch as it moves forward and returns on its own, and only through this does it seem to retain something real. The value of the reference to Hogarth and of this reading of Hogarth is that it frees us from the trap of affect, as though, from a Kantian perspective, the beautiful consisted only of feelings, whereas it is necessary, in order to find it, to go to the writing that underlies it. Short of arriving at the destination, Hogarth at least begins to show the way. We can now see that it is not only the transcendental aesthetic that needs to be rewritten, but also the *Critique of Judgment* in his "Analytic of the Beautiful" and it is indeed, each time, by turning to English philosophy that these changes can be brought about. Against Kant, who, if one doesn't mind the analogy, asserted that it isn't because the knot is a knot that it is beautiful, we should affirm that, to the contrary, it is because beauty has close ties

---

[3] J. Lacan, *Sinthome, op. cit.*, seminar of January 20, 1976.

[4] Lacan, who read *Being and Nothingness*, the grandeur of which he knows to recognize, certainly does not use the adjective *obscene* without having in mind Sartre's remarkable analysis of it. A body becomes obscene when it submits to laws other than its own. Sagging flesh (*chair*), subject to gravity rather than to its own muscles or innervation, is obscene. Thus, submitting to a reality that is not its own, for the sign, is obscene.

to the knot that it [T.N.: beauty] is beautiful. Lacan, at least, does not reject this idea: "Why not?"

THOMAS MORE

A quite lengthy Thomas More development occurs in *Seminar XVI*. The author is used, allusively and not surprisingly, as the inventor of the term *Utopia*; as such, for Lacan, his function is comparable to Plato's in *The Republic*. It is therefore quite obvious that Lacan is not apprehending things at a very detailed level. The context is that of a discussion on freedom of thought. Lacan denies a freedom of the Sartrean kind. Nevertheless, Lacan recognizes two things that limit his negation of freedom. *First*, desire relates to norms which it is possible to obey, sometimes without realizing it, but also, as a consequence, that it is possible to transgress. This room to maneuver regarding the norm means that we speak of *freedom*; the norm imposes an authority, it does not exercise a power that leaves no latitude. However, it remains to be known who is free, and relative to what is free agency. *Then*, if there exist norms that regulate or claim to regulate desire, if it is possible to transgress them, it is also possible to change them to a certain extent; in these two ways, the idea of *freedom* can acquire a meaning:

> On the objective side, the idea of *freedom* does have a core around which it emerges, and which is the function or, more exactly, the notion of *norm*. From the moment this notion comes into play, the correlative one of *exception*, if not *transgression*, is introduced. In a word, it is through thinking up utopia, which, as its name denotes, is a nowhere place, a *no place*;[5] it is from utopia that thought is free to contemplate a possible reform of the norm. This is how it has gone in the history of thought from Plato to Thomas Morus. Relative to the norm, to the real place where it lives, it is only in the domain of utopia that freedom of thought may be exercised. Indeed, this is what results from around the works of the latter among those I just mentioned, namely the creator of the term *utopia*, Thomas Morus, as well as going back to the one who consecrated the term *norm* under the function of the Idea, Plato, who also builds you a

---

[5] This resembles J. Wilkins' *nulliquity* or *nullibiety*.

utopian society, the Republic, where freedom of thought is expressed in the face of the political norm of that time.[6]

Here, we are not very far from Bentham, who does not make much of *freedom*, but who recognizes that the notions of *exception* and *transgression* only give it meaning and gravity when it becomes possible to replace existing laws with laws that, resulting from calculations, allow the calculation of utility. Furthermore, it is interesting that, in conformity with the word *utopia*, Lacan outlines the kind of space in which this freedom emerges and develops. Utopia raises the question of a space that envelops the real and operational space of the city; since Desargues, Pascal, and Leibniz, mathematicians know how to envelop a space with another that has other properties than the preceding one. Freedom does not consist in not having any norm; rather, it is another use of norms or it treats norms differently. We don't know much more than that about the way the real is inscribed in utopia, or the reverse.

---

[6] J. Lacan, *D'un Autre à l'autre, op. cit.*, seminar of April 23, 1969.

6
CONCLUSION

While it is lacking in numerous areas that could have been of use to him—after all, it wasn't Lacan's job to learn and teach classic English philosophy—his knowledge of the authors (I mean those he uses) is astute and perfectly pertinent. It is not impossible that the *Seminar* participated in a rediscovery of English philosophy, the neglect of which was obvious, outside the works of Bergson, who was quite aware of it and took it seriously (even though he tended to reject its claims), and a few sporadic translations—those of André-Louis Leroy, in particular—and some rare studies like those of M. Guéroult on Berkeley. In any case, the ideas developed in the *Seminar* could only seed and make reading Hobbes, Locke, and Hume plausible, despite the absence in Lacan of any direct allusion to them, and, even more so, fertilize the authors he cites, and, to a certain extent, rehabilitate them—this is the case with Bentham, whose utilitarianism one "knew," magically, how to refute without having read a single line of it, before he was buried anew, for the second or third time, under the weight of the odious and untenable Panopticon.[1] It may be that, as he said upon Merleau-Ponty's death, quoting him: "If creations amount to something, it is not only that, like all things, they pass, it is also because they have almost their entire lives in front of them."[2] This horizon does not occur on its own; there need to be other works sturdily built in the present in order to impose it. The *Seminar* had this function for what Lacan himself called "English philosophy," which was also, which is, and which will continue to be, like "German philosophy," although in another way and with other goals, a Francophone's fantasy.

---

[1] About which a quick reading got, from Foucault, everything one needed to read and know of Bentham. I should add that Foucault himself went farther in his interpretation of Bentham than a quick reading would reveal.

[2] J. Lacan, "Maurice Merleau-Ponty," *Autres écrits, op. cit.*, 184.

"German philosophy," such as it was known by the educated French reader of the third quarter of the twentieth century, when it amounts to a few pages or a few works, mainly from two authors, Kant and Hegel,[3] could not have helped him much to grasp the theory of language he needed, nor to produce it. Kantian transcendental dialectics hardly claims to be a critique of language,[4] even though it is one and can only be applied very unequally to a rationality expressed in one language rather than in another. The interest that Kant has in languages and in their specific ways of saying does not extend to the theorization he applied to many other areas. The *Critique of Pure Reason* obviously suffers from the absence of a critique of language. And how can one uniformly critique languages that, like French, through their too great separation of verb and noun, are sensitive to transcendence, in other words, to objects outside themselves, and languages that, like English, can erase the division between noun and verb, easily transforming a verb into a noun, without losing their capacity to express movement, and, as a result, making their speakers less vulnerable to the transcendental illusion of forming realities that are beyond words? As for Hegel, who placed language among the highest achievements of thought, while he inspired the counterintuitive link between language and the death-drive,[5] since designating is in some sense killing the thing, he did not allow going as far as the innumerable variation found during the same period in Bentham, and even earlier in Locke and Berkeley.

It remains to be seen whether we have progressed in answering the double question, made up of distinct but linked elements, that we said would guide our investigation. While we see how a language that grants the analysand many functional and factual facilities may allow diluting and eroding all the obstacles encountered in other languages, and through this masking its presence to the analysand and the analyst himself, we do not see why the extreme ductility of English, since English is concerned, would present any difficulty for the analyst in his

---

[3] Leibniz, Fichte, and Schelling were more or less ignored by Lacan.

[4] Even though the *Anthropology* seems to suggest several paths in this direction. (Part 1, Sect. 39).

[5] Stressing the act of dividing, that is, the strength and the work of the intellect, Hegel writes, in the preface to *The Phenomenology of Mind*, that "life carries death and maintains itself in the very death that is the life of the mind."

task of theorization. We should probably distinguish three different levels of the question: is the English language an obstacle for a speaker who wishes to become an analysand? Is it an obstacle to analysis? Is it an obstacle to the theorization of analysis? While the answer to the first two questions remains unclear, it is less so for the last, if one is to believe the fruitful attempts to use certain philosophies to benefit analytical theory. If, on the triple front of the theory of fictions, the theory of language understood in broader terms than usual, and the need for ternary logic, Lacan was led towards philosophies expressed in English—which at least had the ability to express themselves in English—on what basis did he complain that English did not allow for the expression of psychoanalysis? Does the fact that that there are bad translations of Freud, bad translations of Lacan, allow indicting an entire language, to the extent it is even possible to assign such an identity? Why not, rather than talking about the incapacity of a language to express the unconscious, more modestly target the quality of the translations? Can we accept that Lacan's 1975 assessment of "difficulties (ordinarily experienced) when translating him into English [T.N.: *lalangue anglaise*]" remains generally true today now that we possess English versions of the *Écrits* and several volumes of the *Seminar* that are far from unsatisfactory, even if the *scholar* [T.N.: English in the original] experiences some difficulty reading them? After all, when Lacan's texts first appeared in French, didn't French academics find it difficult to absorb them? And wouldn't many Francophone intellectuals have agreed with Angus Fletcher's emotional critique after Lacan had finished his February 1966 Baltimore lecture?

Should we believe—each language only accompanying conceptualization over small segments, and not necessarily the same ones—that English would not accomplish this task as well as German or French, a little the way any metaphor does, any concept name, and help the concept over a shorter or longer trajectory, but harm it everywhere else? Thought about in this way, the preceding question of the resistance of a language to the expression of the unconscious is less awkward and depends on a balance between the advantages and disadvantages it presents for the psychoanalytic project.

Finally, there is another difficulty. The use of the philosophies according to the axes Lacan follows, or that we have followed ourselves in the course of the preceding study, always leads to contradictions, even if Lacan's choice of authors masks these conflicting discourses:

the intuitive versus the symbolic; the affective versus the linguistic; the subjective (the intentional) versus the syntactical. Philosophy by itself seems incapable of settling these antinomies, which it knows how to identify and develop, but which it can neither resolve nor go beyond, without arbitrarily choosing one side over the other. Lacan was able to take advantage of its ability to shed light on small sectors, without being able to extract from it evidence of what psychoanalysis—such as he conceives of it—asserts. Can he go further with these questions? Will it be by invoking *experience*, the kind of *experience* that is psychoanalysis', "our experience"? Will it be with arguments based on the findings of other sciences? But on these latter points, philosophy is, now, strong enough to show that it would be a waste of time; experience only proves what the activity in which we are engaging has it prove and cannot, therefore, without subterfuge, be turned into an ultimate recourse; moreover, the privilege granted a science that would give us the meaning of all the other sciences would not be convincing without giving its reasons, and these could only be given in philosophical terms. If it is for sociological reasons that sociology gives itself primacy, it is not convincing; but if it is for other reasons, it grants then that another kind of knowledge, a reflexive knowledge, establishes it, and again we encounter the difficulties we thought we had resolved.

II
SEVERAL ELEMENTS OF LOGIC AND LINGUISTICS

This particularly brief section can be seen as an appendix to the preceding one, since it deals with the philosophy of language and the philosophy of logic. We have seen how much Lacan's attitude instrumentalized philosophies, excerpting the authors' theses according to the needs of the moment, and cultivating them for themselves and in the abstract, without the least concern for the balance and the articulation of their doctrine. He is even more apt to use Boole, Whitehead, Lévi-Strauss, Chomsky, and Jakobson to provide tools susceptible of favoring his own work. At least that is his displayed ambition, because overall his discourse here remains allusive, frayed, and disappointing.

The thesis according to which *the unconscious is structured like a language*, even though it stresses the *like*, could not fail to particularly call upon linguistics and theories of language. We already caught a substantial glimpse of it in the preceding section with the philosophers we cited. But we also saw that Lacan seemed particularly anxious to distinguish his research from that of linguistics; when he speaks of his *linguisterie*, it is not out of the modesty of a researcher who feels incompetent to talk about a science that progressed considerably during the second half of the twentieth century; it is really in order to distinguish himself from it. One wonders whether, although he would make little mention of it, like many researchers during this period, Lacan wasn't sensitive to the Husserlian warning to those who labor in the social sciences: they should be careful to avoid thinking that their specialty is the foundation of every other—sociology being for the sociologist, psychology for the psychologist, history for the historian, the key, the foundation, and the measure of all the other sciences. We know that Husserl attacked what he deemed to be a prejudice he castigated as sociologism, psychologism, and historicism, respectively. Might Lacan, wanting to rectify the philosophers' error, have sacrificed to what might be called *linguisticism*, a term that would allow faulting the structuralism with which Lacan found himself in palinode.

7
CLAUDE LÉVI-STRAUSS

Claude Lévi-Strauss[1] is likely the author associated with structuralism who has been the most rigorous in the use of mathematics adapted to his aims and who, even though he did not limit himself to tinkering, showed a great deal of caution in this regard. Desanti had good reasons to take an often rash structuralism to task for gaudy displays of scientificity:

> I wonder whether 'structuralism' really existed, or whether it was no more than an ideological fantasy in the heads of those I will gladly call the "circulators".... In its ideological usage, broadcast for a time to the public (what student, in the early sixties, didn't feel obligated to talk about "structure," under threat of unworthiness?), the concept was defined in the vaguest terms, exported, universalized, and weaponized against the philosophies of the subject and the philosophies of history, and everyone (or so it was thought) was forced to choose sides. You were either backward, still attached to archaic ideas (the "*subject as project*" was obviously one of them) or else you were avant-garde, on the side of science in the making, and you had to talk about "system," "model," "synchrony," "structure." This was how a body of theses of justification, exclusion, and closure was constituted. These only retained a distant relationship with the precise (and up to a certain point necessary) procedures that had led linguists and ethnologists to use the concept of *structure*.

For this ideological practice of the notion of structure, Desanti intended to substitute "a serious practice of structural analysis."[2] Almost all the "structuralists," whether Foucault or Lacan himself, dis-

---

[1] One may be surprised to find Claude Lévi-Strauss considered an Anglophone author, when he wrote most of his works in French. We treat him as such in light of a text he wrote in English in *The Journal of American Folklore*, in October–December 1955, and to which Lacan refers explicitly.

[2] J.T. Desanti, *Le philosophe et les pouvoirs* (Paris: Calman-Lévy, 1976), 119–120.

tanced themselves—sometimes too slowly—from what had become a rallying cry rather than a collection of sufficiently determined theses.

It is less a question of indebtedness than affinity, where Lévi-Strauss is concerned, in the treatment of myths on the part of both the ethnologist and the psychoanalyst. It is in the April 10, 1957, lesson (*The Object Relation Seminar*) that this "meeting of methods" that Lacan expresses in his own concepts is most visible:

> If we follow what is for us a golden rule, and which rests on our notion of symbolic activity, the signifying elements first have to be defined for their articulation with the other signifying elements; and it is in this that the parallel with the recent theory of myth such as it established itself in a manner singularly analogous to that which a simple understanding of the facts also forces us to articulate some things the way, for the moment, I am articulating them.

And Lacan refers us to the October–December 1955 article Lévi-Strauss wrote in the *Journal of American Folklore*. Lacan summarizes the method in these terms: "The first step in the structural analysis of myth is to never consider any of the signifying elements independently of the others that emerge and in a certain sense reveal it; but I mean to reveal it and develop it through a series of oppositions that are first and foremost combinational." The structural method is meant to make a clean break with the projective and empathetic interpretations that use myths as lures to grant intelligence a cheap and consequently bogus unity and universality. Lacan is particularly focused on Lévi-Strauss' statement against emotional participation: "We cannot be satisfied with vague emotions." During this period, Lacan used equally harsh words for those in psychoanalysis who claim to be able to stop at affects, as he wants to erase affectivity from the lexicon of analysis. Maybe a bit prematurely moreover since, while in general the *senti-ment* [T.N.: feelings lie], it turns out nevertheless that certain affects do not lie, in particular those that constitute anxiety; this exception incidentally perhaps being a problem in the Lacanian conception of analysis.

One of the features that Lacan retains in particular from his reference to structuralism resides, as might be expected, in the critique of the subject, who is not the support of the play of signifiers, but rather its product: "The play of the signifier takes hold of the subject and carries him well beyond anything he can intellectualize about it."³ The subject is a certain illusion of the signifier, and, if he believes himself to be autonomous, the reality of this autonomy is found in the laws belonging to the play of signifiers. It would nevertheless be a mistake to view this outcome as strictly philosophical, even ideological, although it also contains this element, since, as we shall have an ample opportunity to see in Part IV, Lacan, seeking purchase for an effective action, will try to determine, under the subject's imaginary, the tougher aspects of the symbolic. A weapon against the philosophies and the psychologies of the subject, it also allows justifying real practices. The real question involves knowing whether Lacan had, to use Desanti's language, a "serious practice" of the notion of *structure*, akin to the one the author of *Le philosophe et les pouvoirs* salutes in the text of Lévi-Strauss' *Structural Anthropology*. What distinguishes Lacan's adherence to structuralism from the adoption of a philosophical thesis constituting one of the two sides of an antinomy, in an antithetic such as that of Kantian transcendental dialectics? Is there, in Lacan, work equivalent to Lévi-Strauss' that allows us to say that he is as distant from a philosophical attitude as the great anthropologist is?

To answer these two questions, Lacan does not avoid here, whatever he may have said, a somewhat ideological philosophy, since, as we shall see, while the repeated formula "The unconscious is structured like a language" sometimes stresses the "like," the stress is displaced from time to time, dangerously, onto "language," which he imprudently understands to mean "tongue," the way we speak of French, English, or German *languages* as opposed to language in general. This is doubly or triply risky, because structure conceived of this way now loses its function of valid fiction that constitutes the whole of Lévi-Strauss' explicative value, the whole of his usefulness. Next, it renders the mathemes useless, which become no more than private formulas for mathematical uses only. Finally, as we shall see, it locks the unconscious into dependency on a single language, which is very strange. Moreover, the structuring is no longer based on the limits of the languages that translate the myths, but it embeds each myth or each unconscious production, in a very reifying way, into the supposed sub-

---

³ J. Lacan, *The Seminar of Jacques Lacan Book IV: The Object Relation*, ed. J.-A. Miller, trans. A. Price (Medford, MA: Polity, 2021), seminar of April 10, 1957.

stance of each language, which misses the entire point of the notion of structure. Lévi-Strauss' methodological elegance consists of building structures based on what appears given in kinships, myths, and finally the body of mores, and then to turn over this induction into a deeper, more real foundation for what appears to be experienced or lived. One might say, with more evidence in favor of Lévi-Strauss than Lacan, that "mathematics are the real," even though Lacan is the one who said it.

The paradox here is that the least philosophical of the two is doing the most philosophy; and it is the philosophy *agrégé* who is doing the most mathematics. Lévi-Strauss spoke of this criss-cross with Lacan, the latter starting from the human sciences to go toward philosophy, the former starting from philosophy to go toward the human sciences; going toward each other for a certain time, it was to be expected that from a certain meeting point, they would move away from one another, through the kind of stellar friendship Nietzsche talks about. But, like Foucault, Lévi-Strauss always kept his philosophical advance over Lacan and realized more quickly than him the dangers of certain positions, like too narrowly tying the unconscious to the fate of a particular language, which deprives the notion of structure of its creative dimension. Despite agreement on a formula that Lévi-Strauss also uses, Lacan gets stuck in problems that neither Lévi-Strauss nor Foucault encounter. And yet, as we have begun to show, Lacan's efforts in the area of logic and linguistics were unstinting.

Meanwhile, our focus on English authors will lead us toward Lacan's use of Whitehead and Boole. But first we need to see what Lacan has to say about two linguists who worked in English, Jakobson and Chomsky, who particularly inspired him.

8

ROMAN JAKOBSON AND NOAM CHOMSKY

Lacan's use of Chomsky is essentially ideological; Lacan attacked one of his theses upon his return from a trip to the United States, where he had the opportunity to hear him in person. It must be said that Chomsky lends himself to all the Lacanian critiques. Because for him "language is itself an organ."[1] "This idea stems from the consideration of something that presents as a body, conceived of as endowed with organs. This conception entails the organ being a tool, a grasping or apprehending tool, and there is no objection in principle to the tool apprehending itself as such. This is how language, among other things, is considered by Chomsky as determined genetically."[2]

In a certain sense, Lacan could consider himself "palmed" by Chomsky's thesis; despite profound differences both end up with almost the same result, since, deeper even than biological structuring, structuring through language remains extremely imperative and truly determining for our passions and emotions; affectivity no more escapes Lacan's linguistic structuring than it does Chomsky's deeper genetic structuring. With the result that can almost be called shared, that their theses concerning language—which belong to the same *batch*—are radically opposed to one another. Declaring his adversary's thesis "irrefutable," to the fullness of Chomsky's language-organ, Lacan opposes the emptiness that is language; according to him: "To my mind, unless the truth principle is admitted that language is linked to something hole-making in the real, it is not only difficult, it is impossible to consider its use. The method of observation could not be based on language without the latter appearing as hole-making in what can be situated as real. It is from this function of hole that language establishes its hold on the real."[3] However, as irrefutable as he

---

[1] J. Lacan, *Sinthome, op. cit.*, seminar of December 9, 1975.
[2] *Ibid.*
[3] *Ibid.*

finds Chomsky's thesis, he still outlines the principle of an objection, since he maintains, but without finding the argument decisive, that "it seems [to him] quite striking that, from this language it is possible to return to itself as organ."[4] In other words, the reflexive relationship that language can have with itself is hardly compatible with the conception of language as a full being. Doesn't the relationship to oneself constitute a split that is difficult to conceive of as a fullness? However, Lacan is sufficiently aware of topology to consider it not impossible for volumes to turn inside out, like the sphere or the torus, which, when inside out, the interior of which cannot be distinguished from the exterior: a situation as characteristic of language as of the body (and of its organs); hence, probably, Lacan's lack of triumphalism at the conclusion of his attempted "refutation" as well as the awareness of his imperfection.

Jakobson, whom we already know was cited by Lacan as the one who had revealed to him little known aspects of Bentham, was, for the psychoanalyst, both a precious friend and, even though Jakobson presented himself as Lacan's "disciple," a great help in giving a more precise meaning to the notion of *structure* and to "find at every moment [T.N.: the wherewithal?] to structure one's experience."[5] In a chapter of his book *Language in Literature*, called "Poetry of Grammar and Grammar of Poetry," Jakobson brings out the key point of the theory of fictions: that fiction is an extremely resistant effect of structure, of syntax, and not some subjective interpretation. And it is not by chance that in a study of poetry, in a poetics, Jakobson invokes above all others an author who had said that poetry was of no greater account in his eyes than the game of pushpin:[6] the poetic effect is an effect that belongs to language, to the structuring of language, and only by this action of language, to subjectivity; but, contrary to the common prejudice, emotion and affectivity must not be the starting point for dealing with the poetic. Commenting on the famous characteristic granted by Bentham to fictions: owing their existence, their impossible but indispensable existence, to language, Jakobson writes: "Linguistic fictions

---

[4] *Ibid.*: "...faire retour sur lui-même...."

[5] J. Lacan, "L'instance de la lettre," *Écrits, op. cit.*, 506: "trouver à tout instant à structurer son experience."

[6] Here, Bentham reprises Malherbe's statement, changing only the game: "a poet is no more useful to the state than a good bowler."

should neither be mistaken for realities nor ascribed to the creative fancy of linguists; they owe their existence actually to language alone and particularly to the grammatical form of the discourse in Bentham's terms."[7] Thus, it is through the theory of fictions that Jakobson establishes that "poetry is the most formal manifestation of language," creating itself its own subjects rather than being their product, and by immediately drawing the conclusion that "the fictions of poetry are entirely lacking insincerity."[8]

If we are invoking Jakobson here, it is not because—although he was a Russian intellectual—he writes in English and on decisive points cites English authors, but because he says something essential about the relationship between psychoanalysis and linguistics, and because he says certain things that may directly shed light on our investigation regarding English. Our task is made all the easier by the fact that Jakobson attended the seminar of February 1, 1967, invited by Lacan, and that he answered several questions that day with exceptional brilliance. The immense import of Jakobson's comments have to do with how, through linguistics, he frees the questions we have confronted from being bogged down in contradictions and that, if he still uses philosophy, it is to make his theses far more operational. Thus, on the question of fiction, he shows with extraordinary clarity how, starting in early childhood, discourse starts "fictioning" and the decisive importance this "fictioning" can have in psychic constitution. Jakobson distinguishes two functions of fiction: that of creating the subjective splintering necessary to role playing, leading to the indefinite variation of roles which makes the myriad subjective appropriations belong as much to the one obliged to enact them as to the other;[9] secondly, that of the modulation of predicates: as soon as the child knows how to say "the cat runs," that "he eats," that "he sleeps," he can say with the same facility, radically freeing language from its moorings, that "the cat barks," invoking a certain unlimited aspect of fiction that obviously has something to do with poetics.

---

[7] R. Jakobson, *Language in Literature*, ed. Krystyna Pomorska and Stephen Rudy (Cambridge, MA: Harvard UP, 1987), 123.

[8] Which is the literal opposite of what Lévi-Strauss said about myths, that they are always inauthentic.

[9] He goes so far as to envision a therapeutic function to learning the use of personal pronouns.

The connections that Jakobson and Lacan never ceased making stem from the concepts' possibilities, produced by each on his own terrain, to act on the other and to combine, without however there being a mixture of the two, which led Lacan to call his own work *linguisterie*,[10] to distinguish it from the linguist's. Once again, let us not be misled by Lacan's apparent modesty: *linguisterie* requires psychoanalysis; moreover "there is no other linguistics beside what I call *linguisterie*."[11] The best example of this "collaboration," constantly revisited and refined by Lacan in his own domain, like an event happening in the register of what he, Lacan, calls the signifier, is the distinction drawn by Jakobson in the field of language, between metaphor and metonymy.[12] But there are others: in *Seminar XII*, for instance, Lacan is interested in *distinctive features*, in the "distinctive features and specifically in the *a* which differs from other vowels, like the compact from the diffuse, other distinctive features being at work on this occasion."[13]

However, for what concerns us, the key question is deeper. Let us begin with an anecdote told by Jakobson to the seminar attendees that is a good way to begin our inquiry. If I am an Anglophone, I can say I spent last night "with a neighbor"; and if my interlocutor asks whether this neighbor is a man or a woman, I can put him off by telling him to mind his own business; a Francophone doesn't have the same options because, if he tells me the same thing, he has to tell me if he has a male neighbor (*voisin*) or a female neighbor (*voisine*), which is unnecessary in English. It is clear that the grammar of our languages creates situations which cannot exist the same way in both. For in the same way as that described by Jakobson, English speaks of a *she-goat*

---

[10] J. Lacan, *Encore, op. cit.*, seminar of December 19, 1972. "*Linguisterie*," which is a word forged by Lacan, is a compound of the "famillionaire" type: it condenses the word "*linguistique*" with "*fumisterie*," which, in French, refers to an activity of little value that barely masks amateuriism, if not complete incompetence.

[11] J. Lacan, *L'insu qui sait de l'une bévue s'aile à mourre, op. cit.*, seminar of March 15, 1977.

[12] Lacan says it in *The Seminar of Jacques Lacan Book V: The Formations of the Unconscious*, ed. J.-A. Miller, trans. R. Grigg (Medford, MA: Polity, 2017), seminar of November 13, 1957: these functions are "tied to something that is expressed very simply in the register of the signifier, the characteristics of the signifier being those... of an articulated chain tending to form firm groupings, that is to say of a series of rings attached to each other to form chains, themselves attached to other chains like rings."

[13] J. Lacan, *Problèmes cruciaux, op. cit.*, seminar of April 28, 1965.

to mean *chèvre*. "Well, adds Lacan, let's call *l'homme*, as is appropriate, a *he-man*,"[14] woman becoming, according to the same logic, a *she-man*, an expression which, retranslated, will yield *hommelle*. But it doesn't stop there, and it becomes apparent that languages are not inert entities, that they react to one another and that they do so around the edges.[15] Jakobson cites the example of Bulgarian, which, under the influence of Turkish, had to change its very syntax. He also speaks of languages that can accommodate other languages—like Russian can be peppered with French expressions—without giving the impression of using another language and without the speaker experiencing the slightest discomfort,[16] whereas he would be not be able to bear, without feeling ridiculous or comical, German making an appearance in his language: either one speaks Russian, or German, but not a mixture of both at the same time. I am obviously getting to my point, about which Jakobson does not say anything directly, but which we cannot fail to bring up: English, as we noted in Rousseau's wake, is a language that is learned twice, written and spoken of course, but also—perhaps more fundamentally—because it interweaves Latin and Saxon, it is itself directly double, without needing to refer to another language.[17] One might say that, in a certain sense, any English speaker is bilingual without needing to leave his own language; he is forced to use two languages. And this can explain a lot about his interaction with the unconscious, since the mesh of a first net can be obstructed by a second. Any translator of English to French, who has a hard time expressing with a single word what English is in the habit of effortlessly expressing with two, knows it well: *republic* and *commonwealth*, *liberty* and *freedom*,

---

[14] J. Lacan, *La logique du fantasme, op. cit.*, seminar of April 12, 1967.

[15] Something Lacan did not always take into account. He would have done well to remember it when he conceived of English as a kind of substantial unit that compromises the expression of the unconscious, unlike French or German, from parts of which English is distantly composed.

[16] "French being but a style of Russian," as Jakobson says in jest.

[17] For, as Jakobson explains to those in attendance at the seminar, February 1, 1967, "no language is monolithic. Each language supposes several subcodes. And, with bilinguals, it is the possibility of speaking two different languages: there is no iron wall between the two languages being used; there is the intersection, the play of the two languages. There is a very frequent, very important phenomenon that plays a huge role: it is how a language of bilinguals is changed under the influence of the other language. There are many possibilities. It's the problem of our diversity of attitudes towards the languages we speak."

value and *worth*. This feature is not only valid for a few word couples, but also for the body of ethical, moral, political, legal, and affective expressions. This double net means that the Anglophone knows he is speaking while he is telling and cannot be the dupe of a discourse that would seem to adhere to things. The relation of citation to things and others is paradoxically a kind of immediacy of the English language—as evidenced by its easier acceptance of the passive compared to French—whereas most other languages only acquire it through contact with foreign languages. No doubt, in any language, "The citations question plays the leading role," as Jakobson says,[18] in other words the primordial role vis à vis the more direct "oratorio," but it seems that English does it more easily than others, as a result of its double origin, or rather from Saxon being covered by Latin. On the other hand, if within a language like English, a sub-code like Latin comes, late in the game but durably, to fill the holes left by Saxon, and if the reverse also happens, this situation risks interfering with the psychoanalyst's grasp of his analysand's discourse.

---

[18] We must point out that Jakobson does not use the words "citation" and "oratio" in their ordinary sense. However, Jakobson hardly innovates compared to the logicians of his time, nor even compared to a great many philosophers of language since the seventeenth century: Locke, Berkeley, Bentham (fictitious entities/real entities), Stuart Mill (connotation/denotation), Peirce (the orders of firstness, secondness, thirdness), Russell (object-language or primary language/languages which presuppose this object-language, which follow in the hierarchy and may be called secondary, tertiary, and so on). The relation of language to itself is the foundation of language's relation to things; in other words, the connection between words makes the reference to things possible, without ever encountering a discourse fully linked to things. There is no language-object that forms the basis of more complex propositions that would suppose simple propositions and would talk about them by citing them. The illusion of language fully engaged with things is another illusion born of language's reference to itself.

Through Jakobson's example in his lecture of February 1, 1967, we are made aware of the question's identity through the authors we cited. Here is the text: "It is a general problem, that of statements that involve citations. To tell the truth, when we speak, either we say outright 'John says this or that,' or 'As John says, it's this and that' (they claim that, etc., etc.); or else we don't cite and we say things we haven't seen ourselves, and which, in certain cases, need suffixes, special verbs (we heard it said. . .); we didn't see how Julius Caesar was killed, but, if we are talking about it, we are citing. If we analyze our statements, we think the citations question really plays the leading role, it's a key thing: [this question is that of] a direct ratio to an oblique ratio." Jakobson immediately adds that this question is typically one "where the linguist and the psychoanalyst must work together."

This seminar has not been published but it is available pro bono at ecole-lacanienne. net/wp-content/uploads/2016/04/1967.02.01.pdf.

9
ALFRED NORTH WHITEHEAD AND GOTTLOB FREGE

It is from an ideological angle that Lacan, in the *Seminar*, most often deals with Whitehead, whose view of religion he did not share. True, Lacan had said, February 3, 1960, that art, religion, and scientific discourse are three ways of contending with the void; art being characterized by "a certain mode of organization around this void," religion consisting "of all the ways of avoiding the void," and, in any case, to respect it, whereas the discourse of science is that of the *Unglauben*, of unbelief.[1] But it is obviously not because they are both connected to the void that it is necessary to "try, as Whitehead does, to divide science and religion into two distinct domains of an objectivity that could have anything in common; their difference is very specifically that of two approaches, essentially and radically distinct, of the subject's position." And he adds: "If I say that psychoanalysis is properly the interpretation of the signifying roots of what, in human destiny, makes up the truth, it is clear that analysis shares the same terrain as religion and is absolutely incompatible with the answers given by religion in this field, for the simple reason that it gives them a different interpretation."[2]

However, there is a homonym of A.N. Whitehead, whose initials are J.H.C and who may have inspired the knot theory Lacan uses. For the author of *Seminar XXIII* cites J.W. Milnor as being at the origin of a fundamental knot in topology, which is true, and it turns out Milnor was close enough to J.H.C. Whitehead to explain his work and accompany his nodology articles.

Of Frege, Lacan retains that he seeks to demonstrate with all his might, against John Stuart Mill, in the *Foundations of Arithme-*

---

[1] J. Lacan, *Ethics of Psychoanalysis, op. cit.*, seminar of February 3, 1960.

[2] J. Lacan, *L'objet de la psychanalyse, op. cit.*, seminar of March 23, 1966. The sentence, which is tautological, is limited to giving a positive spin to the term "interpretation," whereas Lacan is generally critical where this notion is concerned.

tic, which *Seminar IV* recommends reading, "that there is no possible deduction of the number *three* on the basis of experience alone."[3] February 28, 1962, in *Seminar IX*, he returns to the same theme:

> to return to a number that it may surprise you I make an element detached from pure intuition, from sense experience, I am not going to teach you a seminar on the *Foundations of Arithmetic*, an English title of Frege's to which I invite you to refer because it's as fascinating a book as the Martian Chronicles where you will see that it is, in any case, evident that there is no empirical deduction possible of the function of number.... The five dots that you can see on a die is of course a figure that can symbolize the number 5, but you would be completely wrong to think that, in any way, the number 5 is given by this figure.... You'll see there that, in any case, the unit and the zero, so important to any rational constitution of the number, are what most resist, of course, any attempt at an experiential genesis of the number, and especially if a homogeneous definition of the number as such is intended. [Frege] dashes all the geneses of the number that can be attempted to be given on the basis of a collection and of the abstraction of difference based on diversity.

Perhaps Lacan is thinking, through his example of the five dots, of the blind English mathematician Saunderson's numeration system, which was the object of Diderot's reflection in his *Letter on the Blind*, which sufficiently shows that this system may well suggest new mathematics and new relationships among the numbers, although he does nothing with it and, from this perspective, does not move beyond simple fantasy. Saunderson does the same mathematics as Newton, whom he succeeded as chair of Mathematics. He would not invent other mathematics by sublimating his blindness and he would be inferior, in his productions, to his illustrious predecessor.

It seems to us rather strange that Lacan was so attached to distancing himself from psychologism and to sacrifice to what could be called a "mathematical Platonism," as if mathematical objects and mathematical operations could become independent of the psychological actions that produce them and underlie them. One wonders here whether it isn't structuralism that prevented Lacan from yielding

---

[3] J. Lacan, *The Object Relation, op. cit.*, seminar of March 20, 1957.

to psychologism, which involves a rather narrow inductivism, whereas the structure involves a certain independence regarding induction. This is where Lacan's otherwise difficult to comprehend interest in Frege may reside.

10

GEORGE BOOLE

Among the English authors of interest to us for this book, it is probably from Boole that Lacan derives several elements of determination that allow him to aspire to formalize a few small segments of knowledge. Let's observe him undertake an attempt at mathematization.

"To quickly light… this lantern, I will state that the Symbolic is on the order of the One, this One that I already stated as constituting the universe, in [Boole's] logical order. I pointed out, at the same time, that that is… a questionable hypothesis, to make the universe something of the One." Lacan goes on to explain Boole's formula: $x(1-x) = 0$.

"Namely: of x and of everything that is not x, that is to say the whole of the Universe from which x has been removed, the product, the intersection, the encounter, is equal to zero.[1] It is on this basis that Boole claims to be able to propose a formalization of the nature of logic."

Then Lacan proposes an interpretation in the terms of his conception of psychoanalysis: "I propose giving the One the value of what phallic *jouissance* consists of," the latter as opposed to the sexual relationship.

Thus, "inasmuch as something is designated in Boole by an x, something is precipitated as a signifier, this signifier is in some sense taken, removed, borrowed from phallic *jouissance* itself."[2]

The key aspect of this research is that it allows, through this interpretation of $x(1-x) = 0$, a way out of the subjective idealism that

---

[1] We had to reconstruct the argument, which, in the version of the May 21, 1974 lesson to which we had access (*Le Séminaire livre XXI: Les non-dupes errent*, unpublished seminar) was scarcely intelligible. We don't know whether we should incriminate Lacan himself, the transcription, or our own ability to understand the one or the other.

[2] J. Lacan, *Les non-dupes errent*, *op. cit.*, seminar of May 21, 1974.

holds that the key boundary is that of the self and the non-self, and that it raises this boundary between the subject and what is not the subject as a boundary among many others, not necessarily the most fundamental one.

What is clear about this formulation when we look at it closely, if we have gotten it right, is that we are dealing with an application that is more metaphorical than conceptual since it does not go beyond the definitions stage and it isn't susceptible of instituting any theorem, though the language gives the impression that it is.

Inasmuch as it attempts to make symbolic elements function, this logic remains more fantasmatic than a bona fide logic of the psychic processes. While Lacan sought to surpass the elementary level of definitions, he nevertheless stuck to schematic fragments, through which he tried to turn little bits of experience into signifiers in order to obtain more powerful articulations. Indeed, what point is there to formalizing if you don't really go beyond the definitions stage, the abstraction of which even risks turning out to be dangerous and mutilating compared to work that could be carried out in the vernacular, with more of a 'spirit of finesse' than a 'spirit of geometry'? Isn't it necessary, for a formalization to demonstrate its value, that it allows transforming the tools that are definitions and axioms into new theorems and propositions that could not have been obtained through any other means—specifically not that of the vernacular—and that impose, through an original precipitate, a new synthesis? Like other thinkers, like the Utilitarians in particular, who threatened their adversaries with many calculations, but took care not to do them or even to say what they consisted of, Lacan had this fantasy; one wonders whether he even reached the threshold of an accomplishment. He made the discourse via mathemes the touchstone of the pertinence of the construction he sought. Did he achieve better success than Bentham, who, in his era, also talked about calculation, indefatigably taking stock of the requisites, to deliver only few or no real calculations that clearly went beyond the status of axioms? Starting with the Klein bottle or the cross-cap, how many desires to obtain, through the inversion of figures, the equivalent of a theorem, whereas one has only created one more figure, and one may only have established its possibility by showing it! These curious mathemes sporadically betray the desire for formalization, which is intense, but the pertinent accomplishment of which is at best uncertain.

11
CONCLUSION

What is certain, however, is that these little elements of knowledge that are the mathemes, which can scarcely claim a greater advantage than that of being the drafts of an access to propositions which, one day, could be put differently, are worth more, despite their imperfections and their sporadic character, than the grand, more or less rhetorical, ambitions of general structure or "general science." More precisely, it is from the former that structures that are, in a sense, receivable can be sought. "I shall call 'structuralist,' in the good sense of the word, and not in the vaguely ideological sense, someone who, having to deal with a range of phenomena presenting the aspects of a system, is able in a manner specific to this range (by practicing 'good' segmentations, the 'good' laws of composition, etc.) put into practice the sequence of procedures" that, in a mathematical conception of structure, Desanti envisaged prolonging, following the four aspects according to which Lévi-Strauss defined structure: "1. A structure has the characteristics of a system. It consists of elements such that any modification of one of them leads to a modification of all of the others... 2. Any model belongs to a group of transformations... 3. The properties shown allow predicting how the model will react, in case one of its elements is modified... 4. The model must be built in such a way that its functioning is able to account for all the facts observed."[1] Desanti added, in a very disenchanted tone, that it seemed to him "that the range of social sciences[2] capable of sustaining this sequence all the way to the end (in other words, to the accounting clause) is extremely limited,"[3] especially when the so-called researchers thought it sufficient to use a vocabulary of analogies in order to produce a "general science." That wasn't the case with Lacan, who, with a great

---

[1] C. Lévi-Strauss, *Anthropologie structurale* (Paris: Plon, 1958), 306.

[2] From this point of view, psychoanalysis falls within this range.

[3] J.T. Desanti, *Le philosophe et les pouvoirs, op. cit.*, 146.

deal of sincerity, used mathematics to produce the mathemes needed to formalize the small parts of the range that interested him.

We should beware of it becoming a question, as his research advanced, less and less of science in his discourse, but rather of a formalization of the symbolic in order to have a practical access to what underlies the imaginary. Desanti defined the conditions according to which structure may be treated scientifically, eventually by incorporating procedures or strategies for weakening the "draconian" form in which he presents it. Less and less did Lacan defend psychoanalysis' claim to scientificity, which did not prevent him from increasingly having wanted to give a mathematical form to his signifiers, which is to say to the substantial elements that can be used in analysis. He may have dreamed of a "general science," at least, he evokes its equivalent when he deals with Boole by assigning himself as a program, on the basis of his algebra, "to come up with more rigorous formulations for locating what we are dealing with, and which merits, from certain angles, to be undertaken in the most general articulation available to us at this time logic-wise, namely: what, of set theory, is locatable."[4]

But this kind of hope seems to fade during the following decade, without any weakening in the ambition of a mathematical discourse, which is not a discourse of knowledge and the elements and articulations of which leave the least space possible for meaning and hermeneutics. Isn't this exactly what Desanti calls an "ideological expression," which simply has the merit of pointing in a direction without being susceptible of confirmation?

Is not the mark of ideology in this domain to remain without fail at the level of the *archaï* (άρχαι), of definitions and axioms, without arriving at the least theorem? The thing that makes one hesitate in Lacan's favor is that he is sometimes able to create tableaus,[5] which—despite their static character—involves a production of ideas that could not be had without them. But, most often, through a strange inversion, the sporadic character of mathematical formalization plays exactly the role the words of the vernacular play inside a mathematical discourse; in Lacan's analytical discourse, mathematization only applies to small

---

[4] J. Lacan, *La logique du fantasme, op. cit.*, seminar of December 7, 1967.

[5] There is at least one that is developed, session after session, during *Seminar* XVII, from at least December 1969 until February 1970, when the four discourses are elaborated.

segments, exactly the way the words of everyday language help the understanding of mathematical notions and operations over short itineraries, beyond which they mislead it or render it impossible.

Finally, it is clear that we are able to answer the question we raised when we began this second part. By speaking of *linguisterie* and by practicing it, Lacan did not provide an opening for a Husserlian-type attack on the basis of linguisticism. The real linguistics being in his view psychoanalytical, it becomes a question, precisely, of whether psychoanalysis is up to the task of moving beyond the philosophical positions themselves, which, generally, are only able to yield unsurpassable contradictions. Let's not forget that Lacan always refused to consider psychoanalysis a human science among others, like Foucault, to whom he may have suggested the idea—and who certainly returned the favor—that psychoanalysis functions as the basis of the other sciences; it is up to it, on every occasion, to prove that it is indeed henceforth the most fundamental knowledge. It is true that the Husserlian threats were not bound to impress Lacan much; he scarcely mentions Husserl, other than to denounce the impossibility of working on affective and psychological questions in terms of intentionality, which tends to derive the notion of object (of desire, for instance) from that of object of knowledge.[6] Moreover, on more than one occasion, Lacan contemplated psychoanalyzing a philosophical attitude, which amounts to granting the former a higher conceptual destiny than the latter.

---

[6] J. Lacan, *Encore, op. cit.*, seminar of June 16, 1973.

III
ENGLISH WRITERS AND THEIR COMMENTATORS

No more did Lacan seek to write a "complete" philosophy—the way Hume, Kant, or Schopenhauer sought to do in their era—with the idea of completeness in mind such as it might have existed at the time, than he sought to construct a logic encompassing some vast field of knowledge. Nor did he want to build a literary aesthetic or science that would rival some theory or canon of literature, even less so of English literature. Lacan could not care less about completeness, at least in the areas we just cited; his choices are deliberately partial, in both senses of the word. He only rarely cites a page; he did it once with a juicy passage excerpted from Swift's *Gulliver's Travels*. While he speaks at length about Joyce, he doesn't say a word about Virginia Woolf or Katherine Mansfield, nor even about D.H. Lawrence or Oscar Wilde. Lacan borrows from the abundance of English literature what is suited to his own ends; he does not compete with university culture, the goals of which he challenges to the extent that they embrace the pompous and ludicrous pretext of wanting to be "complete." The way Lacan does philosophy, logic, or literature even allows questioning this so-called completeness, if not the simple desire to achieve it. Indeed, how many pages of filler and boredom have resulted from the ardent obligation to link real discoveries? Nietzsche remarked that we only retained tiny details from great works, not the secondary elaborations that bound them together. Lacan knew how to repeat and hammer home definitions and formulations, but he also knew how to spare us the indigestible plasma supposed to link his most precious discoveries; the *Seminar* does without filler between remarks, which does not mean that it is without rhetoric or construction. While the re-transcription, the rewriting, if not the writing of the *Seminar*, are necessarily a betrayal, they have the merit of existing, of often ringing true, to always bring to the surface an impeccable and powerful construct that would have gotten away without the admirable Le Seuil[1] publications, which are henceforth available to those, and they are many, who were not able to attend a session of the *Seminar*. But, with Lacan, construction never stifles the salient character of studies that, one way or another, have literature as their object; like the philosopher-reader, who has the impression of flying from fragment to fragment, the lover of literature, while reading the *Seminar*, goes from one small insight to the next, to considerations of works, without getting lost in the scaffolding, always with the feeling that his comments have the ring of someone who has truly read what he is talking about.

The pinnacle of Lacan's work in English literature occurs in his examination of three authors, and it may be better to speak of three works: Joyce's *Ulysses*, Shakespeare's *Hamlet*, and Poe's "The Purloined Letter."

In 1971, when Lacan wrote "Lituraterre"—a theoretical text on the relationships between literature, literary criticism, and psychoanalysis—he hadn't yet dealt with Joyce. Certainly, he rejoices that "[his] teachings find their place in a configuration shift displayed by a slogan promoting the written word"; but the author of reference, here, remains Rabelais, whose increased readership, and the progress it represents, Lacan celebrates.[2] In 1975, Joyce takes up all the space devoted to the question of writing.

The obvious presence, much earlier, of *Hamlet* in Lacan's work corresponds to another concern: that of radically escaping from the sacrosanct psychobiographical pseudo-analysis and showing *in concreto* what it is possible to do after leaving it behind. It isn't a matter of finding, in Shakespeare's words, some description of the character Hamlet, as if he had a kind of actual existence, but to show how the

---

[1] This applies to the first publications of the *Séminaire*, which will be followed by others, because it is only too obvious that, at certain points, the text is questionable; at others, allusions that were transparent for Lacan's contemporaries have become quite opaque for succeeding generations—whether they involved references to political or social events of the moment or to personalities clearly identified by the context who have become obscure over time. As merciless as Lacan could be regarding scholars and their techniques, it is necessary to consider, in the not so distant future, critical editions of the *Séminaire*, the context of which is becoming increasingly incomprehensible to a growing number of readers.

[2] J. Lacan, "Lituraterre," *Autres écrits, op. cit.*, 12.

disposition of the signifiers creates this illusion, which it is then out of the question to accept at face value.

Earlier still, Poe's key presence in Lacan's work forced an admission on the part of "Lituraterre's"[3] author: that of having authentically engaged in literary criticism in the way he thinks psychoanalysis could be of use to it. "My criticism, if it is held to be literary, only addresses, to try my hand, what Poe does as a writer putting together such a message about the letter." Here again, ordinary "biographizing" and "psychologizing" criticism, seeking the author's intentions, risked disappointment, even if it were not ill-disposed towards psychoanalysis, which it misconceived and from which it expected a disservice. If it expected some psychoanalysis of Hamlet, of Leopold Bloom, of Stephen or of Molly Bloom, if not of Joyce or of Shakespeare, it would have been left hanging. Psychoanalysis did not help literary criticism where it expected help. Far from starting out with characters cutout by the imaginary, which believes they substantially exist, it is necessary to begin with logic in the folds of which one has the impression they emerge. It is in "The Seminar on 'The Purloined Letter'" that there appears "the method through which psychoanalysis best justifies its intrusion: for if literary criticism could effectively renew itself, it would be from psychoanalysis being there so that the texts could take its measure, the enigma being on its side."[4]

As for the other authors, it could be that "Lituraterre" gives precious information regarding the choice of one of them. We examined the case of Dean Swift, even though he was only cited twice in the *Seminar*, simply because his presence seems to illustrate particularly well the work that psychoanalysis *could* do in politics, but that it lets, it must be said, merely shimmer, always giving in to the doubt that the job remains, in this area, quite fantasmatic. It is, perhaps, unfortunate to be able to rely on Swift alone to fill this position; at least he does so sumptuously and for our greater pleasure.

Even as we have insisted on his implantation in the French language, Lacan's works are so rich in English literature that one might wonder what makes the taste of this cultured man tend toward English rather than toward any other foreign language, where literature is con-

---

[3] *Ibid.*
[4] *Ibid.*, 13.

cerned. I shall hazard a hypothesis: literature is intimately bound to the language of which it seems the fruit. When you look at the works of Joyce, Swift, or Sterne,[5] you see the work of an author who is not content to tell a story, but who intervenes in the narrative at every level, like the Bayesian subject who strangely intervenes in the way of doing mathematics. The author does not absent himself from his stories, as he appears to in ordinary stories so as to give them the credibility of the real. And it seems that the English language, through its own way of making the speaker conscious that he is speaking it (by using, for example, passives more easily, which in French are experienced as heavy), intimated a certain type of literature, the idea, the result, the outcome of which are less easily found in other languages. Lacan has a way of intervening in his texts that, through humor and the unexpected, is not unrelated to a Sterne or a Swift. Far from being self-effacing, he, too, deliberately plays his role of author. If we are stressing this point, it is because it seems that we may have a hypothesis concerning the—supposed?—difficulty English has expressing the unconscious.

---

[5] Who is not often mentioned directly by Lacan; we barely glimpse an allusion to the beginning of *Tristram Shandy* in his discussion of the homunculus.

12
JAMES JOYCE

While it is difficult to identify a work like Joyce's *Ulysses*, and maybe even more so *Finnegans Wake*, it is much more complicated to identify the work Lacan bases on his lengthy reading of Joyce in *Seminar XXIII* entitled *The Sinthome*. Even if he is mistaken about the dates of his first contact with *Ulysses*, which happened during a public reading of fragments of the work, it is certain that this encounter was long past when, in 1975,[1] Lacan decided to teach this *Seminar* on Joyce. The term "on Joyce" is inappropriate from the outset, because it is more a question of a discourse according to Joyce, which certainly encounters Joyce or his work, but takes neither as its object. In concert with the work of speaking and writing interlaced with Joyce's writing, Lacan works on knots, in a sector of topology little studied at the time he tackled it, but which belongs to the extension of the mathematical reflection or accompaniment undertaken since the beginnings of the *Seminar*, which gradually led him toward places increasingly less frequented by specialists. In both cases, the investigation was so perilous that Lacan, who for a long time no longer had to prove the authenticity of his creation in psychoanalysis and its theorization, relied on two mathematicians to ensure his comprehension of what happens when you tie and untie ropes[2]— P. Soury and M. Thomé—as well as on the presence of Jacques Aubert to read Joyce and help a voice to progress along the length of this text.

Let us begin by noting that, in Lacan's eyes, there is no contradiction between a literary activity and a mathematical reflection or

---

[1] This encounter is remembered in small, very precise allusions. Thus, the *Écrits* (on page 25) features the Joycean wordplay *A letter, a litter*, with the specific reference to "what it ambiguously evoked [*équivoqué*] in Joyce's circle about the homophony of these two words in English."

[2] On this point, he followed a wise lesson from Descartes' *Regulae* that advised the researcher to understand knits.

occupation. The intimate link between the two enterprises is found in the writing of a language, which is to say in the inscription of signifiers that are not necessarily those that are already known, but which can be the invention of a language. The works of Joyce, and not only *Finnegans Wake* where wordplay rules, tend toward this invention, like those of the mathematician who solves new problems and seizes new sectors. Lacan was obviously not the first to notice this, and the affinity between treatises on mathematics and treatises on writing was recognized as early as the age of French Neo-classicism. Fontenelle's *Essai sur les infiniment petits* [Essay on the Infinitely Smalls] is a treatise on writing that shows how close to the constitution of new series from older ones is the literary act of inscription in the gaps and the holes of preceding works. Moreover, whether in Peirce or Pascal, the creation of symbols is tied to a break in the usual progression of a first discourse to which we are forced to substitute a second.[3] The mathematical methods and their different intersections are modes of writing; for, in language as well, there has to be a "break" that allows it to lose, for example, with Joyce, its "phonic identity" for it

---

[3] F. Recanati, in his June 14, 1972, contribution to Lacan's *Seminar*, pointed out that, according to Peirce, to make a symbol emerge, it was critical that there be a before and an after: "There can only be an access to what came 'before' through the simple analytical operation that consists of removing what there was 'after,' everything that makes up the character of this 'after.' Because the 'before' that is then determined is only the before of this 'after,' it is only an imaginary specification of this 'after.' As such, the 'before' is no more than a crossed-out 'after'; it is even the inscription of this 'before' based on this crossing-out that is the foundation of, that characterizes, the 'after' as such. The 'after,' therefore, only differs from the 'before' thanks to this particular inscription. But the fact that the before is inscribed in the after does not mean that it can be found there, since the only thing that characterizes the before is *precisely* the fact of not being inscribed, which is to say of not being inscribed as non-inscribed either. To put it another way, the *before* is that which is not inscribed, is nothing, and the *after* is the same nothing, but inscribed." *Scilicet* 4 (1973), 56. Is it by chance that Lacan took an interest in Pascal's comparable articulation of the calculation of parties? After playing with a comical interpretation of *to be or not to be* in *Seminar II*, Lacan is interested in the paradox that Vuillemin attributed to Diodorus Cronus; he treats it from the standpoint of a comical version of the fearsome expression "better not to have been born": "It's true. It can be at the time we say it, *it would be better if I hadn't been born*. What is ridiculous is to say it and launch into probability calculation." *The Seminar of Jacques Lacan Book II: The Ego in Freud's Theory and in the Technique of Psychoanalysis*, ed. J.-A. Miller, trans. S. Tomaselli (New York: Norton, 1991), seminar of May 19, 1955. Of note is that Oedipus' tragic words are not very different from the cry at the very end of Act 1 in *Hamlet*—"The time is out of joint: O cursed spite / That ever I was born to set it right"—as Lacan points out in his April 29, 1959 lesson.

to prevail and succeed as writing.[4] It is more or less equivalent, to understand how a writing [T.N.: une écriture] functions, to consult a mathematician or an author who creates his language. The mathematician pours out his signs,[5] like the writer pours out his, with perhaps, in literature, the more affirmed *jouissance* of drawing the edges of holes in knowledge.[6]

For Joyce creates his language and causes us to doubt that the language "in" which he writes has an identity other than precisely the one he is writing; even when it's *Ulysses*:

> Joyce writes English with these particular refinements that amount to, the English language, in this case, he dismantles it. Don't think that it starts with *Finnegans Wake*. Well before, most notably in *Ulysses*, he has a way of breaking up his sentences that is already headed in this direction. It's really a process that tends toward giving the language in which he writes another usage, in any case a usage that is far from ordinary. This is part of his *savoir-faire*.

On the same page, Lacan ambiguously deplores his "lack of practice, call it [his] inexperience in the language in which he writes." It would be hard to know to which language he is referring, to the English language or to Joyce's, if several lines later on he had not contrasted this "inexperience" with Jacques Aubert's "practice," which "goes well beyond [his], not only of the English language but of Joyce in particular."[7] Joyce speaks in a language he deconstructs to reconstruct otherwise.[8]

---

[4] J. Lacan, *Sinthome, op. cit.*, seminar of February 17, 1976.

[5] J. Lacan, "Lituraterre," *Autres écrits, op. cit.*, 17: "Writing like surveying are artifacts to dwell only in language. How can we forget it when our science is only operational from the outpouring of little letters and marks combined?"

[6] *Ibid.*, 14: "The edge of the hole in knowledge, isn't this what it (the letter) traces?" Hadn't the myth of Pandora designated it as *Elpis*?

[7] Lacan, *Sinthome, op, cit.*, seminar of January 20, 1976.

[8] Oddly, Bentham's contemporaries asked themselves the same question about his English; Hazlitt in particular. This desire to belong to no language in particular and to be able to be expressed in each one is present in Bentham. It is just as odd that Lacan, who does not cite Hazlitt's text to which we just referred, cites another, from his *Essays on Shakespeare*, about Hamlet, with which he finds himself in agreement, in a chain of approbations that begins with Goethe, continues with Coleridge, and arrives at Hazlitt. Indeed, March 11, 1959, Lacan says: "For Goethe, the character of Hamlet is action paralyzed

From the opening lines of *Seminar XXIII*, Lacan addressed this point, perhaps leaving us a precious clue for solving, if only partially, one of the problems central to our investigation. "Joyce had to write in English, undoubtedly, but as Philippe Sollers… said, he wrote in English in such a way that the English language no longer exists."[9] This is a trait that brings him closer to Lacan when he writes in English, if not when he expresses himself in French. What does Joyce Hellenize, when he says "*to Hellenize*" Gaelic?[10] English? In the same way that, as Lacan had seen by reading Hegel, who had written it before him, words destroy the things they talk about, Joyce destroys or erases the language in which he writes. And, Lacan adds, speaking explicitly about the English language: "This language did already have little in the way of consistency, which does not mean that it is easy to write in English, but through the succession of works he wrote in English, Joyce added that something that makes [Philippe Sollers] say we should write *l'élangues*."[11] Joyce deconstructed an inconsistent lan-

---

by thought…. Hamlet is, in short, the man who sees all the elements, all the complexities, all the patterns of the game of life, and who is suspended, paralyzed in his action by this knowledge. As for Coleridge,… he agrees wholeheartedly, but in a much less sociological, much more psychological way. There is something, in my opinion, that dominates Coleridge's entire handling of the question and that I like to remember: 'I have to admit that I feel in myself some taste of the same thing.' It is what in him traces the psychasthenic character, the impossibility of committing to a path and, once there, staying committed. The discussion of hesitation, of multiple motives, is a brilliant piece of psychology that, as far as we are concerned, gives us the key, the motive, the quintessence, in this remark of Coleridge's said in passing: after all, I have a taste of this. Which is to say, I see myself in this." Perhaps Lacan is alluding to the remark found in the chapter of *Shakespeare and the Elizabethan Dramatists* (*op. cit.*, 207) on *Hamlet*: "For its commonness in ordinary conversation tends to produce the sense of reality, and at once hides the poet, and yet approximates the reader or spectator to that state in which the highest poetry will appear, and in its component parts, though not in the whole composition, really is, the language of nature. If I should not speak it, I feel that I should be thinking it; the voice only is the poet's—the words are my own." This is exactly the point Lacan notes as being shared by Hazlitt: "We have been so used to this tragedy [*Hamlet*], he says, that we hardly know how to criticise it any more than we should know how to describe our own faces." *Characters of Shakespeare's Plays* (Cambridge: Cambridge UP, 1908), 85.

[9] Lacan, *Sinthome, op, cit.*, seminar of November 18, 1975.

[10] "That he knew bits of, enough to get around, but not much more." *Ibid.*, 166.

[11] *Ibid.*, 11–12. In issue 29 of the journal *Essaim* (02/2012) F. Pellion, under the title "Quelques remarques sur 'lalangue' et sur le cas particulier de la surdité prélinguale" [A few remarks on 'lalangue' and on the particular case of prelingual deafness] authors an excellent synthesis concerning this notion of *lalangue*, which appears in Lacan probably

guage. Does this mean it doesn't hold up? Does he mean that, differently from what happens in Japanese, according to Lacan,[12] English is not directly affected by its being written, absent a writer's hand being involved? Is he talking about the fusion of functions which means that each grammatical being can easily replace another? In other words, is English this language where words are polyvalent, where verbs can easily become nouns or adjectives, and nouns verbs? By dissolving the frontiers of every function, by undermining the system of denotation

---

for the first time in the November 4, 1971, lesson: "Henceforth, I will write *lalangue* as a single word."

Lacan's idea, which owes nothing to a slip of the tongue, as is sometimes stated, is to distinguish what the psychoanalyst calls language, when he says "the unconscious is structured like a language," specifying that he means by that, French, English, German, or some other language, from what the linguist means. It's a question of going beyond what remained analogical and metaphorical in the formulation "the unconscious is structured like a language," to distinguish the unconscious the psychoanalyst works with from the linguistic unconscious, and thus to be in a position to grasp the link between the unconscious and what does indeed maintain a relationship with (the linguist's) language but remains distinct from it. This way of writing *lalangue* is programmatic and involves a deep recasting of what is understood by language [*langue*] and signifier, which were equivocal up to that point since, while it seemed that the *language* [*langue*] and *signifier* Lacan talked about were not exactly the linguist's *language* [*langue*] and *signifier*, it wasn't known whether they were distinct. Yet, the way our unconscious is inscribed, is written, is not exactly the way a language exists, is inscribed, is deposited in a speaker, even if the two processes have something to do with each other.

F. Pellion quotes the lovely November 1, 1974, text, of which we only reproduce a fragment here: "*Lalangue*, what needs to be conceived of it, is that it is the deposit, the alluvium, the petrification that is the mark of group's handling of its unconscious experience…. Language is not to be called living because it is in use. It is far more the sign's death that it traffics." *Lalangue* is, in a certain sense, the dead part of us, what we have inherited and what we bequeath to others in an absolute unconsciousness. "From the outset," Lacan says in *Encore* (seminar of January 9, 1973), "there is a relationship with *lalangue* that warrants being called the mother tongue for good reason because it is through the mother that the child receives it. He doesn't learn it. There's a slope." *Lalangue* isn't learned; it is transmitted by being written, so long as we don't take the term "written" too literally. Nothing can be added to or subtracted from *lalangue*: "All *lalangue* is a dead language, even if it is still being used"; what is dead in us is extremely important to the structuring of the unconscious. The psyche only exists and only lives through something that is dead in it and was originally transmitted to it. A writer's writing could have as much to do with *lalangue* as with language. A great writer never writes in a language without transforming it. If a language can be transformed, it is because it belongs to *lalangue*.

[12] "I would like to bear witness to what happens to an already marked fact: namely that of a language, Japanese, inasmuch as it is reworked by writing." J. Lacan, "Lituraterre," *Autres écrits, op. cit.*, 19.

with connotations that are too easy, this language is supposed to put an end to illusions of transcendence and offer protection from dialectical effects, but at the price of any linguistic firmness; and the apparent gains would end up being dispersed.

The phenomenon Lacan wants to particularly study, where Joyce is concerned, is the way a man belongs to the language, to put it in phenomenological terms; in truth, there exists no belonging of this kind, and language does not give rise to some simple appropriation. What do we possess when we possess a language, to the extent that it is ever possessed? Because the one we possess belongs to so many others at the same time, while our initial appropriation of the language occurred through processes which, to the contrary, have sometimes excluded the other.[13] Despite the fantasies speakers may harbor regarding this subject, language does not exist in and of itself, it is not a substance; it is a phenomenon of interference, of transfer, of edge, of collar. Lacan says so in his June 16, 1975,[14] lecture:

> Joyce said that in Ireland you have a master and a mistress, the master being the British Empire and the mistress being the Holy Roman and Apostolic Catholic church, both being similar kinds of plague. It is indeed what one observes in what makes Joyce the symptom, the pure symptom of where the relation to language is, inasmuch as it is reduced to a symptom—namely, to what it has as an effect, when this effect is not analyzed.[15]

Joyce's language is a symptom of interference.

The same intermediary status is found in *Ulysses* between the written and the oral, between writing and speech: "It is through the intermediary of writing that speech decomposes and asserts itself as such, namely in a deformation where knowing whether to free oneself of the speech parasite remains ambiguous… or, on the contrary, to let oneself be invaded by the essentially phonetic properties of speech, by the polyphony of speech."[16] The long sequence without punctuation

---

[13] As Jakobson established in "experimentations" that were of interest to Lacan in *Anxiety, op. cit.*, seminar of June 5, 1963.

[14] June 16 is "Bloomsday"—the day all of *Ulysses* is set.

[15] J. Lacan, *Sinthome, op. cit.*, seminar of June 16, 1975.

[16] *Ibid.*, seminar of February 17, 1976.

that stages Molly Bloom's thoughts at the end of the work, is it some written transcription of the oral? Some capture of the oral by the written? The ultimate triumph of speech over writing? Or the opposite? The wedding of writing and speech against the backdrop of Molly and Bloom's failed wedding? The ambiguity is as perfect as the engraving is fascinating and, in any case, evades Saussurian categories by virtue of their too well-defined distinction between speech and language.

In a page of *Seminar XXIII*, Lacan shows that consistency is a fantasy that only stems from the imaginary and has nothing to do with the symbolic reality that underlies it. In topological language and under the title of R. Adams' work *Surface and Symbol: The Consistency of James Joyce's Ulysses*, Lacan analyzes how "*consistency*" should be understood, and it is in the vein of the critique of substance, such as English philosophy has undertaken it, from Hobbes and Locke to Bentham then Russell, that we should read this text, which uses as paradigm the false consciousness we have about the unity of our own body:

> Consistency, what does it mean? It means what holds together, and that's why it is symbolized by the surface. Indeed, poor of ourselves, our only idea of consistency is of what is bag-like or rag-like. It's the first idea we have of it. Even, the body, we feel it like skin, holding in its bag a bunch of organs. But the capacity for imaginative abstraction is so weak that, of this rope—this rope shown as the residue of consistency—it excludes the knot.[17]

The lived consciousness of our body is to the reality of the system of organs as the rope is to its knots: "The knot does not constitute consistency. Consistency and knot must even be distinguished. The knot ex-ists[18] for the rope element, for the rope-consistency."[19] The way we experience consistency, whether it be that of the language or that of the body, is not at all the way it is underpinned. We must learn to theorize without this impression of consistency and beyond it, for

---

[17] *Ibid.*, seminar of January 13, 1976.
[18] Ever since the *Écrits*, this term indicates, for Lacan, being [*l'être*] in an eccentric location. "Séminaire sur 'La Lettre volée," *Écrits, op. cit.*, 11.
[19] *Ibid.*

this impression does not have, and is not its own key. For, "In a rope the knot is all that ex-sists, strictly speaking."[20]

Writing is not in a relationship of servility to the imaginary that aligns itself on the conventions and clichés the latter seems to promote—that there are characters in a novel, that they come in contact with one another, that there is an intrigue that is resolved, and a few other habits of the same kind. Writing deconstructs this imaginary in order to reconstruct it. There is, in the May 11, 1976, lesson a ray of light concerning this, a blinding blitz, an almost excessive probe: "Why is Joyce so unreadable? We have to try and picture why. Maybe because he doesn't awaken in us any sympathy."[21] The statement is excessive, since the characters of Molly, Stephen, and Bloom, while they present surfaces and edges such that it is still possible to speak of characters, are not without eliciting waves of sympathy from the reader of *Ulysses*. But it is true that these characters are so little "in" a context, enter so little "into" relationships with each other, present so few objective borders and asperities, their ectoderm being so fractalized, that sympathy is eluded, defused, discouraged in *Ulysses*, which gives us writing to read more than it tells a story. *Ulysses* still performs on the edge of sympathy, which this novel elicits, as though out of nostalgia, an inscription in the ancient avenues of other novels. In a certain sense, in "English" literature, *A Confederacy of Dunces* by J.K. Toole, without the premature death of its author, was more clearly going in the direction of a reading that requires no sympathy for the protagonist. *Ulysses* did not reach this point through all of its tendencies.

Nonetheless, in the ways that interest Lacan the reader, for his own work on language, and in particular for the construction of a novel language, *Ulysses* far exceeds Toole's book, which Lacan could not have known. And it is through work that echoes, that mirrors Joyce's book, that follows its perspective, that Lacan seeks an attitude for the reading of *Ulysses*. Leaving aside the question of whether Joyce compensated for sexual impotence through literary activity,[22] whether he wanted to make a name for himself in literature to replace that of a

---

[20] *Ibid*.

[21] J. Lacan, *Sinthome, op, cit.*, seminar of May 11, 1976.

[22] Lacan does, however, note that: "As his cock was a little limp, his art made up for his phallic posture. And that's how it always is." *Ibid.*, seminar of November 18, 1975.

father who was a failure, or replace the father himself[23]—all this being only hypothetical, for Lacan humbly admits it: he was not able to psychoanalyze Joyce and Joyce's attitude toward psychoanalysis resembled anything but a request[24]—there remains the singular attitude of Lacanian analysis towards Joyce's work. This attitude is related neither to scholarly technique[25]—foolishly sure of its mastery, whereas it is, at best, only one statutory way of dealing with texts among an infinity of other procedures, while it only owes its consistency to its repetition and its power—nor to some art of inductive and psychologizing guessing, nor to contemplation. It is not at all a question, for example, of knowing what Joyce "really" believed and thought of himself, based on clues that he might have left.[26] It is apparently bizarrely, with competing witticisms, puns, and rebuses, that Lacan places himself and us in an "adjusted" relation, so to speak, to the text, by trying to impose as little as possible some pre-existing identity on what might be a reading of Joyce.[27] Lacan goes so far as to write, most paradoxically, that the verbal slip-ups—those committed reading him—are not without interest to have access to a work, so long as they are in the nature of a co-

---

[23] "Joyce has a symptom that comes from this, that his father was deficient, radically deficient—that's all he talks about. I've centered the thing around the name, and I thought—do as you wish with this thought—that it was from wanting a name that Joyce compensated for paternal deficiency." *Ibid.*, seminar of February 17, 1976.

[24] "What's terrible is that I am reduced to reading him, since it is certain that I haven't analyzed him. I regret it. Anyway, it's clear that he wasn't well disposed toward it. The terms Tweedledum and Tweedledee to respectively designate Freud and Jung came to him naturally. This does not show that he was inclined to be analyzed." *Ibid.*, seminar of February 10, 1976.

[25] Even though, and Lacan does not omit this, Joyce "deliberately wanted this [scholarly] tribe to spend time on him. The amazing thing is that he succeeded beyond his wildest dreams. It lasts and will continue. He wanted it to last for three hundred years. He said 'I want to keep the critics busy for three hundred years,' and he will, so long as God doesn't atomize us first." *Ibid.*, seminar of November 18, 1975.

[26] *Ibid.*, seminar of February 10, 1976: "In particular, reading Joyce, how can it be known what he thought of himself?" On the preceding page, Lacan had asked: "The question, in short, the following one—how can we know, according to his notes, what Joyce believed?"

[27] Generously, Lacan also shares other people's inventions. Thus, *Scribbledhobble* is borrowed from Norman Conolly to characterize a Joyce manuscript (*ibid.*, seminar of February 10, 1976); or *eftsooneries* is taken from *Surface and Symbol* to designate these disorienting expressions the effects of which will only be understood later (*ibid.*, seminar of January 20, 1976).

incidence,[28] either with the text, or with readings of the text. The slips are, after all, elements of an entire language that asserts itself on the margins of another language, the latter being sure of its status. In the same way an author's comments are considered, in a certain sense, to belong to that author, the slips can be considered, in a certain sense, to belong to the text from which or on which they are committed.

The writing I am reading is the symptom of what? This could be the crux of any reading. And writing alone, with its own resistance, allows maintaining the demands of this question which stem from an art of reading. Let's not imagine, however, that this *Leitfaden* leads us to the possibility of analyzing Bloom, Molly, Stephen, or the author of *Ulysses*; if there were some contradiction between the declaration of this impossibility and the interest in literature of psychoanalysis—an interest reciprocated by literature and literary theory in psychoanalysis—we should respond by stressing the great difference there is between claiming to analyze "someone" based on their function as author or character, which is sharply contested, and taking advantage of literature as a *thought experiment* susceptible of perfecting given conceptual components or of creating an articulation between them.

But, for Lacan, while the preceding maxim bespeaks prudence—for zealous analysts who may want to apply their methods to authors of the past or to the characters who populate their works—it is not the best lesson to come from his long reflection on Joyce. If Lacan invites Jacques Aubert, who is probably the best possible translator of *Ulysses*, to his seminar, it is probably to certify the impossibility of translation, if what is meant by that is rendering in one language what is expressed in another. All translations are off-kilter and only become remarkable, creative, and great, when they govern the imperfection

---

[28] Thus, committing a slip of the tongue by referring to Joyce's work *Portrait of the Artist as a Young Man* as *Portrait of an Artist*, Lacan notes his slip before saving it—as is his habit, a little later, by extending it with a voluntary pun meant to show the fusion between Stephen and Bloom, who is seeking a son, representing Joyce's own fusion with a father he rejects: "There is an entire chapter in *Surface and Symbol* that is only about this. It is to the extent that it culminates in a Blephen and Stumm who meet in the text of *Ulysses*. This shows manifestly that it isn't only that they are made of the same signifier, but really of the same substance. *Ulysses* is the testimony of that by which Joyce remains rooted in his father while rejecting him. That's what his symptom really is." *Ibid.*, seminar of January 13, 1976.

without removing it. Hence the strange idea about the slips coming from the readings and commentaries belonging to the work. To translate is to be at odds with the work, not to turn your back on the truth but because it is impossible for there to exist something like a truth to this undertaking. The text creates a place of mirages; the language into which it is translated does as well. There is no chance that these mirages will coincide, however it may seem to us as translators.

This, in large part, sheds light on what we reproached Lacan for when he writes in English: he translates himself; he presents in English as an author producing French; he then becomes more or less incomprehensible to the English reader, while annoying the Francophone who reads him in English, since he does not seem to place his remarks in the ordinary context of English. He cultivates the off-kilter, the side-step, the impossible coincidence. He absolutely refuses to make what he says in English "naturally" coincide with what he says in French. His English isn't English, and isn't identified as such by either English speakers or by himself; it is a *situs* that allows envisaging the conceptual work he does when he invents new concepts in analysis. Thus it would be absurd to reproach him his lack of ease—his mannered style—when he expresses himself in English; not only because something prevents him from expressing himself "naturally," fluently, in English, but because what he has to say, in this discontinuity between French and English, is absolutely constitutive of what he means by *analysis*. Analytical discourse does not refer directly to objects; it concerns them, if you will, through linguistic detours, which neither fade away nor even arrive. Lacan's English discourse is filled with pitfalls; it exists only wrestling with and competing with French, with his French that is untranslatable. The English he uses does not vanish before objects in such a way that French is forgotten: French is in the foreground, even in English, and it prevents English from constituting its own objects, simply because the true objects of analysis are linguistic objects, without correspondents that are not. In his lectures and articles in English, Lacan installs his French discourse, without seeking to make it vanish, quite simply because it is the material that needs to be said and that cannot be said otherwise. Joyce's untranslatability closely resembles Lacan's; he identified this untranslatability to his own. Basically, he has the same style in French and English, and the difficulties of his style are not "faults"; as he says himself in the November 13, 1957, session: "There is, in the difficulties of this style, something that corresponds to the very object at hand."[29] "Correspond" may not be the best word, because what corresponds to the difficulties of his style does not exist as such, at least not as counterpart.

But as much as the difficulties of Lacan's style in French appear rich and stand out, the "same" difficulties of style, translated into English, are dull, artificial, fallacious, and hardly appear outstanding to the English speaker.

The passage into English killed them, but is there a passage into English that could bring forth the Lacanian text from its entrails rather than reflecting it in some mirror?

---

[29] J. Lacan, *Formations of the Unconscious, op. cit.*, seminar of November 13, 1957.

13
WILLIAM SHAKESPEARE

"It is to the fool, O Shakespeare, as much in life as in letters, that
destiny gave the task of keeping available over the centuries the
place of truth that Freud would bring to light."
—Jacques Lacan, *Écrits*, 661.

The references to Shakespeare in the *Seminar* occur much earlier than those concerning Joyce. No doubt, the expression "writing on
Shakespeare" is as bad as the utterance we have already criticized: "to
write on Joyce." Lacan no more practices literary analysis in the 1950s
than he does about Joyce in the 1970s; and it could be said that he
writes "with Shakespeare" or "according to Shakespeare," by allowing
the author and his admirable language to work on him, as much as we
said that he wrote "with Joyce" or "according to Joyce." Nevertheless,
the references to Shakespeare bear the mark of the concerns of the
first years of the *Seminar*, which will fade over the following years.[1]

Thus, at the end of the 1950s it was still a matter of breaking
with the notion of *intersubjectivity*, whether understood as being between conscious subjects or unconscious subjects and to substitute it
with, as much as possible, the notion of *structure*, which Lacan would
later gently deride.[2] *Hamlet* is analyzed in order to understand the
fascination it holds for most spectators. It isn't Hamlet the subject who
touches us and with whom we will sympathize through his words;
from the outset Hamlet is a collection of signifiers working on what

---

[1] Lacan may have wanted this retreat, since he situates in 1956 an event that caused
him to "give up on references to Shakespeare's savage dramas, which have become com-
pulsive in analytical circles, where they play the role of *savonette à villain* [figurative
expression—a soap that washes away the stain of low birth] for philistinism." "L'instance
de la lettre," *Écrits*, *op. cit.*, 503 (n. 1.).

[2] When it becomes clear to him, perhaps belatedly, that it has become a slogan
rather than a useful tool.

may well be called subjects, those of the spectators, on condition of calling *subject* an interplay of replacements and contrasts of signifiers:

> We cannot account for the experience of analysis by working from the premise that the signifier is, for example, a pure and simple reflection, a pure and simple product of what are currently called inter-human relations.... Hamlet is the image of this level of the subject where it can be said that it is in terms of pure signifiers that destiny is articulated, and that the subject is only in some sense the reverse of a message that isn't even the subject's.[3]

And this is precisely what makes your blood run cold and constitutes the real ghost. Hamlet's father's ghost's speech is less received by the subject Hamlet than it constitutes this subject, who is the mode according to which this association of signifiers is lived, and no doubt comes across multiple others. But, one might object, while it is perfectly clear that, as Lacan says, "The hero is only there, present through the words he bequeaths to us,"[4] while his "subjectivity" is fictional and exploded, it needs at least to be held, built, embodied by actors who lend their living subjectivity to the operation of the tragedy, who, by delegation, communicate, to our own subjectivity, an author's subjectivity. During this period of the 1950s, phenomenology was pervasive and intersubjectivity was considered a real notion like sympathy had been in the excessively "realist" readings done of Hume. Lacan uses Shakespeare's theater in order to challenge this way of representing the play's effect on our unconscious:

> That the mode a work uses to touch us, to touch us specifically in the deepest way, which is to say on the level of the unconscious, is something that owes to an arrangement, to a composition of the work which, without a doubt, causes us to be interested at the unconscious level; but this is not because of the presence of something that really supports in front of us an unconscious. I mean that we are not dealing, contrary to what is believed, with the poet's unconscious; even if its presence is felt in certain

---

[3] J. Lacan, *The Seminar of Jacques Lacan Book VI: Desire and Its Interpretation*, ed. J.-A. Miller, trans. B. Fink (Medford, MA: Polity, 2019), seminar of March 18, 1959.
[4] *Ibid.*

non-concerted traces in his work, elements such as slips of the tongue or symbolic elements unnoticed by the author.[5]

Lacan does not believe in the *subject* any more than Hobbes or Hume and he does not grant him any substantial reality; on the other hand, he deciphers what we take for sympathy, whether it be with Hamlet or, through him, with the play's author, as a kind of concatenation that allows us to situate and insert a part of our own signifiers in the play's signifiers. We "come to terms with" the play's structure and insert our signifiers so successfully, although in very different ways, that we harbor illusions of communication and identification with the characters. In fact: "The leading status that Hamlet takes on for us is that which gives us his value of equivalent structure to that of Oedipus." *Hamlet* interests us because we find a role to play there.

From this perspective, it is regrettable that Lacan did not use Hume's conception of the psyche as a theater able to link up to other nested theaters, in such a way that it creates, with these others, a composite system, certainly, but one in which it is impossible to tell if such and such an actor, that are, in turn, impressions and ideas, belong to a certain fraction of the system rather than another. Is it by chance that Hume writes about tragedy and accentuates the role of language to resolve the famous paradox to which philosophers have devoted their attention since Antiquity?[6] In any case, it is indeed the idea of *theater*, of the articulation of scenes, that is held by Lacan to explain our interest in tragedy: we place our signifiers on a scene that is not ours but that we can easily appropriate. It isn't some psychology of a character or an author that captivates us:

> It is quite obviously the articulation of tragedy itself that is what interests us.... This is true of its organization, through what it establishes in the way of superimposed frameworks inside of which the dimension of human subjectivity can find its own space. And this means that, if you will, in this machinery, or even in its clothing racks, to put it metaphorically, in the need for a certain number of superimposed frames, the depth of a stage, of a hall, of a room, the depth is given inside of which can be posed

---

[5] *Ibid.*

[6] How is it that we feel pleasure at watching what, in real life, would or should horrify us? Hume insists, to resolve this paradox, on the role played by language.

in the simplest way the problem for us of the articulation of desire.... If we are moved by a play, it is by reason of, I will reiterate, the dimensions of the development it offers to the place that is ours to take of what strictly speaking our own relationship with our own desire contains that is problematical.[7]

The topic of desire is the key to what we experience, without necessarily understanding why, as an emotion of sympathy for the character whose existence we wish for beyond words. In truth, the play's signs capture a certain amount of our psychic material and compel it to organize itself in a certain way, sheltered from the action, but not from affective investments.

Far from sympathizing with such and such a more or less supposed aspect of the author's biography, we rush headfirst, without even realizing it, into a place the author prepared through his writing to trap our desire, by capturing or stunning it:

> That there is a Shakespeare drama behind Hamlet is secondary in light of what composes *Hamlet*'s structure. It is this structure that accounts for Hamlet's effect, and this all the more since Hamlet himself is after all a character whose depths are not unknown simply because of our ignorance. Indeed, he's a character who is made up of something which is the empty place in which to situate—and this is the important part—our ignorance.

In a great author of tragedies there is the equivalent of a Desargues in topology; and, reciprocally, if we are so trapped by problems in topology, and if Desargues' theorem, for example, has such an effect on us, it is because it encounters in us a structure comparable to what we can enter into or inhabit in a tragedy: "*Hamlet* is a composition, a structure such that desire can find its place correctly enough for the

---

[7] *Ibid.* In a certain sense, by transcribing it, Lacan adopts Hazlitt's analysis of Hamlet: "Hamlet is a name; his speeches and sayings but the ideal coinage of the poet's brain. What then, are they not real? They are as real as our own faults. Their reality is in the reader's mind. It is we who are Hamlet." *Characters of Shakespeare's Plays, op. cit.* The text goes on to show, through a multitude of examples, how we assimilate, through numerous traits, to Hamlet, who is not just a character of which the only being consists of existing in front of us. We know, as we saw in the preceding chapter on Joyce, that Lacan read this text, since he subtly quotes a detail from it, and that the passage we cited is just before this detail.

problems of the subject to desire to be able to be projected there; it's enough, in some sense, to read it."

As for the actors, who seem to embody the signifiers and, so to speak, subjectivize them so that they don't remain simple gears powering a structure, are they, through their function, what they seem to be? "Of course, this dimension added to the play, namely the actors who are going to play this *Hamlet* is strictly analogous to that through which we ourselves are interested in our own unconscious." They too cast their signifiers, those they constituted with their own history, into the structure, in such a way that we—the audience—feel that our place there is pointed out. The analogy that's involved is that "the actor lends his limbs, his presence, not simply as a marionette, but with his quite real unconscious, namely the relationship of his limbs with a certain history that is his." Good or bad, "The actor is there; it is to the extent of the concord of something that can, indeed, have the closest relationship with his unconscious, with what he has to portray for us, that he gives it a touch that adds something, but that is far from constituting the crux of what is being communicated to us: the drama's performance." The actor comes to cross his own signifiers with those of the "character" we figure he embodies, or that he figures he embodies, and with those of the audience, with each member of the audience. "The signifier, we are the ones who provide the material for it; it's with our own limbs—that's the imaginary—that we make the alphabet of what we say that's unconscious, and of course each one of us in diverse ways because we don't use the same elements to be caught in the unconscious."[8]

The play scene, "the scene of the play that Hamlet has performed, with which he surprises and captures the king's conscience, and where everyone's anxiety mounts regarding his, Hamlet's intentions," is there to remind us that the scene is a structure destined to capture the viewer, who won't take long to be fascinated by it.

Nonetheless, where is English in this entire adventure, which might as well be Oedipus' or Antigone's, but does not particularly or specifically signal an English play as such? At this time, Lacan did not seek to settle this question, as we thought we noticed some tendency that he did when he speaks intensely about Joyce: does Joyce write En-

---

[8] J. Lacan, *Desire and Its Interpretation, op. cit.*, seminar of March 18, 1959.

glish? How to identify the language he uses? Etc. No questions of this kind for Shakespeare: "His language—whether Shakespeare's or the English language's—is admirable." The privileged contact with English seems to reside in *two* major moments, if not in *three*, if it is appropriate, as we believe it is, to take into account a detail.

The *first* consists in the fact that Lacan speaks less about Hamlet's *fantôme du père* than about the *ghost*. What difference is there between saying *le fantôme du père* and saying *ghost*, using Shakespeare's English term in a text written in French without visible or even audible quotes, for Lacan doesn't even appear to be citing when he says *"le ghost"*?

Lacan does not directly answer the question himself; he exploits this difference beautifully and he practices it very effectively to methodically get his results, but fragments of his work need to be gathered in order to glimpse several consistent elements of doctrine relating to this point. The best places where we have seen him theorize such a use of language are those where he examines, with the exclusive help moreover of English authors, the status of proper names, which is of interest to the analyst from the outset, who is spontaneously vigilant to the way the analysand names himself, the way he names those with whom he lives, and to the toponymy of the places he frequents. He treats the question prior to his use of *ghost*, in *Seminar IX* and again in *Seminar XII*. But what is the relationship between the question of proper names and that of the use of *Das Ding* or of *ghost*, neither being a proper name, where we might have legitimately expected one.[9]

It consists precisely in this remark, more suggested than explicitly stated by Lacan at the time he said it, that the proper name and the common noun are only noun functions rather than intrinsic characteristics that could be definitively and inherently attributed. It then becomes possible to render a noun proper by undermining its plural, which is what happens when you go from *"fantôme"* to "ghost." When in French I use the word *"fantôme,"* even for Hamlet's father, it easily finds its place among the *"fantômes,"* whether or not one believes in their existence; *le ghost*, used in English in a French text, does not

---

[9] Let us point out here, in order to avoid any ambiguity, that we are not going in any detail into the dialectic of the theses of Stuart Mill, Russell, and Gardiner, but that we are using pieces or articulations of theses that we can be certain were known to Lacan, no matter how he may have made use of them in *Seminars IX* or *XII*.

make me feel like saying *les ghosts*, which could probably be very easily said in English, on condition of saying *the ghosts*. *Le ghost*, with its French article, becomes a kind of syntagm that is almost as difficult to pluralize as *the old man*, a term adolescents sometimes use to refer to their father. The fact of writing—writing here plays a crucial role, even if spoken—the word in a foreign language, appending an article from the host language, gives it a singular conceptual rigidity and fixity that separate it from the individuals and collectives that it would have a right to call its own. Become *le ghost*, Hamlet's father is no longer a ghost like any other; he is susceptible of taking on a totally specific history, loaded with all the details that are found in Shakespeare's play. Lacan's stroke of genius, who imposes his reading of *Hamlet* by coining *le ghost*, is that Hamlet's father loses his name—whereas he has one in the play, the very one his son has—in exchange for a noun, but which, bound to a French definite article and left in English inside the French, reclaims its proper name and thus becomes everyone's father's name, explaining in the process the play's fascination and intromission or immixing in each of us.

The theory of *le ghost*, which is necessarily the ghost of someone very specific, is not the same as would be a theory of the ghost or of ghosts. *Le ghost* immediately introduces us to Hamlet's fantasies, to the constitution of his psyche, as the play's composition structures it, is its structure. *Le ghost* is less a character than an identification, a personification, for it is the strangle knot into which Hamlet cannot fail to fall; it is the slip knot that constitutes Hamlet, as is clearly shown by the encounter atop high walls from which there is no escape. Like Antigone, but in another way, Hamlet is walled in, this time by ramparts. The dead father is constituted by *le ghost* in a kind of eternal singular that does not completely exclude the plural, for many are the men who live with their dead father, but such that this plural seems almost impossible, for it is the debate of any mental structure with the father (with one's father) that is captured by this, centered and open to being invested by identification, rejection, in attraction and terror. Locke was able to identify this aspect of paternity, with his refutation of Filmer, when he speaks of "this strange kind of arrogant ghost called paternity which, when you have caught it, soon procures you empire and an unlimited absolute power."[10] This

---

[10] F. Lessay, *Le débat Locke-Filmer* (Paris: PUF, 1978), 272.

business of Shakespeare's ghost and the ghosts that Hume knew to criticize, bears a striking resemblance, in his helicoidal tourniquet, to that of the *Nom-du-Père* [Name-of-the-Father], launched by Lacan in 1958, with upper case, dashes, and in the singular, before reappearing in 1963, for a single session in the singular, although with no certainty as to the upper case and the dashes, then, later on according to the entire range of singulars and plurals, without the voice ever allowing us to be certain about the inscription.

The *second* point relates specifically to this helicoidal tourniquet, the same one to which Adam Smith has recourse in his *Theory of Moral Sentiments* when he distinguishes in a theoretical vortex, a notion understood in its subjectivity, then in its objectivity, before being picked up again, afresh, in its subjectivity, in a movement that one suspects is able to be prolonged for a long time, if not indefinitely. Thus, merit, the love of praise, authority, are caught and composed in this spiral of which Smith only considers a segment.[11] Lacan finds this movement, which is so closely related to some Pascalian reversal of the for and against, which is not unrelated to that of Adam Smith's reader that Hegel was, in Shakespeare's *Sonnets*, when he prepares to read them by risking a translation of certain words at least. He notes, for example, in the April 29, 1959, lesson, that *dépit*, which tends to be translated as *spite*, has the disadvantage of being experienced as "subjective" in French, whereas its meaning tends to be objective in Shakespeare:

> *Spite* is everywhere in Shakespeare's sonnets. For us, *dépit* has a subjective meaning; our first step in an introduction to the Elizabethans ought to be, for a certain number of words, to rehabilitate their ability, too, to turn on their hinges, in other words to situate *le dépit* somewhere between objective *dépit* and subjective *dépit,* in something to which we seem to have lost reference, which is precisely what happens on the level

---

[11] Lacan often has recourse to this Smithian tourniquet, to which we should attribute the November 1, 1974 remark (The Third), where he cites an example of subjectivization/objectivization: "Lalangue, is what permits that the *voeu* [wish], we consider that it is not by chance that it is also the *veut* [wants] of *vouloir* [to want] (third person of the Indicative), that the negating non [no] and the naming nom [name], it isn't either by chance that d'*eux* ("d" [of] before that "eux" [them] designating those of which we speak], is shaped in the same way as the number *deux* [two], it isn't by chance nor is it arbitrary as Saussure says."

of the order, namely of the terms that can be at the same time between the two, between the objective and the subjective.

Thus, in Hamlet's complaint:

O cursed spite!,[12] it's what he has *dépit* of; it is in what way time is also unjust to him. We no longer know how to articulate these words that are at play at the center of what is the subject's lived experience, or everything that it can designate as injustice in the world. Perhaps you recognize in passing the misguided *belle âme*, which we have not left behind, far from it, despite our best efforts, but which the Shakespearian vocabulary transcends.[13]

Nothing is therefore missing in the analysis of this spin from the subjective to the objective, with return to the subjective, not even the allusion to Hegel, who, we know, where this method is concerned, owes everything to Adam Smith.

This engraving, around which subjective and objective are distributed, like a Moebius strip, which, at the same time, binds and separates interior and exterior, is a veritable trope of Shakespeare's writing such as Lacan reads it. The way he investigates *spite* is also how he examines *conceit*. The ghost asks Hamlet to "Step between her"—the Queen—"and her fighting soul," adding, "Conceit in weakest bodies strongest works."[14] Lacan remarks that *conceit*, which signifies at the same time *vanity* and *witticism*, is ambiguous; he retains the latter, for *conceit* is what French calls in the plural *concetti*, borrowing, without modification, from the Italian the term for these "subtle and affected expressions, witticisms in sometimes dubious taste, that one encounters in a literary work or in a conversation," as defined by the Klincksieck dictionary; in other words, the quips that leave a mark in the mind and the body.

Let us conclude with three short remarks, the third of which coincides with the little detail we announced to punctuate the preceding observations. *Firstly*, we invoked Hume by regretting that Lacan was

---

[12] "The time is out of joint: O cursed spite / That ever I was born to set it right." *Hamlet* 1.5.189–190.

[13] J. Lacan, *Desire and Its Interpretation, op. cit.*, seminar of April 29, 1959.

[14] Act III, Scene IV.

unfamiliar with his work and by speculating that he could have put it to good use. Nonetheless, these regrets need to be nuanced because, in fact, Lacanian research and findings have made it so that we can no longer read Hume the same way, and that aspects that would remain invisible without reading Lacan now jump out at us and become absolutely essential. We are convinced that the Lacanian theory of the subject, that of the signifiers to which it is related, the theory of the scene, constitute points of reference from which to reread Hobbes and Hume and to transform what could easily be taken for simple metaphors into quite consistent conceptual frameworks that now stand out. *Secondly*, since Lacan defines psychoanalysis as a deciphering of enigmas,[15] he could have addressed Goethe or some other German author; one cannot help but notice that he does so much less often and that he clearly leans in an Anglo-Saxon direction. While he devotes a lesson to *Elective Affinities*, we do not find anything with *Faust* or *Pandora* of equivalent magnitude to what he undertakes with *Hamlet* or *Ulysses*. *Finally*, how can we avoid the thought that Lacan's attitude toward English may have changed? All his analyses surrounding Shakespeare leave him captivated by this language, and it is hard to tell whether it is Shakespeare's or English itself. And this is not the last text that we will pick from the March 11, 1959, lesson to help us decide. Talking about the percussive power that each line of *Hamlet* has in English, Lacan allows himself to say, to the clear detriment of French: "Through a very odd kind of thing, I think I can say, based on my own experience, that it is unperformable in French. I have never seen a good *Hamlet* in French. Nor anyone who plays Hamlet well, nor a text worth hearing." There is, nevertheless, an element that sneaks in here and must not get away, urging us to be cautious: the disparity of the two languages, French and English, be it, here or there, to one or the other language's advantage. *Unperformable*: the term is very strong and it detonates strangely, immediately accompanied by the idea of *untranslatable*. *Hamlet* cannot be translated, while the French audience is affected by the text as well as the English audience, or rather, is available and susceptible of being affected by the text in the same way. Soon it will be the turn of Francophone psychoanalysis

---

[15] And even "the answer to an enigma." J. Lacan, *Sinthome, op. cit.*, seminar of January 13, 1976.

to be reputed unable to be expressed in English: the valorization of one language over another, or the affective connotation that modifies their appreciation in one context and another, does not change anything. What counts is the non-encounter, or rather—because there is never a non-encounter—the bad encounter, the impossibility of making things coincide, the failed rendez-vous, and there are others in Lacan, starting with that of the sexes engaging in sex. This little clue of *Hamlet* reputed to be unperformable in French is obviously the distant, analogical announcement, and the connecting thread, of the idea of a language unsuited to the expression of psychoanalysis. When languages are as disjointed as English and French, it's that their relationship to the unconscious is different, heterogeneous. It becomes understandable, then, that the relationship with analysis cannot be the same. Has anyone thought about the fact that French speakers who learn English the best can neither speak it nor write it well enough to be mistaken for English speakers? Thus, details about the difference between French actors, unable to play the role of Hamlet, and English actors, who see it as the pinnacle of their career, must be properly understood. It is as impossible for a French actor to make the role of Hamlet and the text of *Hamlet* (translated into French) his own as it is for an English analysand to make his unconscious his own through the English language, which is an absolute impediment, and probably for the same reasons. But we should be careful: the fact that an English speaker resists analysis or that English is an obstacle to analysis is no more a "fault" of English than the fact that Shakespeare's English—or Joyce's, for that matter—is untranslatable into French and that what is at play in Shakespeare's language cannot be played in French. In truth, it isn't certain there is a change in attitude, although there appears to be, because to say that the English language prevents the English speaker from being an analysand is not necessarily to denigrate the English language: we need to pinpoint, without the depiction having been completed, the aspect of the English language that makes it unsuited to the production of an analysis.

14
EDGAR ALLAN POE

The allusions to Edgar Allan Poe are only interesting to the extent that Lacan turns his attention to the tale called, since its translation by Baudelaire, *La lettre volée* [*The Purloined Letter*], the debatable[1] title of which participates in the title of a masterful seminar that serves as the entrance to the *Écrits*. As with *Ulysses* and *Hamlet*, it's the tale's structural operation that constitutes the object of Lacan's study in this work. The two remarkable things about the "Séminaire sur 'la lettre volée'" ["Seminar on 'The Purloined Letter'"] derive, first, from a strong affirmation on Lacan's part, and, secondly, to discussions of Baudelaire's translation, of which Lacan, as he claims to reveal Poe's logic, endeavors to show the weaknesses.

The strong affirmation is that "The Purloined Letter" "demonstrates"—this is the word Lacan chose; it is strong because it is the one that would be used to characterize the work of the mathematician—"in a story, the major determination the subject receives from the path of a signifier." We do not think that the term *demonstrate*, used in this context, is a kind of inadvertence: he uses it again explicitly in 1971, speaking insistently of a "literary demonstration."[2] Once again, it is a matter of demonstrating that "it is the symbolic order that is, for the

---

[1] [Translator's note] As we shall see, Lacan contests Baudelaire's translation of *purloined* as *volée* [stolen]. He employs etymological gymnastics to assert that *purloined* should have been translated as *détournée,* meaning, in English, *diverted.* Beside the fact that Poe could have used this term but chose not to, and that *purloined* seems above all an elegant way to say *stolen* in English, Webster's dictionary does point out that while *to purloin* is a synonym of *to steal,* it "stresses removing or carrying off for one's own use or purposes." Perhaps *La lettre dérobée* might have come closer to Poe's title, but this would not have suited Lacan's overall reading. His criticism of Baudelaire's translation strikes one, here and elsewhere, as unfounded; French simply has no exact equivalent to the word Poe chose so judiciously. Might Lacan's animus toward Baudelaire, in the midst of his otherwise extraordinarily perceptive reading of Poe's tale, be motivated by jealousy directed at an unmatched master of *lalangue*?

[2] J. Lacan, "Lituraterre," *Autres écrits, op. cit.*, 15.

subject, constitutive." The subject is not what he imagines himself to be, nor what he is imagined to be; it is the action of the signifiers, from which he is offset but of which he thinks he is at the origin, that makes him what he is, without his ever being able to coincide immediately with himself or with others (through some sympathy). What does "The Purloined Letter" demonstrate? That the structure that binds subjects is deeper than the idea that each might have of being at its foundation and that it evolves according to its own logic, which has nothing to do with what the subjects might imagine.

The queen is in possession of a compromising letter; we will never know more than this about its content. The king does not know the letter exists. The minister knows about it, suspects that it is "compromising," but does not know its content. He invents a scheme to remove the letter and replace it with another one under the noses of the protagonists, who, fooled or paralyzed, cannot intervene: under that of the king who sees nothing and knows nothing; of the queen next, who sees everything, understands everything, sees that she is being shown everything, but who cannot say anything nor do anything to stop the minister without compromising herself; of the minister himself, protected by the royal power, which he surpasses thanks to his knowledge. Through his story, Poe shows that the situation can only evolve in a way that eludes each of the protagonists, who can only calculate, when they have the information to do so, with the calculations supposed to be those of the others. The letter's recovery only becomes possible thanks to detective Dupin who, informed of the affair by the police commissioner, who happens to be one of his friends, undertakes, this time against the minister, an operation comparable to his, to the point of being no more than its repetition. The plot twists are such that the subjects only enter it and participate in it as passive elements in what could be called a "structural marcottage." They only exist through the implacable action of what Lacan calls the *signifiers*, which cause the subjects to submit to their own laws. Poe solves a problem in game theory, the structural complexity of which includes a reflection on space and time. *On space*, because the problem thieves always face is where and how to find their target and then of knowing whether they will be able to hide their goods for any length of time; improvisation would be dangerous, but logic is no less, for all the protagonists can seize upon it as well. *And on time*, for the moment things must be done is as though dictated to the protagonists, whenever they act rationally in a situation; under these conditions it is necessary to grasp in time how the other party cannot fail to understand a situation and structure it. We can see someone we do not think knows they were seen, but care must be taken to avoid being caught in the same situation as that through which we imagine reducing the other to a seen object.

The cynic—the minister—who turned the situation for a time to his own advantage, can see his advantage removed by the same logic that allowed him to acquire it in the first place: the situation develops according to its own logic, which is that of none of the protagonists.

What Lacan shows is that the letter travels: it *always* arrives at its destination, sooner or later, whatever journey it has had to make, and whatever ambushes and traps it has had to evade to get there. The letter is the cipher of the psychic material carried in "the train of the signifier as arms and baggage,"[3] as Lacan puts it in the *Écrits*. This understanding of the letter's trajectory allows Lacan to condemn Baudelaire's translation, which he considers flawed in several ways, beginning with the title. "Baudelaire, despite his devotion—we would gladly add: thanks to it, or because of it—betrayed Poe by translating as "La lettre volée" [The Stolen Letter] its title, which is *The Purloined Letter*, in other words a title that uses a word that is rare enough to make it easier for us to define its etymology than its usage. *To purloin*, the OED tells us, is an Anglo-French word, a composite of the prefix *pur-* found in *purpose, purchase, purport*, and the Old French word: *loing, loigner, longé*. We recognize, in the first element, the Latin *pro*, insofar as it is distinguished from an *ante* by what it supposes of a behind before which it goes, eventually to protect it, if not to vouch for it (whereas *ante* goes forth to meet what is coming toward it). As for the second, the Old French word *loigner*, verb of the attribute of place *au loing* (or also *longé*), it does not mean *au loin* [in the distance] but *au long de* [alongside of]; it is therefore a question of *mettre de côté* [to set aside] or to refer to a familiar locution that plays on both meanings, to *mettre à gauche* [to set to the left]. Thus are we confirmed in our detour by the very object that takes us there: for it is indeed *lettre détournée* [diverted letter] that we are dealing with, a letter the trajectory of which has been *prolonged*, or, to reference

---

[3] J. Lacan, "Séminaire sur 'La Lettre volée," *Écrits, op. cit.*, 30.

postal vocabulary, the *lettre en souffrance* ["dead letter," in English, but literally "suffering or pending letter."][4]

The finesse of his reading, ensured by the logic of Poe's demonstration thus revealed—thanks to the head start he has on the poet—allows Lacan to correct Baudelaire at his leisure and to appear exquisite in English when he takes the time to pinpoint what he considers several of Baudelaire's lapses, leading to mistranslation. The only one we shall examine, because it deals directly with the logic we described, is found as early as the second page in

> a cleverly worded comment by the narrator, who tells us that "the minister's upper-hand depends on the knowledge that the thief has of the knowledge the victim has of his thievery," in Poe's text: *"the robber's knowledge of the loser's knowledge of the robber."* Terms of which the author stresses the importance by having Dupin literally repeat them right after the narration of the scene of the letter's theft. Here again, we can say that Baudelaire floats in his language by having one character question, the other confirm, with these words: "Does the thief know...?" then "the thief knows..." What? "That the person robbed knows her robber." Because what matters to the thief isn't only that the said person knows who stole from her, but indeed with whom she is dealing as thieves go; it's that that she thinks him capable of anything, meaning that she confers upon him the position that no one is capable of fulfilling in reality because it is imaginary: that of absolute master.[5]

March 17, 1971, Lacan comments again on his translation, comparing it favorably to Baudelaire's: "The block format of the phrase I quote must be kept," before adding, "This element of knowledge that knows, in other words, to have imposed a certain fantasy of self—what the minister was able to impose on the queen's psyche—to be indeed the man who dares everything, is, as Dupin says right away, the key to the situation." It is indeed the same "block" aspect that he defends against Baudelaire's translation where this famous man is concerned *"who dares all things, those unbecoming as well as those becoming a man."* Baudelaire translates it as *"ce qui est indigne d'un homme,*

---

[4] *Ibid.*, 29. In March 1971, after having reread himself, he maintains the same commentary. J. Lacan, *D'un discours qui ne serait pas du semblant, op. cit.*, seminar of March 17, 1971.

[5] J. Lacan, "Séminaire sur 'La Lettre volée," *Écrits, op. cit.*, p. 33.

aussi bien que ce qui est digne de lui" [what is unworthy of a man, as well as what is worthy of him]. Now, Lacan insists, at this point, to literally translate: "*ce qui est indigne aussi bien que ce qui est digne d'un homme*" [what is unworthy as well as what is worthy of a man], because it is as a block that the phrase should be taken. Phallic power is at play here, and if you break up the phrase, as Baudelaire does, the idea is lost at the same time.[6]

One only translates a text to the extent it is understood; here and elsewhere it should be the one who has best understood its log-

---

[6] [Translator's note] Both of Lacan's critiques of Baudelaire's translations here seem unfair, at best. In the case of "*the robber's knowledge of the loser's knowledge of the robber*," translating it as a "block" is not workable in French because of the possessives, particularly in the context of the narrative. Far from "floating in his language," Baudelaire's solution of incorporating it into the dialogue is actually brilliant. The second "block" Lacan insists on does not respect French syntax or is based on an ignorance of English syntax: "*those unbecoming as well as those becoming a man*" is read or heard by English speakers as "*those unbecoming a man as well as those becoming a man*." In French, the "block" separates the two terms into: 1) unworthy things in general, and 2) things worthy of a man in particular. Baudelaire's translation might be called "structuralist" in that it calls upon the structure of each language to perfect his translation, thus his "*ce qui est indigne d'un homme, aussi bien que ce qui est digne de lui*" [what is unworthy of a man, as well as what is worthy of him"] actually recreates in French what an Anglophone pre-reflexively fills in when reading the phrase. It remains to be seen, in any case how much any of these translations heighten or diminish the already clearly phallic nature of the language and the situation. Below are examples of the passages written by Poe and translated by Baudelaire that are discussed here by Lacan. Those with enough French can judge for themselves the quality of Baudelaire's translations.

Poe: "But this ascendancy," I interposed, "would depend upon the robber's knowledge of the loser's knowledge of the robber. Who would dare—" "The thief," said G., "is the Minister D--, who dares all things, those unbecoming as well as those becoming a man."

Baudelaire: — Mais cet ascendant, interrompis-je, dépend de ceci : le voleur sait-il que la personne volée connaît son voleur ? Qui oserait... ? —
Le voleur, dit G..., c'est D..., qui ose tout ce qui est indigne d'un homme, aussi bien que ce qui est digne de lui.

Poe: "Here, then," said Dupin to me, "you have precisely what you demand to make the ascendancy complete—the robber's knowledge of the loser's knowledge of the robber."

Baudelaire: voilà précisément le cas demandé pour rendre l'ascendant complet : le voleur sait que la personne volée connaît son voleur.

ic who is in the position to produce the best translation. It certainly seems that exposure to game theory is helpful in understanding the logic of "The Purloined Letter." But, as Lacan's problematical remarks regarding Baudelaire's translation indicate, in judging a translation, other factors, including the degree to which the original language is understood and issues of translatability, are involved as well.

Lacan does explicitly point out the importance of game theory to Poe's composition, but he uses the contested language of the "precursor" in doing so: "Poe, as the good precursor that he is of the research into combination strategy that is in the process of renewing the sciences, was guided in his fiction by an objective similar to our own."[7] As far as we are concerned, we think it is in no way necessary to have recourse to the very fallacious concept of *precursor*, which the very philosophy Lacan salutes in Peirce or Recanati allows us to condemn. Let us say instead and more modestly that game theory illuminates the signifiers of the writing of "The Purloined Letter." While the mathèmes do not coincide with what Lacan did not dare call *littérèmes* or *littéra-turèmes*, but which would be frameworks as consistent as them and as efficient in their consistency, each nevertheless opens the door to the other in such a way that if one is missing, the other is also. We should not, any more than Pascal, oppose the *esprit de finesse* to the *esprit de géométrie*; it is enough that one should be lacking for the other, as well, to be touched with imperfection. But, curiously, these two types of balanced effectuation, which are also two types of reading, evolve over time at such a different rate that the same text, characterized by the identity of its signifiers, so long as these have been conserved, can no longer be read at all in the same way over time. The evolution of the mathèmes no longer allows situating the leading edge of the *litérèmes* where it was, in the course of a move that renders us radically amnesiac, for we can absolutely not rediscover the way an author could be read at the time he was writing. It is thus that Lacan, who sees Poe as a precursor, is the first to challenge the avatars of the remains of the philosophy of sympathy that led the English author to interpret the supremacy of a player of the odds and evens game as resulting from his ability to put himself in the other's place and to think and feel like him. This divination is

---

[7] *Ibid.*, 61.

pure hokum, which, at best, might work for a turn or two, but which would become completely impossible beyond that against a player of average intelligence, in other words, against anyone other than a complete idiot.[8]

---

[8] Lacan seems to forget here—at least this is what J. Houis, who translated this text, suggests to me—that the problem lies in detecting the adversary's tendencies, which can be done by observation of the adversary's behavior, not by pure sympathy, but indeed by putting yourself in his place. It is then precisely after a certain number of observations that you can gain an idea of the adversary's habits. The method is not only applicable to odds and evens, but also to poker, or to rock, paper, scissors; how would it be possible, if this were not so, for there to be champions?

15

LEWIS CARROLL, JONATHAN SWIFT, WILLIAM WORDSWORTH, ALDOUS HUXLEY, HENRY MILLER, WALT WHITMAN, VLADIMIR NABOKOV

If we are addressing several renowned names in literary history, it is simply because Lacan cites them and uses them directly; but we are aware, in so doing, that we are playing a dangerous game, since Lacan tends to use wordplay or create neologisms that are winks to the reader who must grasp, between the lines, what author is involved, thanks to a little sign perceptible only to the one with whom he is complicit. It is thus that, as we have said, the author of *Tristram Shandy* is never directly cited, which does not mean that allusions to his work do not percolate here and there. But we will limit ourselves, on principle, to a few authors, directly cited.

Lewis Carroll

The fifties and sixties were a strange time, when the most important authors did not find it unbecoming—and almost found it their duty—to attempt an interpretation of *Alice in Wonderland*. Deleuze has one in his *Logique du sens*.[1] True, Carroll is rarely cited by Lacan, compared to the authors previously studied. He is cited once, to illustrate identification to the rule that no one can avoid. The text is in *Seminar III*:

> Starting with an utterance, a game ensues, in every way comparable to what happens in *Alice in Wonderland*, when the servants and other characters of the Queen's court start playing cards by dressing up as cards, becoming themselves the King of Hearts, the Queen of Spades, and the Jack of Diamonds. An utterance commits us to support it with our words or to renege, to recuse it or confirm it, to refute it, but even more so, to yield to many things that are in the rules of the game. And even if the queen

---

[1] Paris, Les Éditions de Minuit, 1969.

changes the rules at any time, the crux of the matter wouldn't change; once introduced into the play of symbols, you have to follow rules.[2]

Language makes rules for us; whether we want it or not, it exercises its authority, compelling us to adopt an attitude toward it. It is this enlistment and this forced identification to its signs that Lacan's text addresses.

Three years later, Lacan advised psychiatrists and psychoanalysts to get acquainted with *nonsense*, in particular by reading *Alice*:

> I must tell you that if I had to recommend an introductory book to what a child psychiatrist or psychoanalyst must be, rather than any book by Mr. Piaget, I would recommend starting by reading *Alice in Wonderland*, because they would immediately grasp this thing that is based on children's deep experience of mental play [*qui repose sur la profonde expérience du jeu de l'esprit des enfants*] and which in effect shows us the value, the incidence, the dimension of the play of *nonsense* as such.[3]

It would be absurd to oppose literature to a scientific activity like psychology; literature conducts "experiments,"[4] certainly not by framing them in a perspective of teleological development such as Piaget wants to develop from the standpoint of the position of the adult who registers the progress of an individual gradually achieving a critical point of view, but by entering into original, discontinuous, and non-deducible points of view, complicit with the child's thought processes, that there is no question of viewing in terms of what separates it from the adult's thinking.

Jonathan Swift

Swift does belong after Carroll because, in the only lesson where Swift is presented at some length, his name is associated with Carroll's. Here is the opening of the April 26, 1961, lesson: "Swift and

---

[2] J. Lacan, *The Seminar of Jacques Lacan Book III: The Psychoses*, ed. J.-A. Miller, trans. R. Grigg (New York: Norton, 1993), seminar of December 7, 1955.

[3] J. Lacan, *Desire and Its Interpretation, op. cit.*, seminar of January 21, 1959.

[4] Speaking of Walt Whitman, he says that it is through a "thought experiment" that he achieves "an epidermal contact with the whole world." J. Lacan, *Ethics of Psychoanalysis, op. cit.*, seminar of January 13, 1960.

Lewis Carroll are two authors whom, without my having the time to provide a running commentary, you would do well to consult in order to find a lot of the material that relates very closely, as closely as possible, as close as is possible in works of literature, to the theme I am currently closest to." Lacan then lingers on a page he reads to his audience in its entirety, a rare occurrence. It's a page of *Gulliver's Travels*, in which Gulliver, on his way to Laputa, visits several kingdoms and pays particular attention to the way informers operate in the kingdom of Tribnia, called Langden by the locals: "They seize the letters and papers of the inhabitants. These papers are put in the hands of specialists who are expert in decoding the hidden meaning of words, syllables, and letters." Then, Lacan adds, Swift has a field day:

> for instance, they can discover a toilet to signify a privy council; a flock of geese, a senate; a lame dog, an invader; the plague, a standing army; a buzzard, a prime minister; the gout, a high priest; a gibbet, a secretary of state; a chamber pot, a committee of lords; a sieve, a court lady; a broom, a revolution; a mouse-trap, a public job; a bottomless pit, a treasury; a sewer, a court; a cap and bells, a favorite; a broken reed, a court of justice; an empty barrel, a general; a running sore, the administration. When this approach fails, they have more efficient ones, that their specialists call acrostics and anagrams. They give all initial letters a political meaning: thus, N could mean a plot, B a cavalry regiment, L a fleet. Or they transpose the letters on a suspect paper in such a way as to expose the most secret plans of a dissident party. For example, in a letter reading: "Our brother Tom has hemorrhoids," the clever transcriber will find in the combination of these neutral words a phrase meaning that everything is ready for a sedition.[5]

It is difficult to avoid thinking about certain political regimes that are particularly efficient at discovering, if not inventing, plots. But what might also come to mind is a certain rigid and allegorical use of the hermeneutics to which Freud contributed—in nevertheless famous pages of the *Interpretation of Dreams*, for example—that seem to deliver a particularly restrictive lexicon of dream signifiers, and, thereby, a conception of the signifier with which Lacan radically broke. However, Swift's slyness is at least double-edged, and, while it shows

---

[5] J. Lacan, *Transference*, *op. cit.*, seminar of April 19, 1961.

the absurdity of the path the informers have to follow in order to satisfy their delirious security measures, it seems to authorize, for our enjoyment, through a boomerang effect, the reverse movement that consists of calling things by their name and of transforming the king's privy council into a toilet seat, the senate into a flock of geese, etc. All censorship causes the return of the banned words, but then their effect becomes catastrophic since everything points to the reverse discourse telling the preceding discourse's truth, the best response to the informers being to reverse their hermeneutics, which become much funnier and much more real. And things are better designated by this method upside down rather than right side up. Inspired by the English tales of Swift and Sterne, the method will be Montesquieu's and Voltaire's, those fervent admirers of English culture: all political authoritarianism, reversed, yields philosophical tales. Isn't it also the case that any hermeneutics, with its back and forth, and in its pretension to go beyond the action of the signifiers, can prove what it wishes, but finds itself thus the target of ridicule? In this case, there would be many different sectors of our culture, decoders of encrypted messages, that stand to be castigated as useless or grotesque curlicues that never lead anywhere other than back to their starting point.

William Wordsworth

In his *Seminar VII*, Lacan reflects at length on a Wordsworth quotation cited by Freud: "If the benefit and novelty of the analytical experience were to be limited to that, it would go no farther than that dated thought that was born well before psychoanalysis, that child is father to the man. This saying, quoted by Freud himself, with respect, is from Wordsworth, an English Romantic poet."[6] The saying is of interest thanks to the inversion of an idea we find in Plato, for example, that the Ancients are our fathers; and while they are genetically, they are not culturally. This idea, which seems natural, is "dated," as Lacan says; it is tied to a history. And, in fact, Pascal, who is mentioned several lines later, had already overturned the legitimacy of worshipping ancestors supposed to be more knowledgeable than us:

---

[6] J. Lacan, *Ethics of Psychoanalysis, op, cit.*, seminar of November 25, 1959.

156

The entire line of men, over the course of so many centuries, must be considered as one subsisting man who is continually learning; whence the injustice of respecting Antiquity in its philosophers: for, just as old age is the age most distant from childhood, who cannot see that old age in this universal man must not be sought in the time closest to his birth, but in the time farthest away? Those we call Ancients were truly new in all things and made up the childhood of man, strictly speaking; and since we have added to their knowledge the experience of the centuries that followed them, it is in ourselves that this Antiquity can be found that we revere in the others.[7]

Thus is the cultural and historical order the reverse of the natural and biological order; while we are born of the Ancients, we are their parents the way our children will be ours through intelligence and culture. Though they may share the same links,[8] the lineages of cultural history, they are not those of natural biology. The cultural order is marked by a break with the natural order, something of which the seventeenth century was wholly aware.

That said, Wordsworth was brought up to go much further. Wordsworth is a nineteenth-century author. And it's for belonging to this period and the England of the Industrial Revolution that he is cited. Lacan's remark opens up very different horizons that give a singular twist to the Pascalian perspective with which it seemed at first to be in harmony:

It's not for nothing that we find him there—that English Romantic poet—with that *je ne sais quoi* that is new, shattering, if not stifling, that is unleashed, at the beginning of the nineteenth century with the Indus-

---

[7] Pascal, "Preface to the Treatise on Vacuum," *Les Provinciales, Pensées et opuscules divers, op. cit.*, 89–90.

[8] Leibniz had used this example to illustrate the relativity and ideality of space: "As the mind can picture an order consisting of genealogical lineages the sizes of which would consist only of the numbers of generations, where each person would have a place, and if we were to add the fiction of metempsychosis and brought back the same human souls, the people could change places. The one who was father or grandfather could become son or grandson, etc. And yet these genealogical places (lineages and spaces), although they would express real truths, would only be ideal things." Leibniz's fifth paper, mid-August, 1716, in *Correspondance Leibniz-Clarke, présentée d'après les manuscrits originaux des bibliothèques de Hanovre et de Londres*, ed. A. Robinet (Paris: PUF, 1957), 144.

trial Revolution, in the most advanced country in the order of its effects,[9] namely England. Indeed, English Romanticism appears with its particular traits, which are the value given to childhood memories, to the child's ideals and wishes, which the poets of the time make the root, not only of the inspiration, but also of the exploitation of their major themes, which distinguishes them radically from the poets who preceded them and especially from this admirable poetry of the seventeenth and early-eighteenth centuries, called metaphysical, I don't know why.

Dickens' *Great Expectations* would give rise to an identical commentary. Why this reversal compared to the previous century? Because instead of taking the adult's point of view regarding the child, the child's point of view regarding the adult is taken. And this reversal is what causes a secondary break, this time of these authors with Pascal, the Enlightenment, the *Aufklärung*, and a certain psychology which, for example, is eminently Piaget's. When Pascal said that the ancients were spiritually our children, and that from this perspective, we were their fathers, it was not to claim the status of these children but indeed to raise the profile of our own position by pitying the Ancients for not being able to reach it and dying in a state of ignorance we no longer have.

Now, "the reference to childhood [in the nineteenth century], the idea of the child that exists in the man, the idea that something requires man to be something other than a child, and yet the requirements of the child as such are perpetually experienced by him, all this belongs to psychology and can be situated historically." Frankly, psychology was only following the fundamental prejudice of any type of pedagogy: turn the child into an adult, sculpt someone who will know to make it on his own, or more specifically, according to the needs of society. It is no surprise that the advice given to psychiatrists and psychoanalysts to read *Alice in Wonderland* should come to mind here.

A man who also lived in the first half of the nineteenth century, a Victorian of the first generation, the historian Macaulay, remarked that at the time, without calling you unprincipled or a complete fool, one disposed of an excellent weapon by accusing you of not having a fully adult mind, of holding on to the traits of an infantile mentality.

---

[9] It is impossible not to recognize, in the expression "order of the effects," the mark of Pascal, which Lacan slips in covertly.

This argument, so datable historically that nowhere in history can it be witnessed before this period, marks a pause, a break in historical evolution. In Pascal's day, to talk of childhood was to say that a child is not a man.[10] If adult thinking is being discussed, there is never a case where it is to find the traces of infantile thinking.[11]

It is the idea of the march of progress, the one that can hierarchize mankind's performance in every field, that makes us prefer our situation to that of the Ancients and makes us regret not being young enough to know about more advances in all those fields. Now, this is exactly what psychoanalysis calls into question: one must learn to see the adult from the child's vantage point. This latter decentering is disconcerting; it is shared by psychoanalysis with the English Romantic current that took a view opposite to that of an Enlightenment prejudice none of its authors sought to question: that it is from the vantage point of the adult that the child should be judged and not the reverse. Let us understand that it obviously isn't a question of going backwards and renouncing any cultivation of reason; but reason itself leads us to regard our adult state[12] from the child's point of view, no doubt to gauge its difference from the current state, but also to grasp its implication in the latter.

It is not a question of returning to the prejudices of childhood and the superstitions intimated by nannies,[13] which Descartes denounced:

> There is a very different tension between the thought we are dealing with in the unconscious and the one we call, Lord knows why, adult

---

[10] Similarly, when Descartes refers to childhood, it's to discover therein the source of our prejudices, which we must obviously give up. See, for example, *Les principes de la philosophie*, 1ere Partie, Art. I (AT, IX, II, 25).

[11] The commentary is gripping, but somewhat incautious, for we know that Hobbes spoke of the wicked as a "robust child," which so shocked Rousseau, who, in *L'Émile*, saw it as a contradictory monster. It is notable, once again, that Lacan missed Hobbes: had he read him, he would not have been so preemptory on this occasion.

[12] We should note here that French has no equivalent to the English word *adulthood* (which appears in 1850). Although it has *enfance* (childhood), it relies on *maturité* (maturity) to denote adulthood, a word that contains a comparison unfavorable to childhood. In French, at least, the state of being an adult is so normal it isn't objectifiable.

[13] Even this presentation is too obviously dependent on the idea of *progress*.

thought.[14] What we are constantly touching upon is that the latter is running out of steam relative to the, now famous, child's thought that we use to judge our adult.[15] We use it, not as a foil, but as a point of reference, a point of perspective, where the incompletions, if not the degradations, converge and conclude. There is therein a perpetual contradiction in the way we use this reference.

As advanced as it is relative to the child's thought processes, "adult thought" might not present a superior point of view relative to it. We should not, in the name of pedagogy and its demands, imagine, in a naïve teleology, that the child's thought processes are so inferior to the adult's;[16] we certainly would not create, under this iron rule and in the service of all kinds of powers that be, a psychology worthy of the name. To what are we referring when we speak of adult thought? "And when we are speaking of the adult being, to what reference do we turn? Where is the model of the adult being?"[17]

It remains to explain what pedagogy would result from this reversal, so deliberately non-adaptive. To what other approach should we refer? If, as he says in *Seminar XXI*, no one has written better than Kant on this topic, it is hard to understand the point of the brilliant, though enigmatic, preceding thought, so open-ended does its horizon

---

[14] It is obviously with this same paternalistic thinking—we should be able to say "adultist"—that Europeans colonized, with the clearest conscience imaginable, other peoples or other people they called "big children." So-called primitive thought also finds its rationale in this facile opposition between the child's thought processes and the adult's. This may also explain Lacan's irritation regarding any idea of stages through which the mind progresses, whether they exist in Auguste Comte, whom he practically does not cite, or Bachelard, whom he (and on many points, no doubt, very unjustly) absolutely ignores. It is clear that a great part of Bachelard's epistemology, which is "psychological" in essence, has as its spine the opposition of childhood and adulthood, as though this strange disparagement, one held onto a reason susceptible of explaining the passage from one mode of comprehension to another.

[15] Elegant term that allows getting around the deficiency of French I discuss in note 12 of this chapter.

[16] There is, in this perspective, in the June 12, 1963, lesson of *Seminar X*, a magnificent discussion of an example drawn from *The Language and Thought of the Child*, in which, far from following Piaget in his undervaluation of the thought of the child, who is capable of reproducing an explanation he was given, but less so able to explain to someone else what he understood, Lacan wonders, not without humor, about what Piaget has understood of the child's thought.

[17] J. Lacan, *Ethics of Psychoanalysis, op. cit.*, seminar of November 25, 1959.

remain. Unless knowing something is never anything more than a pedagogue's invention, the key being that the supposedly long gradual process of knowledge in reality occurs in a flash.[18] It is not impossible that, on this point, Lacan is profoundly Leibnizian, since the author of *Meditations on Knowledge, Truth, and Ideas* saw no contradiction in considering symbolic knowledge as superior, by virtue of the freedom of its operations, to Cartesian evidence, but nevertheless placed intuitive knowledge above knowledge that is built "blindly" with symbols.

Aldous Huxley

Aldous Huxley is summoned to remind analysts that the importance of the whip in a sex-life should not be underestimated. The construction of a world of pleasure with no suffering may be what we fantasize as being the best of all worlds, but it does not necessarily constitute the most enviable reality. In a certain way, in the interpretation that Lacan gives, Huxley proposes a kind of inversion of the myth of Pandora: the happiness we would like to save for ourselves at the bottom of a bottle or inside some secured space is not superior to the suffering that can exist outside in the vast world where it is widespread:

> Mr. Aldous Huxley depicts a future world where everything will be so well organized as far as the instinct of reproduction is concerned that little fetuses will quite simply be put into bottles after having chosen those that are destined to provide the best seeds. Everything goes well and the world becomes particularly satisfying. Mr. Huxley, as a result of his personal preferences, declares it boring. We shall not take sides, but it is interesting that while tending to these kinds of anticipations to which we ourselves do not attach the least importance, he has the world he knows and we[19] know as well being reborn, through a character who isn't run of the mill, a girl who manifests her need to be whipped. There is no doubt that it seems to him that there is something here that is closely tied to the humanity in the world.[20]

---

[18] This is indeed what the February 24, 1969, lesson holds, in *D'un Autre à l'autre, op. cit.*

[19] The "we" refers to the analysts, who, like novelists, have a certain experience of sexual matters.

[20] J. Lacan, *Formations of the Unconscious, op. cit.*, February 5, 1958.

The partisans of a world without pain have simply forgotten masochism and the perversions. This version of the condemnation of the worlds that have achieved happiness is a variant of what can be found in Nietzsche, who preferred to use the argument that, since there have been men for so long who figured that happiness was the ultimate goal of their existence, they would have achieved it long ago if this project had ever had any consistency. Which proves that the thing is not possible.[21]

Henry Miller and Vladimir Nabokov

It is indeed with the perversions that we have to conclude. Lacan is particularly harsh with these two authors. He considers the first, author of *Plexus* and *Nexus* as falling way short of Sade. The second, author of *Lolita*, "a work bearing the stamp of our contemporary period," sees his work summed up in a murderous sentence, in which Lacan evokes "this couple's miserable trip through beautiful America." The crux of his remarks might reside in the turn of phrase "beautiful America" [*la belle Amérique*],[22] which it is difficult not to hear as bitterly ironic.

We shall see that he also has harsh words for England, but, as singular as this country's history is, it is somewhat commensurate with the rest of Europe. He does not travel to the United States, represented at first as a concentrate of the modern world's vicissitudes, until quite late, since it is not until February 1966 that he first travels there (a trip that went quite well, moreover, according to him). But even though he refuses to pass judgment on a country he admits to not knowing, he can't help noting his first impressions: "a really crushing impression of what there is that can be heavy to lift in our world." That's saying it all: it is as though *the American way of life* were only bearable on condition of planning to change it drastically. In the United States: "I seem to have encountered a past, an absolute, compact past, a past you could cut with a knife, a pure past, a past all the more crucial

---

[21] Lacan had, in his way, spotted this weakness of utilitarianism, which is linked, through certain aspects, to the ideology of pleasure, very much in vogue during the eighteenth century. See the first lesson of *Ethics of Psychoanalysis, op.cit.*, seminar of November 18, 1959.

[22] J. Lacan, *Desire and Its Interpretation, op. cit.*, seminar of June 24, 1959.

Carroll, Swift, Wordsworth, Huxley, Miller, Whitman, Nabokov

that it never existed, neither where it is, for now, nor from where it is supposed to have come, namely from us." Lacan wants to break the myth of America as the New World, land of all possibilities, and absolute presence of the future. He talks about himself, about his feelings, and one wonders if he isn't missing the point; he doesn't talk about the United States that a certain number of French intellectuals in the 1960s know has already taken the lead from European thought, and that the only ways of pursuing science and philosophy henceforth—and certainly for a long time—go through American philosophers and scientists.

16
CONCLUSION

In New York's Museum of Modern Art, there is a work by the conceptual artist Marcel Broodthaers that consists of nine plaques, one of which is empty and one of which recapitulates dates; the other seven are, strangely enough, made up of the names of Jonathan Swift, Edgar Allan Poe, William Blake, Oscar Wilde, Charles Dodgson, Lewis Carroll,[1] and James Joyce, accompanied by their dates of birth and death. For some,[2] he noted their "dimension," for others,[3] their "turpitude"; and for the last,[4] their "mind." It seemed arresting to us that this work from 1973 cites the English authors that most interested Lacan.[5] That a francophone conceptual artist, who spent twenty years as a surrealist poet, arrives at the same selection as Lacan (setting aside Shakespeare) is not without holding our attention and shows that, despite the frontier constituted by language, the selection of what is important leads to the same result.

What Lacan expects from literature is like what he said about Sade,[6] but the remark can extend to all literature of interest to him: *a thought experiment*. From this perspective, literature may well not use empty space in the way physics does, for example; but, by putting into place *experiments* that we would do well to call *writing*, it comes close. Just as it comes close to mathematics, if we accept saying that

---

[1] Marcel Broodthaers does not mention the fact that Charles Dodgson and Lewis Carroll are one and the same author.

[2] Swift, Poe.

[3] Wilde, Dodgson, Carroll.

[4] Blake, Joyce.

[5] It is true that Blake is not cited outside of *The Marriage of Heaven and Hell*, in the April 23, 1974, lesson, most appropriately but in a way that remains quite allusive and marginal.

[6] J. Lacan, *Ethics of Psychoanalysis, op. cit.*, seminar of March 30, 1960: "Sade appears... in the order of what I would call experimental literature. Here, the work of art is an experiment."

it carries out experiments and considering mathematical texts as treatises of writing (an idea that did not have to wait for conceptual art
to be operative, since we find it at work, as we have pointed out, in
Fontenelle, whom Lacan does not cite).

By becoming so vividly interested in English literature, Lacan
does not only display his culture. We have had sufficient opportunity
to show that literature, by displacing signifiers, by articulating them
in new ways, stirs the affects and other psychic actions; while it is not
medicine, it is not nevertheless without curative value. It's an old idea
that philosophy has value as care and a medical dimension: despite
their disagreements, Epicureans and Stoics shared this idea. More recently, England had, in the eighteenth century, physicians, like Mandeville, the author of *The Fable of the Bees*, and Arbuthnott, who did
not conceive of their work without a privileged relationship with language, in its function of conversation. To treat his patients, Mandeville
did not speak to them "strictly about their sickness"; as for Arbuthnott,
the queen's physician, partisan of the theory of climates and great
probability specialist, he treated Hume by letter (for his neurasthenia
tied to overwork, stemming from the writing of *The Treatise of Human Nature*) and diagnosed him as suffering from the "disease of the
learned." In this case, Hume, sickened by literature, was healed by it.
In Locke's tradition, himself a physician and talented surgeon, English
medicine did not neglect the link between knowledge, the know-how
of care, and language, even in its literary form. But, one might ask,
wouldn't these remarks apply just as well to literature in general, without having to do with any particular property of English literature? It is
true that we must go further.

If languages, considered impermeable units—which they are
not—are incapable of linking the themes that circulate among authors,
be they writers or philosophers, then what is that link? How does it
function? How does it allow people who think quite differently to relate to each other? This is the question that Lacan seems to have confronted, never trying to hurry the answer; maybe he never formulated
it himself and left it open.

It is odd that in English, where one can speak of Hamlet's father's ghost, who requires of the son a revenge that will break him
inescapably through a destiny that surpasses him as it defines him, and
of the *Holy Ghost*, the Holy Spirit, the use of the same word, *ghost*,
precipitates dizzying depths of unification and identification, where

French only sees difference and distance: *Saint Fantôme* cannot be imagined. At most, one might speak of spirits to tone down the specifically morbid, dangerous aspects of ghosts.

It is strange that the ghost is invoked even by the person who no longer attaches any signified to it. We can read in Bentham, for example, in a text attacking *The Book of Common Prayer*, this fragment that we are isolating, where all the cultural elements we just mentioned are visible: Bentham does not believe in ghosts, to whom he denies any reality, but that does not stop him from making the word *ghost* function and fully exercise its real effects:

> [In the name of the Father, and of the Son, and of the Holy Ghost]. Here we have a short string of sounds—sounds that are in use to perform the office of names—and by the texture thus given to a mouthful of air, note well the effects produced! A human being rescued or not rescued from a state of endless torment! And, to such an operation, in the character of a cause-by whom- by what- have such effects been attached?- by the deluded and deluding imaginations of a set of presumptuous and domineering men.- Under the name of magic, or some such name, state the same conceit as issuing from a heathen brain, execration or derision, instead of awe and veneration, are the sentiments it calls forth.[7]

Lacan's relationship to his own culture—dare we call it French?—is of this kind. Lacan plays with belonging to a culture well beyond the oppositions among authors: whether or not some believe in ghosts is not of the utmost importance; what *is* important is that it be possible for *ghost* to play a role in one culture even though it belongs to another. Lacan's introduction of the impermeable and relatively immutable thematics of the *name-of-the-father* in our culture has something as strange sounding as the uses of *ghost* to the ears of a French speaker

---

[7] J. Bentham, *Church-of-Englandism, op. cit.*, 53: "[*In the name of the Father, and of the Son, and of the Holy Ghost.]* -Here we have a short string of sounds -sounds that are in use to perform the office of *names* -and, by the texture thus given to a mouthful of air, note well the effects produced! a human being rescued or not rescued from a state of endless torment! And, to such an operation, in the character of a *cause*, -by whom -by what -have such effects been attached? -By the deluded or deluding imaginations of a set of presumptions and domineering men. -Under the name of *magic*, or some such name, state the same conceit as issuing from a heathen brain, -execration or derision, instead of awe and veneration, are the sentiments it calls forth ».

in an Anglo-Saxon culture, which includes not only the word, thus the appearance of the thing, but also everything needed, and more, than in French, to criticize any substantiality to the strange imperial relationship that the word *ghost* weaves with other words.

Thus, it is not necessarily through rejection of and disgust with the English language that Lacan states the paradox that it is not a language suited to psychoanalysis. It has excellent reasons not to be, the main one being that it does not hide—as we have pointed out—the narrator's placement in his narrative (in the broadest terms).[8] Literature is, from this angle, an excellent clue. We do not have the leisure here to compare a page of Swift or Sterne to a page of Diderot, for example. They are so close in the vivacity of their tone. Yet, even in *La Religieuse*, Diderot withdraws from the narrative and leaves it to his heroine, while he hides in his role of puppeteer, pulling the strings of his character. Sterne and Swift do the opposite: their characters are given as creations whose relation to their creator is visible through the latter's multiple interventions.[9] This is the literature that Lacan likes, and that in a certain sense he practices when he writes his own work. Thus, in so doing, this language, full of wit, with a stage-craft so varied and composite, creates a less deceitful narrative, a pure phenomenon of language, a production of signifiers with unreliable signifieds and referents. The French narrative is, from start to finish, because of the author's disappearance, a deceit; the author's disappearance that the lived language seems to demand of French may be more propitious than the apparent disorder and impromptu of the "subjective" interventions in the "English narrative." What Lacan gives us to understand is that a language that, by its very functioning, takes the analyst's place, saturates all the analyst's positions, does not allow receiving the unconscious, at least not as easily as a language that does not allow this "topology." We now need to verify this point, first brought up through philosophy, then through our literary considerations, by examining the English psychologists and psychoanalysts. Does one do a different psychology when one does it—and a different psychoanalysis when one attempts to do it against head winds and tide—in the English language?

---

[8] I mean that even the position and resolution of a mathematical problem is a narrative.

[9] This point is made in R.A. Lantham's excellent book, *Tristram Shandy: The Games of Pleasure* (Berkeley, CA: University of California Press, 1973).

IV
PSYCHOLOGISTS AND PSYCHOANALYSTS
READ IN ENGLISH

English is obviously a working language for psychologists and psychoanalysts, as it was clear in the 1950s, when the *Seminar* began its research. Almost every meeting included readings of Anglophone authors, whether Lacan directly introduced them or whether it was done through some *Seminar* participant. The text thus presented was critically sifted through. This rhythm and ritual of the lessons, especially during the first years of the *Seminar*, accompanied the installation of the three-part system of the imaginary, the symbolic, and the real. The contributions appeared to be invariably measured by this yardstick: either the authors are making progress on one of these axes, but haven't seen the whole; or they have seen a particular articulation of these axes, but again they are missing the whole; or they missed the problematics altogether, and the latter's superiority is detailed in order to account for what Lacan called "the experience," if not "our experience" (when he addressed an audience made up of psychoanalysts).

From the first years of the *Seminar*, what is of greater interest to the philosopher than to the Anglophone (or the student of English) stems from the construction of a psychoanalysis that does not start with objects, as almost all authors of books of psychoanalysis do,[1] and does not base its interpretations on the traditional philosophical opposition between "subject" and "object," but which starts rather with desire, with desire that is neither satisfied nor leads to any object, and which holds the subject's splitting without being contained by it or in it. This latter, very general, conception does awaken certain echoes in

---

[1] To begin with Balint, who "defines the object relation as the satisfaction of a need to which the object corresponds in a closed, finished manner, in the form of primary love, of which the first model is furnished by the mother-child relationship. . . . Once set, such a definition of the object, no matter how you vary the qualities of desire, from oral, to anal, and then to genital, you will need an object to satisfy and saturate it." J. Lacan, *Freud's Technical Papers, op. cit.*, seminar of June 2, 1954.

philosophy; Lacan knows this and it is quite indifferently and without dealing with their contradictions that he refers to Spinoza as well as Pascal[2] and Hegel, because each in his own way saw that desire desired itself and that it only fooled itself when it thought itself to be the desire for such and such an object. This thesis was followed to its conclusion, as its author read not only philosophers, but in even greater number psychologists and psychoanalysts,[3] the latter receiving, however, a philosophical reading.

But, one might say, even though it is often impossible to read them in another language, how can it be important or specific to read these psychologists and psychoanalysts in English? Couldn't we find the "same ideas" if they had written them in French or German? Clearly not, as can be seen when the texts he presents, the concepts he points out and critiques, are kept in the language in which he discovered them, followed or not by a translation or an attempt to translate them. It isn't only the words that are presented in their language, which does not necessarily coincide with French; even their syntax is different: a subject doesn't dream, doesn't think, doesn't act the same way according to whether he can say something or not because the place is smooth in his language, presents no hole, no edge, one might fill or catch. It is thus that, reinterpreting a dream already interpreted by Ella Sharpe, Lacan notes that the dreamer talks about a woman whom he says wants *"to get my (his) penis."* Now, *to get* has no equivalent in French: *"To get,* is *obtenir,* in all the possible ways of the verb *obtenir.* It's obtain, catch, seize, be done with. And *to got,*[4] if the woman is able *to got my penis,* this would mean she has it." What is clear is that the subject, even in its splintering, is not said in one language the same as in another, and its splinters do not coincide in both. The same slips of

---

[2] Is it by chance that the same Pascal shows that no object will ever satisfy desire and writes the problem of points, which, on the occasion of a break in a game's ordinary conditions, introduces a new symbolism? It is on top of something broken, in a world where the fit of subject and object is off kilter, that symbols take place.

[3] What is striking, when one reads Lacan, is the very strong presence, always impeccably erudite, of philosophers in his work. However, as far as English-language authors are concerned, there is no doubt that the most numerous and the most often cited are not the English philosophers, but rather the Anglophone psychologists and psychoanalysts.

[4] Obviously, *to got* does not exist in English. Without "to have," the expression is not correct.

the tongue would not occur either.[5] What does it matter, some may say, if the signifier Lacan speaks of, which punctuates the life of the psyche, does not coincide with the Saussurian signifier, which only applies to spoken languages?[6] We must be aware that while the two types of signifier do not coincide, they nevertheless share a very active linguistic component; and it is not without importance that the subject/object axis is not inflected in English the way it is declined in French. At the time when, during the 1950s, Lacan analyzes the scansion of sexual life from the perspective of the phallus, each, man or woman, possessing it in his or her fashion, and being situated in relation to it, he notes that the roles that are distributed around the phallus cannot be the same in a language that for "*se masturber*" can say "to masturbate" as in another where the verb necessarily takes a pronominal shape. The phallus is not the penis: the penis is the biological organ; the phallus is its symbolic function. And, while the symbolic does not boil down to its linguistic function, Lacan nonetheless stresses that "if the phallus relates to the subject's being, it isn't with the subject's being pure and simple... it's with a speaking subject, with a subject inasmuch as it ensures his identity and, as such, I would say—that's why the phallus plays its essentially signifying role—that the subject at the same time is it and isn't it. The speaking subject is and isn't the phallus." He is inasmuch as language attributes it to him, and he isn't inasmuch as the same language deprives him of it or attributes it in multiple ways to others. Thus, even if we admit that an analysis occurs by selecting signifiers deemed to count more than others,[7] it would be rash to think that they would be the same in French and English, considering that these languages are only contingent clothing expressing something essential that eludes them.

With Ella Sharpe, the idea can even germinate—all the more since Lacan declares his general approval of the way she conceives of

---

[5] The English-speaking subject analyzed by Ella Sharpe, then in an analysis reinterpreted by Lacan on the basis of what Ella Sharpe says, commits this slip of the tongue, of which it is difficult to see how it could be committed in French; he speaks of "travel with my wife round the world." He evidently wanted to say, "travel round the world with my wife." Wordplay seems as untranslatable into one language as into another.

[6] See Chapter 2, note 1.

[7] This is how Lacan reports Ella Sharpe conceives of analysis, in his February 4, 1959, lesson.

the work[8]—that an analysis would benefit by going from one language into another, for an analyst can then grasp in another language what is hidden in his own.[9] Thus it is that Ella Sharpe is set right on a point she did not notice in *The Book of Common Prayer*, though Lacan is ready to recognize she knows it better than he does. Sharpe notes as equivalent two different phrases "We have left undone those things which we ought to have done" and "We have done those things which we ought not to have done," whereas they are not equivalent, especially when the subject's very problem is precisely that of being unable to do anything at all for fear of succeeding too well.[10]

The treatment of Ella Sharpe's way of conducting analysis is unusual. Most of the time, leaving Freud himself aside, when Lacan finds himself in harmony with a colleague, which does happen to him from time to time, he does not draw much attention to it. This is why we will not examine Spitz, despite his important contribution to psychoanalysis, which Lacan defends against Smirnov in *Seminar VII*: "far from being harsh with Spitz, I am, on the contrary, coming to his defense; I'm not saying he's right. But it's very strong and really stands out."[11] At this time, he is mainly interested in *rooting*, the oscillation of the head the child does upon approach of the breast, and in which Spitz, in *Yes and No*, claims to find the pattern of *no*. Otherwise, aside from a succinct allusion to the primal cavity and the dream screen, Lacan doesn't have much to say about Spitz. He is amused by an anecdote where he has a funny role in a female patient's transference.[12] Lacan spends more time exploring the disagreements—which is, moreover, intrinsic to the primary action of criticism—and is far more eloquent when it comes to them than he is when he has no objection to make. We are going to verify this next with the Balints, since Alice worked as a team with her husband.

---

[8] J. Lacan, *Desire and Its Interpretation, op. cit.*, seminar of February 4, 1949: "There is, in her interpretation of analytical theory, this kind of giving real value to the signifying dimension of things. She highlighted metaphor in a way that is not absolutely dissonant with the things I am explaining to you. And, the entire time, she knows how to emphasize that element of the substrate that is linguistic, strictly speaking, in symptoms, which she brought to her literary analyses that make up an important part of her work."

[9] Which Freud did not hesitate to do, since he was able, with patients who were able as well.

[10] See *ibid.*

[11] J. Lacan, *Ethics of Psychoanalysis, op. cit.*, seminar of February 3, 1960.

[12] J. Lacan, *Four Fundamental Concepts, op. cit.*, seminar of May 6, 1964.

17

MICHAEL AND ALICE BALINT

While Lacan does not contest Michael Balint's practice,[1] he does critique his way of accounting for what he does.[2] This reproach is frequent with Lacan; we saw Ella Sharpe narrowly escape, we shall see other analysts fall under this condemnation. Lacan can recognize in another analyst an undeniable effectiveness while profoundly differing with him on the explanation of this know-how. The areas of disagreement with Balint are many and are concentrated around three poles: the question of primary love; ego psychology, of which Balint is one of the founders; and the question of the end of analysis.

Primary love is the reciprocal love of the mother and child during the first months of the child's life. The Balints view it as a kind of pre-established harmony between two object relations. According to Alice Balint, in particular: "the characteristic of the mother-child relationship is that the mother as such satisfies all of the child's needs. This does not mean, of course, that it is always realized. But it is structural to the situation of the human child."[3] The terms *mother's love* and *love for the mother* should be understood as Stephen does in *Ulysses*, as the compassion of a difficult pedagogical relationship with a student of somewhat obtuse intelligence, in other words, uniting in the *amor matrix*, of which the genitive can be taken as object as well as subject. What matters then, in a puritanical ethical conception, and, in any case "more than normative, moralizing,"[4] of which Lacan

---

[1] Lacan even relates an interesting anecdote, which casts Balint in a good light, in *Freud's Technical Papers, op. cit.*, 351-352.

[2] *Ibid.*, 357.

[3] *Ibid.*, 323. Indeed, we read from Alice Balint, in the book *Primary Love and Psycho-Analytic Technique* (London: Maresfield Library, 1994), 120: "Maternal Love is the almost perfect counterpart to the love for the mother."

[4] *Ibid.*, 315–316. He added on the same page: "If the article ("Pregenital love", excerpted from *Primary Love and Psycho-Analytic Technique*) were not from 1932, I would say that we owe it the diffusion of a certain puritan moral ideal. There are in Hungary

contests the legitimacy in psychology, is making this mother-child re-lationship good, because, if it is, the child's entire life, and that of the future adult, will be off to a good start.[5] It is as if the mother were necessarily and always—or at least should necessarily and always be—a block of love for the child, who, himself, is a block of love for the moth-er, or, rather, "feels the need to be the object of the love, the care, the affection, the interest of another object."[6]

It is this primary love that the Balints hypothesize and—in the fa-mous slippage, pointed out by Hume, of *is* to *ought*—almost make the duty of analysis, when it is requested, to restore: to be loved, to be the object of care, such is, indeed, in Balint's eyes, the goal of the cure[7] and the atmosphere in which the cure must develop.[8] As though it went without saying that everything that was good for the patient was good in and of itself, for anyone; as though the idyllic atmosphere of the cure were the very model the real needed to espouse.

It is easy to see that Lacan's basic criticism stems from the un-balanced structure the cure sets forth between the imaginary, the sym-bolic, and the real. It is clear that the Balintian cure grants too much to the purely imaginary elements of harmony, the possibility of which is never doubted and which are even seen as being able to constitute the real, the supposed real of the "egos." Nothing points to the harmony of the "egos" being possible; nothing says, either, that it is possible for it to constitute the real and that it is necessary to orient a subject re-questing treatment toward such a conception of the real. Why should what works for one person work for another? Why would one person's satisfaction be saturated by the other's and vice versa? The real con-fronted by the analysand in the Balintian cure is totally inconsistent and improbable.

---

historical Protestant traditions that have precise historical ramifications with the history of Protestantism in England. Thus we can see a singular convergence of the thought of this pupil of Ferenczi, led by his teacher, with his fate, that ultimately integrated him so well to the English community." Lacan exaggerates somewhat the moralism of the Balints, who, in *Primary Love*, speak of intra-uterine life and its restauration in terms of *good* or *bad* rather than *right* or *wrong*.

[5] *Ibid.*, 324.

[6] *Ibid.*, 285.

[7] "Balint says exactly this: the entire progress of analysis consists of the subject's tendency to rediscover what he calls primary love" (*ibid.*, 285). For "the child does not love but is loved" (*ibid.*, 194)

[8] *Ibid.*, 317.

To the cure understood as two loving objects that always fit together, without either really wanting this fit, or as two bodies that correspond to each other, an idea is added, which can seem contradictory at first and which will become the leitmotif of ego psychology: the ego needs to be reinforced. The ego must be convinced that it has a right to *jouissance*.[9] But, here again, to the illusions of two-body psychology are added, without solving anything, those of *autonomy*; for, in presenting one of the goals of analysis as "reinforcing the ego," doesn't one risk throwing the person who participates against a wall? This works the same way as in Kantian ethics, which proposes your achieving a subject whose author has made sure to show you ahead of time could not possibly exist. "The progress of an analysis does not depend on an enlargement of the ego, it is not the ego's re-conquest of its unknown fringe, it is a veritable overturning, a displacement, like a minuet executed by the ego and the id."[10]

The apparent contradiction comes from two aspects of the question. The *first* is that the concept of idyllic fitting together, less of two loves than of two egotisms, incidentally, involves an "objective" conception of two things that fit together, for it is impossible to achieve such a fit between an object and a subject, or between two subjects:

> The analysis becomes the relation of two bodies between which a fantasmatic communication is established where the analyst teaches the subject how to see himself as object; subjectivity is only admitted in the parentheses of the illusion and speech is reduced to a search for experience which becomes its supreme goal, but the dialectically necessary result appears in the fact that the psychoanalyst's subjectivity, being freed of any restraint, leaves the subject vulnerable to all the intimations of his words.[11]

The accusation is serious: the Balintian cure weakens the symbolic to the point of reducing it to a simple and pale description of

---

[9] Lacan waxes ironic about certain consequences of this reinforcement of the ego maxim, when Balint sees in it a treatment for premature ejaculation, "because this reinforcement would permit him a more prolonged suspension of his desire." "Fonction et champ de la parole et du langage," *Écrits, op. cit.*, 250 (n. 6).

[10] J. Lacan, *Freud's Technical Papers, op. cit.*, 357.

[11] J. Lacan, "Fonction et champ de la parole et du langage," *Écrits, op. cit.*, 304.

the imaginary, to a paltry philosophy of language,[12] which even turns out to be disastrous and dangerous since, in this decay of the symbolic, psychoanalysis subjects the patient to its power and only leaves him, as horizon outside of the cure, that of submitting to others.[13] But there is *a second aspect to the question*, which appears to contradict this "objective" conception: it is the claim of *autonomy*, the right to be a subject; but what subject is being claimed, when the symbolic and the real have been so weakened? And, especially, "to what internal necessity does the fact that there must be an autonomous ego respond?"[14] Why make of *autonomy* an incontrovertible dogma, as though it were the indisputable end of all ethics as well as all analysis? Doesn't the ideology of the *strong ego* and the *weak ego* stem from this dogma that, although it features no content and does not cover anything that isn't imaginary, is never challenged?

There is more, and this time it is the very goal of analysis that is at stake. "The end of analysis would be—according to Balint—to identify with the analyst." Lacan adds, "as far as I am concerned, I don't think so. But it is what Balint thinks, and it's very surprising."[15] In 1960, in a page of the *Écrits*, Lacan discussed this Balintian conception to which *Seminar XXIV* alludes. The analysis ends in "a narcissistic effusion where he [the subject] signals himself the end of his analysis."[16] In this triumph of the imaginary, where the latter, at the height of its illusion, becomes the law, of the subject as well as of the analysand, subverting the power that the analyst could have on him (through

---

[12] In *Freud's Technical Papers, op. cit.*, 317, Lacan speaks of "Balint's ignorance of the symbolic register."

[13] It is true that some of Balint's phrases are a little suspect. On page 232 of his *Primary Love*: "I think it may therefore be accepted that the 'language' is always highly cathected by libido; the use of his own language is an important gratification to the analyst," even when "conscious or unconscious gratification [would] contribute to the building up and shaping of the psycho-analytic situation."

[14] Lacan asks the question about Heinz Hartmann in *The Ego in Freud's Theory, op. cit.*, seminar of November 17, 1978.

[15] J. Lacan, *L'insu que sait de l'une bévue s'aile à mourre, op. cit.*, seminar of November 16, 1976.

[16] J. Lacan, *Freud's Technical Papers, op. cit.*, already reported it in these words: at the end of the analysis, "there occurs, in the subject, a state of narcissism that goes to an unbridled exaltation of desires. The subject is intoxicated with a completely illusory sensation of absolute mastery of reality, but one that he needs in the post-terminal period" (285).

the weakening of the symbolic that we recognized as inherent to the doctrine), "the patient believes, according to Michael Balint, that he exchanged his ego for the analyst's."[17] "Let's hope for his sake that isn't so," Lacan starts by saying, dryly, before commenting a little later, "it was necessary [for him] to sweep away the imaginary for being too prized in the technique."[18] To become the other—even if this other is the one supposed to have understood the processes that led me to analysis, to its effectuation and its denouement—cannot be the end of analysis. Even supposing that an "event" of this kind might have concluded it, this conclusion must not be confused with its end. And even if the analyst were to use this illusion of fusion or of identity with the analysand, "those are not the means to the end [of analysis]."[19]

From this brief analysis of the Balints' examination by Lacan, two conclusions can be drawn. The *first* stems from the identifying of the helicoidal structure at the center of their contention, as we have seen with Hume and Adam Smith. The spinning of the subject/object axis on itself in space-time is the method that makes the Balints the inheritors of the Enlightenment philosophers. It is with feelings of self-interest that values transcending self-interest are dialectically produced. Hume had tried to show how self-interest, well understood, takes the self-interest of others into account, and, while remaining self-interest, has the effect of altruism.[20] Lacan shows that, in the same way, "Balint goes on to say [not without reason] that intersubjectivity, meaning the experience of the other's *selfishness*,[21] comes from the pre-genital stage, from which he excluded him previously." That is to say from a *selfishness* that was totally ignorant of the other's *selfishness*. Fine. But in this case, one must no longer speak of primary love. The construct must be open as much on the side of the future as on the side of the past; indefinite constructs must be preferred to closed circles.[22]

---

[17] J. Lacan, "Remarque sur le rapport de Daniel Lagache," *Écrits, op. cit.*, 681.

[18] *Ibid.*, 682. In 1954, he already said: "Don't you have the impression that this is an extraordinarily unsatisfying game, a utopian ideal?—which surely disappoints something in us." J. Lacan, *Freud's Technical Papers, op. cit.*, 285.

[19] J. Lacan, "Remarque sur le rapport de Daniel Lagache," *Écrits, op. cit.*, 681.

[20] David Hume, *Treatise of Human Nature*, B. III, Part II, sec. V.

[21] In English in the original.

[22] In the language of intersubjectivity that he is soon to reject, Lacan focuses his argument in terms that Hume or Bentham would have gladly used against the contractualists, Locke and Rousseau: "We must [much more in conformity with our experience] start from

The *second* is a conclusion we have seen before: it comes from the desire to account for genital love stemming from primary love in the form of a fusion-like return to some origin. Once again, we witness the triumph of the imaginary, which leads, in this instance, to contradictions pointed out by Lacan as early as *Seminar I*. How—so long as the mother and child form, according to Alice and Michael Balint, a single totality of needs[23]—is this unit closed on itself, presented as the origin of genital love? How could this relation—so complex in regards to the other, through which copulation becomes love—that involves idealization and tenderness derive from such a simple relationship without any subjectivity? Balint falls into the trap of the philosophers who try to explain things by their origin rather than by their history; through a mirage, they attempt to derive the most complex from the simplest. These philosophies are quite close to the myths that, like Pandora or the Golden Age, are incapable of explaining, since humans were happy before some catastrophe or fall that they nevertheless initiated, how they could have forfeited this happiness. Very old belief systems orient mindsets in psychology. To each subject an object needs to correspond and the correspondence needs to be happy, or, if it isn't, then it should be; no one can conceive that the symbol is essentially in the breakdown of these relationships, always fallaciously thought to be idyllic between subjects or between subjects and objects, that the relations between subjects and objects such as they conceive of them are rather in the *fading* of any symbol.

It is apparent: when Lacan questions English-speaking psychologists or psychoanalysts, he touches on philosophical problems that were of particular interest to English thinkers; it is even on these philosophical problems that he makes the former stumble, often in the same terms as the English critics, who, in every domain, had such success tracking down false origin narratives (origin of the social in the conflicts of nature, origin of the political in a social contract, origin of

---

a radical intersubjectivity, from the total acceptance of the subject by the other subject. It is retrospectively, *nachträglich*, from experience, from adult experience, that we must approach original, superimposed experiences, terracing the degradations, without ever leaving the domain of intersubjectivity. So long as we remain in the analytical register, we must admit intersubjectivity at the outset." *Freud's Technical Papers, op. cit.*, 335.

[23] According to the expression in J. Lacan, *The Object Relation, op. cit.*, seminar of December 12, 1956.

property in some inaugural gesture). We shall see it again in the case of Lacan's analyses of the work of Melanie Klein.

Let us finish with two notes of caution. The *first* is that, in citing Hume with some precision, we do not mean to suggest that Lacan has inherited his thought. Probably, Lacan did not know Hume that well. On the other hand, it is probable that a good number of Hume specialists in France, starting in the 1960s, by direct or indirect filiation, would never have been interested in certain aspects of his thought—beginning with his critique of the subject or of substance—without the Lacanian research that allowed these to emerge from the shadows.

But that hardly changes the terms of our problem: if the critique of the psychologists never does more than return us to the antinomical conflicts of the philosophers, one can scarcely expect to supersede them (something so useful to put into practice) by adhering to the thesis or antithesis, the conviction in favor of one or another. It is overcoming these basic adherences that must be accomplished, as much—as we have seen—through a certain use of linguistics as through ways of shaping psychology or psychoanalysis.

The *second* is to rectify a wrong impression we may have given. We are not suggesting that the Balints were the only ones behind Ego Psychology, since it distinguished itself through the "triumvirate" of Heinz Hartmann, Ernst Kris, and Rudolph Loewenstein.[24] What Lacan notes, in Kris, is the promotion of an Ego the patient would need to construct autonomously; the misfortune of such a moralizing theory is that the autonomous ego, thus promoted, takes on "all the *petitio principii* to which the psychologist, without awaiting psychology, puts an end, but which unambiguously deliver the figure of its promoters' ideals." The argument of these promoters[25] of the autonomous ego is obviously to rely on Freud's declaration "*Wo Es war, soll Ich werden.*"[26] But Lacan soon locates, in this way of using autonomy, a kind of behaviorism, through which, under the term *autonomy*, things are arranged in such a way that the subject follows the norms of a given society, sometimes having recourse to the introjection of the psychoanalyst's ego.[27]

---

[24] J. Lacan, "Réponse au commentaire de Jean Hyppolite," *Écrits, op. cit.*, 393.
[25] J. Lacan, "Situation de la psychanalyse et formation du psychanalyste en 1956," *Écrits, op. cit.*, 490.
[26] Literally, "Where It was, shall I be," or "Where Id was, I shall be."
[27] J. Lacan, "Réponse au commentaire de Jean Hyppolite," *Écrits, op. cit.*, 398.

Kris, who is more than a little proud of his therapeutic method via Ego Psychology, explains a case of plagiarism that he intends to treat by "the means of truth": his patient, who accuses himself of copying others' ideas, does not copy them, and does not use, contrary to what he thinks, livelier and more alert brains than his to produce new ideas. Kris attempts to convince him of this and, in the acting out that follows, Kris receives as his only answer that his patient has taken to seeking out and consuming fresh brains! If the psychoanalyst wants his patient to "become himself," and the patient could not care less, it becomes clear at once that this is not the way to treat him. To bring someone to, or back to, the path of autonomy is not necessarily appropriate in the resolution of an analysis if only because *autonomy* is among the more obscure and contradictory of notions.

While it is Melanie Klein's turn to find herself called a good prac-
titioner but a bad theorist,[1] she does not earn the same reproach
from Lacan as Balint. She does not harbor any *primary love* that fuses
the child with the mother beyond any words or possible symbols. With
her, it is the relation to the symbolic that is primordial, and Lacan was
able to say, in the February 5, 1958, lesson, that Melanie Klein "presented the most articulated position on the role of the symbol in the
Ego's position."[2] He returns to this theme a year later, still stating his
complete agreement with the author: "the inaugural process, taking
place at the beginning of the subject's life, it's that the reality of the
first apprehensions of the object, such as Madame Klein shows us,
comes from this: it's that the object—beyond the fact that it can be
good or bad, profitable or frustrating—is meaningful."[3] Lacan goes
on to specify the terms of his agreement as well as the extent of that
agreement:

> What Melanie Klein brings us is a kind of primitive algebra about
> which we can say that it relates completely to what we are trying to high-
> light here under the term "function of the signifier." What Melanie Klein
> describes are the primary, primitive forms of this function of the signifier.
> With the points of reference that are ours, we can see that what is involved
> is something that restores this primitive relationship, this schism—as she
> herself put it—of object as good or bad to this other register of the inside
> and outside of the subject.

---

[1] This mode of attack is also used against Nunberg, in *Freud's Technical Papers, op.
cit.* and in *Transference, op. cit.*, seminar of March 1, 1961.

[2] J. Lacan, *Formations of the Unconscious, op. cit.*, seminar of February 5, 1958.

[3] J. Lacan, *Desire and Its Interpretation, op. cit.*, seminar of June 17, 1959.

In other words, despite the strong resemblance of his research with Melanie Klein's, Lacan keeps his distance from the moral discourse of *good* and *bad* and substitutes for it the more topological discourse of the Moebius strip, of the subject's inside and outside.

However, it is not only a "moral" discourse that Lacan attacks through the play of "good" and "bad" objects, nor is it only the very realist expressions that Melanie Klein uses to account for symbolic processes, but it is also the way she envisages the genesis of the function of the real in children. In a manner that is very consistent with her positions on the primacy of the symbolic, she starts off with a kind of delirium, against the background of which the child gains favorable objects and is subjected to unfavorable ones; then he plays with that, constantly winning new objects that he submits to more or less the same classification, but that no longer concern the narrow sphere of vital needs. Here, Klein resorts to the classic eighteenth-century genesis blueprint, whether it is the one Rousseau uses in his *Discourse on the Origins of Inequality Among Men* or that of Ferguson, who, in the *Essay on the History of Civil Society*, showed how, by loosening the strait jacket of needs, Man obtained increasingly sophisticated cultural objects, which gradually superseded the former and situated them in a completely different way. It is worth taking a closer look at these things.

Melanie Klein tells us the following:

> What we call *objects* are successively conquered by the child inasmuch as, the more the objects are farther from the child's needs, the more they become charged with the anxiety tied to their use in the aggressive, sadistic, fundamental relationships that are those, at the start, of the child with his entourage, as the consequence of any and all frustration. It is to the extent that the subject displaces his interest onto more distant objects—which in turn become charged with the same anxiety—that the extension of the child's world is conceived as such. It is through a progressive extension of the world of objects in a contraphobic dialectic [that reality is conquered].[4]

Without denying the plausibility of the process, Lacan does not think that this is how the conquest of reality is constituted.

---

[4] J. Lacan, *Desire and Its Interpretation, op. cit.*, seminar of June 17, 1959.

He explains his reticence to follow Klein all the way. Certainly, Lacan stresses, with Klein's student Susan Isaacs, that the child manifests early on its ability to discern the symbolic, by distinguishing a slap from the shock caused by a fall,[5] for example. In *Seminar II*, Lacan repeats this as an observable fact:

> The same blow, the same knock, the same slap is not received the same way depending on whether it was punitive or accidental. As precociously as possible, earlier even than the subject's fixation with his own image, than the first structuring image of the ego, the symbolic relation is constituted, which introduces the dimension of the subject in the world, capable of creating a reality other than what presents as brute reality, like the shock of two balls.[6]

Even though she accentuates the role of the symbolic starting in the earliest childhood, it is more to a mode of Humean explication that she has recourse: indeed, one finds in Hume, in particular in Book II of the *Treatise of Human Nature* concerning the functioning of human passions, a veritable logic of the imagination, if not a metrics of the imagination, on the foundations of the constitution of human objects and, especially, their valorization. Distinguishing *imagination* from *fantasy*, Hume distinguishes an *imagination* that, although it has a tendency to prefer objects contiguous to the subject (B. II, Part III, sec. III.), moves just as well from the far to the near and from the near to the far; from *fantasy*, which gladly propels us into the distance (B. II, Part III, sec. VIII), Hume constructs a veritable dynamic of these effects that appear, at first sight, contradictory, but that enjoy, on closer examination, a paradoxical regularity. It is thus on the delirious mode of the imagination that objects are conquered, by being cast from what is closest to what is farthest away. Lacan identifies this word *fantasy*, used by the Kleinians, and which shares an august destiny among English authors, because often, for them, it is what builds the world, even what the world has that is most reasonable:

> It is, for example, around the fundamental aggressivity of the subject that is ordered, in a series of projections of the subject's needs, this world

---

[5] See J. Lacan, *Freud's Technical Papers, op. cit.*, 279–280.
[6] J. Lacan, *The Ego in Freud's Theory, op. cit.*, seminar of June 1, 1955.

of *fantasy*, such as the concept is used in the Kleinian school. It is at the surface of this world that a series of more or less happy experiences intervene, and it is desirable that they be happy. In this way, little by little, the world of experience allows a certain reasonable identification of what, in these objects, is, as they say, objectively definable as corresponding to a certain reality, the background of unreality remaining absolutely fundamental.[7]

The reasonable world is gradually won against a backdrop of delirium.[8] Expressing, in philosophical terms, the English psychoanalyst's view, Lacan writes:

In the Kleinian perspective... any apprenticeship, so to speak, of reality by the subject is primordially prepared and undergirded by the essentially hallucinatory and fantasmatic construction of the first objects classified as *good* and *bad* objects, inasmuch as they set an initial primordial relationship that, during the rest of the subject's life, will yield the major types of modes of the subject's relation to reality. This is how we arrive at the notion that the subject's world is based on a fundamentally unreal relationship of the latter with objects that are only the reflections of his fundamental drives.[9]

Lacan then summarizes the situation in one stroke: "A normal subject is, then, in short, a psychotic who turned out well [and whose] psychosis harmonized successfully with experience." The turn of phrase is stellar, but this Humean world of psychosis that evolves and ends well does not convince Lacan:

The notion that the child lives in a world of delirium, which seems to be involved in the Kleinian conception, is one of the least admissible things there is, for the simple reason that, while this psychotic phase is necessitated by the premises of the Kleinian perspective, we have no experience of any kind in the child of anything that corresponds to a transitory psychotic state.

---

[7] J. Lacan, *Formations of the Unconscious, op. cit.*, seminar of February 5, 1958.

[8] It was the reading of Hume that Deleuze proposed in *Empirisme et subjectivité* (Paris: PUF, 1953).

[9] J. Lacan, *Formations of the Unconscious, op. cit.*, seminar of February 5, 1958.

It is thus—quite dangerously, to our eyes, since he seemed to us to have criticized the notion—on *experience* that Lacan relies in order to distance himself from the Kleinian flights of fancy. He has recourse to *experience* again to contest the supposed enclosure in a tight circle of the primitive world that the child constitutes with the mother: "In fact, everyone knows, and you only have to watch him live, the very young child is not at all auto-erotic."[10]

Lacan understands that, with Melanie Klein, we are in the heart of English philosophy; but, in the name of experience, he rejects the tendencies of this philosophy—which has so often been called *empirical* and has so often called itself as much—by showing how, rather than following experience, it built through imagination and affect. The wit of this insight is worthy of note. It is in any case interesting to locate the derivation of a certain English psychoanalysis, whether it is aware of it or not—in any case, what Lacan shows allows us to take note of it—from the philosophies of the seventeenth and eighteenth centuries.[11] Whether he knows it or not, it is through his critique of Melanie Klein that Lacan differentiates himself most clearly from certain themes of English philosophy and demystifies its supposed "empiricism," which is an ideology like any other, no more concerned with *experience* than any other, despite aligning itself with it, or claiming to.

In other words, when an author is too "philosophical," Lacan turns to traditional methods of refutation: *calling upon experience*, which has the flaw—as we shall see—of not being the best way to convince an adversary.

---

[10] *Ibid.*

[11] We have already noted that Freud adhered, concerning a detail but a really important one, to Hobbes.

19
ERNEST JONES

Jones confronts us with another myth, and Lacan does not fail to note that he, like Balint, is Protestant.[1] This time, the problem is that of the differentiation of men and women, which psychology cannot posit easily, *first of all* because of the moral and juridico-political constraints immediately imposed by questions of equality between the sexes, as if the latter were imperiled by Freudian investigations. It must be that the obstacle is a substantial one and that the terrain is heavily mined (and has been for a long time!) for a mind as subtle as Derrida's, in his *Carte Postale*, to indict the sexism of Lacanian psychoanalysis, and perhaps have forbidden himself to understand what was at play in the thematic of the phallus. And then, there is *a second obstacle*, also religious in nature, concerning the fitting together of the two beings that are man and woman, supposedly "made for one another," in such a way that the conjunction is idyllic, and that when it isn't, it is thought that it is supposed to be. At least the essence of the phenomenon of the difference between the sexes is that of coincidence and concordance; the avatars of splits, breaks, and discord, be they numerous, being only contingencies, are unable to affect the essence:

> Jones was not without a certain orientation; he may have only had one flaw, which was to think that God created [human beings] man and woman. It is with this phrase that he concludes his article on the *phallic phase*, revealing the biblical origins of his convictions. Since God created them man and woman, they are therefore made to go together, and that is how it has to end up or it has to be said why.[2]

---

[1] J. Lacan, *Anxiety, op. cit.*, seminar of June 19, 1963. Lacan reveals "the Protestant mischief of this Welshman" on the occasion of the article "Madonna's Conception Through the Ear." Lacan pays close attention to everyone's religious affiliation, specifically because it is for the most part kept secret the better to play its role.

[2] J. Lacan, *Formations of the Unconscious, op. cit.*, seminar of March 26, 1958.

The snag in this egalitarian interpretation is Adam's rib, which shows that, even in the Bible, things are not so simple and don't provide many arguments in Jones' favor.

The question of sexual difference is such a minefield that any statement put forth on the psychological terrain meant to attempt to understand it is immediately interpreted in terms of the effect it may produce on the principle of equality between the sexes. And it is true that the literature produced on this theme by those who are still sometimes called "the great philosophers" is mind-boggling,[3] calling their seriousness into doubt, on this subject at least (and, consequently, on many others) for all those whose research specifically addresses sexual difference, which is the case of psychoanalysts. The misogyny of most philosophers of the past does not need to be demonstrated. The misfortune is, when one thinks one can reply to this misogyny with some counter-attack, worthy sentiments and morality in psychology lead to where they lead to in literature, blind alleys, if not the impossibility of posing problems in the first place.

> Mr. Jones, whose utility and function in analysis will have been in direct proportion to what he did not understand,[4] very quickly tried to articulate the castration complex by giving it an equivalent.... The best thing he has written, which culminates in his article on "The Phallic Phase," consists of saying: why this darned phallus that is always underfoot, why privilege this incidentally inconstant object, when there are things that are just as interesting? The vagina, for example. And indeed, he's right, this man. It's clear that this object is no less interesting than the phallus, this we know. Only, what surprises him, is that both do not have the same function. He was strictly destined to not understand anything, to the extent that, from the outset, from his first cast, as soon as he tried to articulate what the castration complex was in Freud, he felt the need to give it an equivalent, instead of retaining what is tough, if not irreducible, in the castration complex, namely the phallus signifier.[5]

---

[3] We devoted an article to this question, under the title, "Les philosophes et la différence des sexes," in *Letterina* 59 (April 2012): 49–69.

[4] This rather cruel remark does not, however, mean that he was radically useless by asking questions he was unable to answer or by thinking that he was blazing trails when he was only losing his way.

[5] J. Lacan, *Formations of the Unconscious, op. cit.*, seminar of March 26, 1958.

Lacan himself is surely not without prejudice; we have stressed that his major guiding principles have been in place for a long time, allowing him to navigate this teeming literature—the famous RSI—and that they function like a weapon of war against those who depart from his diagram or like a machine to record instructions when an author seems to have progressed on some axis. Perhaps the thematic of the phallus is false and leads nowhere; but it has the advantage of pointing to the problem, of maintaining its edge and avoiding an antinomy of the philosophical kind where we would see, in one thesis, one sex dominate the other and, in some sense, organize the other, whereas the other thesis would be content to reverse the first affirmation. Lacan installs the research in asymmetry from the outset and bases sexuality on this insurmountable asymmetry. It is in any case absurd, even if tempting, to speak of Lacan's "phallocentrism" by implying that it leads straight to sexism, if it isn't its direct product. True, the affirmation is tempting, for one could say, by putting the vagina in place of the phallus, through a kind of antinomical conflict of which philosophical dialectics have the privilege, that the difference is as well or as little explained. But this kind of reversal is similar to the illusions novices in mathematics may have, when they think that in order to solve a difficult problem, it's enough to reverse the terms. One might say that if the irrational number in mathematics is hard to deal with, if $a\sqrt{2}$, length of the diagonal of the square of side a, is a cumbersome notion, it would be enough to call it a and one would then eliminate the difficulties. In reality, this would just postpone the difficulties because the sides would then be what would be divided by the irrational number. If truth be told, the phallus is forged like a reality on the order of the irrational in mathematics; it is at the heart of a relationship of incommensurabilities. Only the relationship counts: to speak of the *phallus* signifier does not mean that any privilege has been granted to men, who are no more privileged by their *possession* than diagonals are in relation to the sides of a square. But they fulfill certain functions under the term *phallus* that women do not, while the reverse is equally true. We need to be able to articulate the logic of this relation. Its problematization is not even accessed by questions that are too quick to moralize and false solutions warranted on principle by an inappropriate egalitarianism.[6] For, to search for a common term that relates

---

[6] *Ibid.*, seminar of February 12, 1958: "What they don't understand is that Freud is

both men and women to their desire, we enter a blind alley, "since, it is to be unaware that, specifically, these relations are fundamentally different and only, since this is what Freud has discovered, by virtue of their asymmetry in relation to the phallus signifier."[7] *Asymmetry* has nothing in common with *inequality* and does not lead to the latter. The girl cannot enter the Oedipal pass the same way as the boy; but it is this, "the very fact that women enter it with a baggage which in fact is not theirs, appears to constitute for him a sufficient difference from the boy, for him to claim something."[8]

It is understandable that, for moral reasons, one might try to avoid what can appear to be a primacy of the phallus. But the risk in renouncing this notion, and failing to understand it as a signifier and nothing else, is that of losing the asymmetry, which is the only way to explain the entire affair.

The term *aphanisis*, coined by Jones, his attempt to impose a certain meaning on the psychoanalysts of his era, is obviously meant to replace the Freudian theme of *phallus*: "literally incomprehensible by almost all those in Freud's circle, even though they go through contortions to make it enter their discourse, because the facts require it."[9] Contortions or not, *aphanisis* plays a double role, the *first* of which can receive Lacan's approval, since it affirms the non-coincidence of desire with its object. As for the *second*, it is, through its will to forge a notion that is applied to masculine and feminine desire alike, an unacceptable sleight of hand.[10]

Let's begin with the acceptable point that removes the idea of desire as a happy, necessary, and spontaneous adequation with its object. Explaining Jones' point of view, Lacan writes in *Seminar VI*:

> The human object undergoes this kind of volatilization which is what we call, in our current practice, the possibility of displacement; which does not simply mean that the human subject, like all animal subjects, sees his desire move from object to object, but that this very displace-

---

positing there a pivot signifier around which turns the entire dialectic of what the subject must conquer of himself, of his own being."

[7] J. Lacan, *Desire and Its Interpretation, op. cit.*, seminar of December 17, 1958.

[8] J. Lacan, *Formations of the Unconscious, op. cit.*, seminar of March 12, 1958.

[9] *Ibid.*, seminar of February 12, 1958.

[10] *"Jeu d'escamoteurs"* is the expression he uses to designate Jones' enterprise in this regard. In *Desire and Its Interpretation, op. cit.*, seminar of February 4, 1958.

ment is the point where the fragile balance of his desire can be maintained.... In the end, it's a matter of preventing satisfaction while always keeping an object of desire.

In fact, the subject's greatest fear is not to be lacking an object, but "to be deprived of his own desire": it's this notion that Jones names *aphanisis*.

But, in short order, this term *aphanisis* is used to "be understood regarding castration." And what he wants to be understood is this, that the boy is at least as lacking regarding the girl as the girl is regarding the boy:

> I would like to relate something about a great number of male patients who present a deficiency in finishing or achieving their virility relative to other men or to other women, and to show that their failure is, in this case, their obstacle, is in the strictest sense,... their need to acquire something from women, something that, with good reason, they can never really acquire. Why? Says Jones. And, when he says *why* in his article and his context, he punctuates it like a vanishing point, an opening, a perspective, a point without guides. "Why?" An act is imperfect. So, it can give a boy the feeling of an imperfect possession of his own penis. I am absolutely convinced that the two things are absolutely intimately linked to each other, whereas the logical connection between these two things is certainly not obvious, in any case not obvious to him.[11]

Lacan concludes cruelly.

Jones has found the only means—there aren't any others—to make *aphanisis* an equivalent of the castration complex, that of defining it the way he does: namely, the disappearance of desire. To refute him, Lacan invokes, as usual—but also with a dubious shortcut—when he contests an analytical or psychological theory, *experience*. "Isn't there something there that is absolutely unfounded?," he asks, when Jones has just introduced his notion of *the disappearance of desire*. Incidentally, wasn't he speaking more about the fear of this desire disappearing? "That this is already something that is of the second or third degree relative to a relationship expressed in terms of need is without doubt, and yet it is what he doesn't seem to doubt in the

---

[11] J. Lacan, *Desire and Its Interpretation, op. cit.*, seminar of January 7, 1959.

least."[12] Lacan certainly would not be one to challenge the right to create fictions, of whatever type, in a scientific endeavor; but it seems that some can be called fallacious, which is the case here. It seems that this fallacious usage is tied here to the concealing of a notion Jones does not want to contemplate: that man and woman are two different relationships to desire. By forging the *aphanisis*, Jones throws castration on a Procrustean bed or out the window and wrecks the idea, through the politico-ethical conviction, most laudable therein, but disastrous in psychology, of the equality of the sexes.[13]

And then, to complete his refutation, Lacan must give his own explanation (I mean: in the terms of his own thesis) of the experience, quite gripping, it must be said, adduced by Jones to make the primacy of the phallus disappear:

> Jones makes of *aphanisis* the substance of the fear. Here, I shall remark that it is exactly the opposite direction that should be taken. It is because there can be castration, it is because there is the play of signifiers implicated in castration that, in the subject, this dimension is elaborated where he can become fearful, alarmed, about the possible future disappearance of his desire.[14]

If *aphanisis* can retain a meaning, it is thanks to a castration deemed more fundamental; in other words, it is the phallus that is central to determining—all moralism aside and all, absolutely legitimate, considerations regarding the equality of the sexes aside—the asymmetry of the sexes.

Beyond the question of *aphanisis*, which is a point of dispute with Jones, there are, to the contrary, at least two other points where Lacan leaned on Jones to constitute his own doctrine.

The *first* belongs to a theme we already encountered, since it appeared when Lacan shared the idea with Ella Sharpe. When submitting an element of dream or myth to interpretation, there is no barrier between languages, which can easily borrow from each other in the form of a rebus, as Joyce demonstrates in *Finnegans Wake*. Com-

---

[12] J. Lacan, *Formations of the Unconscious, op. cit.*, seminar of March 26, 1958.

[13] The *Écrits* (in "Du sujet enfin en question") treat this point in more or less the same terms, 232.

[14] J. Lacan, *Desire and Its Interpretation, op. cit.*, seminar of February 4, 1958.

menting on an idea of Jones, Lacan notes that "The *horse* is a rather rich theme in mythology, legends, fairy tales, in what is most constant, if not most opaque, in oneiric thematics. The *cauchemar* in English is a *night-mare*. Mr. Jones' entire book concerns this. He shows us that it isn't by chance that the night mare is not only the harrowing apparition of the night witch, that the *mare* is a substitute for the witch."[15] Here begins the critique to which Lacan subjects Jones, who, according to him, does not know how to distinguish signifiers from signifieds: "following the good habit, Jones looks on the side of the signified, which leads him to finding that everything is in everything"; which leads him to granting too much importance to the imaginary as compared to the symbolic; and it is no doubt true that the imaginary provides limits to the symbolic, but the symbolic must be granted all of its possible imaginary extension without restricting this imaginary to narrow bounds. That is when Lacan begins, on the side of the signifiers, a process that erases linguistic borders: "It is not difficult to show that the root MR, which is at the same time *mère*, *mara*, but also *mer* in French, contains, on its own, this meaning, all the more easily found in that it covers just about everything." Thus have we gone from *mare* to *nightmare* to *mère* to *mer*, which is *sea* in English, although *marine* and *maritime* are frequently used, by virtue of English's double origin. This remark is, when one considers it, decisive for casting doubt on the soundness of Lacan's reservations regarding English's ability to express the unconscious. To be able to advance such a thesis, languages would need to be impermeable entities, which they are not. For we see the unconscious take hold of languages by disregarding their so-called frontiers and treating them as though they were a single language.[16] Lacan might have remembered his remark at the time of his attack against the English language.

The *second* has to do with research, mostly begun by Lacan on the father, the name of the father, which intersects with Jones' remark, stressing that it is absolutely impossible for any human intelligence to

---

[15] J. Lacan, *The Object Relation, op. cit.*, seminar of May 8, 1957.

[16] Jalil Bennani highlights this point with pertinence in his *Entretiens avec Ahmed El Amroui*, when he says "in the unconscious, all languages are articulated through the words of each of them, as if this plural formed a single language. Unconsciously, a language is worked on by another." *Un psy dans la cité: Entretiens avec Ahmed El Amroui* (Casablanca: de la Croisée des chemins, 2013), 108–109.

ignore that there had to be intercourse for the woman to bear a child within a precise time-frame. True, adds Lacan, but "what is important is not that people know perfectly well that a woman can only give birth when she has had intercourse; it's that they sanction with a signifier that the one with whom she has had intercourse is the father." The father is not the father through intercourse, but because he is instituted, in one way or another, as the one who had intercourse. "For otherwise," Lacan adds, "the way the order of the symbol is naturally constituted, absolutely nothing prevents the something that is responsible for procreation from continuing to be maintained, in the symbolic system, as identical to just anything, namely a stone, a fountain, or the encounter with a spirit in a remote place."[17] This addition is essential and shows the relative independence of the symbolic vis à vis the biological, the order of the symbolic being able to behave aberrantly toward the natural and, in any case, institute it, even when they seem to be working together in a necessary dependency. What is true of the *symbolic* is true of *authority*, which, Hobbes tells us in chapter XVI of *Leviathan*, that it can be that of any object we want;[18] what appears *natural* is so little that it has to be instituted. The natural is only the mask of the institution. The proximity of Lacan's remark with that of the author of *Leviathan* is uncanny.[19]

Several conclusions remain to be drawn regarding Jones. The *first* has to do with the difference in the way Lacan treats the English language when he is interested in Jones and is very critical of him. When he attacks his *aphanisis*, it's to denounce an idea "that made its way [through the analytical community] and led to failures, principally among

---

[17] J. Lacan, *Formations of the Unconscious, op. cit.*, seminar of January 22, 1958.

[18] In Chapter XVI, Hobbes in fact adds this detail: "There are few things that are incapable of being represented by fiction." The Latin specifies: "that cannot have a *persona*." Inanimate things, a church, a hospital, a bridge, can be personified by a rector, a director, a controller, who can, in some sense, speak in their name. Hobbes' bridge can have a *persona* the way a stone, a fountain, a spirit encountered in an out of the way place, can stand in for a father, for a mentality that is often too quickly characterized as primitive.

[19] Hume, the philosopher his contemporaries took, not without reason, to be Hobbesian, got it right in his analysis of paternity: men are willing to be fathers on condition of being instituted as such and obtaining thereby some guarantees regarding their spouse's fidelity. See *The Treatise of Human Nature*, L. III, Part II, sect. XII. This critique parallels Bacon's of the notion of *nature* and Bentham's of the notion of *law*, a term that seems particularly inappropriate to him once it leaves the confines of the judicial.

English authors."[20] The incomprehension is attributed to an influential author who contaminated English authors; for the time being, however, there is no attempt to search, as Lacan will later, in the English language itself for some principle that renders it resistant to psychoanalysis.

And yet, there is a very thin stem in *Seminar IV*, in which we cited page 306, which could have given us some ramifications of a connection with the future themes of *lalanglaise*. It is found in the reproach addressed to Jones of not distinguishing the signifiers from the signifieds. But, in fact, is the question of the sign as easily stated in these terms to an English speaker as it is to a French speaker? The French are, one might say, quite spontaneously Saussurian in their conception of the sign, since they distinguish without difficulty, and are supported by their language in doing so, what belongs to *langue* and what belongs to *parole*. Such is not the case in English, which does not dispose of a word[21] to make room in the language, to the *langue*, as a code or a system of signs. One has to say *English language*, whereas one would not say *le langage français*; and one can talk about *English speech* without the expression being heard with the aftertaste of nationalism that *La parole française* would have. *Langue* is not as distinct from *language* in English as from *langage* in French; and the efforts to distinguish them, as Bentham does, by using the

---

[20] J. Lacan, *The Object Relation, op. cit.*, seminar of March 13, 1957.

[21] We need to be very careful with this type of statement. We could, for instance, state that French does not have an article able to distinguish the universal from the particular. Thus, the definite article *le* is used for the definite in *où as-tu mis le lait?* [*where did you put the milk?*] as well as the generic in *j'aime le lait* [*I like milk*]. It is obviously the context, which is structural in nature, that conveys the meaning here. The same goes for language in English. Language equals *langage* in the examples, "Language is a particularly human trait," "the language of film," etc. Language equals *langue* in the examples "the French language," "the language of rogues and riddlers," etc. It is only when these words, intended for a technical usage, use a single term for a given concept that the difficulty appears, and this when it is time to translate French to English or English to French. As far as *parole* and *speech* are concerned, they are discussed here in the Saussurian terms frequently privileged by Lacan, even though he is aware that they can be referenced outside of Saussure. Thus, English speech vs. French *parole* raises all sorts of questions. True, an Anglophone linguist could easily have used the terms *language* and *speech* in order to create the Saussurian distinction, since *language* has two meanings in English, *langue* and *langage*; but there is, in this decision—once again, when it concerns a word denoting, for a technical usage, a concept, which is a situation that often involves theory—a part of convention: the two languages do not coincide in the distribution of meaning among *language, speech*, on the one hand and *langage, langue*, and *parole*, on the other.

term *tongue* for *langue*, seem artificial and forced. This point may not be without importance for the understanding of the difference between *signifier* and *signified*, including how it is understood by Lacan. Be it Saussurian or Lacanian, the balance between the ideas of imaginary and symbolic cannot occur in the same way for a Francophone and an Anglophone, who enjoys a high degree of freedom when it comes to determining what constitutes *la langue* and what is left to *la parole*, since the frontier is entirely lacking precision. The Francophone imagines there exists a clear frontier between the code and the use of the code; which is not the case with the Anglophone, who cannot even *tell* the difference.

The *second* concerns fictions. Be it in Balint, Klein, or Jones, Lacan highlighted the use of fictions; hasn't he had vast recourse to them himself? How many so-called experiments that he promoted, only exist as fictional experiments![22] There is no point in turning the argument he uses against his predecessors against him. Rather, the question is: how to tell an acceptable fiction from one that isn't? This Benthamian question pops up again here without an obvious solution. That Balint's *primary love*, Klein's initial psychosis constitutive of the world, and Jones' *aphanisis* are fictions hardly constitute an argument against their admissibility; but why should we dismiss them? Can one go so far as to define one or several general principles to do so? These questions are only dealt with piecemeal; and when they are, they leave the impression that objections stemming from the use of fictions have to do with getting in the way of Lacan's position or at least not conforming to it. For the recourse to experience in these areas is vague and lacking in credibility, being itself not decisive and to such an extent composed of other fictions in the name of which the former are condemned as fallacies.

We can see here that, if, as Lacan says, truth has the structure of fiction, if knowledge is a certain architecture of fictions, the true epistemology of the type of truth and the type of knowledge sought or forged in psychoanalysis requires that the project of the theory of fictions be taken up again. Not only in literature, although it is perfectly suited and creates there, but in the psychoanalytical task itself, when it is the analysand's job.

---

[22] What is the reality of the "mirror experiment" when one is aware of the extreme latitude that must be granted to the notion of mirror and when one knows the variations that Lacan has imposed on this so-called "experiment"?

As might be expected, the discussion is concentrated around the transitional objects of which Winnicott is, in some sense, the inventor. Lacan in no way disputes him this invention, which moreover is well known and highly regarded;[1] instead he turns to his favorite maneuver of relating it back to the terms of his own theory, to transcribing it in the Real-Symbolic-Imaginary, and annexing everything that is compatible with it. It is even interesting to follow in detail the history of the annexations. Thus, in *Seminar X*, on anxiety, when the thematics of the *objet a* are put into place, the transferable character of the transitional object[2] becomes of interest, whereas there was no mention of it previously, when, at the end of the 1950s, the transfer of the object did not appear to be an essential idea. Nothing new, then, compared to the treatment of preceding psychologists and psychoanalysts; simply that, in the previous discussions, it was the ignorance of the symbolic or that of the articulation of the symbolic and the imaginary that were in question, and that focused the criticisms, this time it is the real that is increasingly in question. Lacan himself notes the connection of the transitional object thesis to a certain current of English philosophy that claims to generate real objects from the imaginary, perhaps dodging the quasi-cataclysmic, in any case unexpected, tearing of the real. Thus, examining Lacan's critique of Winnicott is of interest because of the additions to the list of authors resulting from the always increasingly confirmed distribution of axes, according to the Symbolic, the Real, and the Imaginary.

---

[1] "Winnicott, of whom we know that the mind and practice cover the full scope of the current development of psychoanalysis and its techniques, up to and including an extremely precise consideration of fantasm systems that are in frontier field of psychosis." J. Lacan, *Formations of the Unconscious, op. cit.*, seminar of June 18, 1958.

[2] J. Lacan, *Anxiety, op. cit.*, seminar of June 26, 1963.

Transitional objects are those objects that appear while the child is in the process of constituting his world, through a game of satisfactions and non-satisfactions of his desire:

> Inasmuch as a world is articulated for the human subject, which includes a beyond of the demand, it's when the demand is satisfied and not when it is frustrated, that what Winnicott calls *transitional objects* appear, in other words those humble objects that we see early on acquire an extreme importance in the relation to the mother: a bit of bedding that the child tugs jealously, a scrap of anything, a rattle.[3]

The status of these objects is ambiguous because, if everything goes well, the object is at the same time a bit of reality, of the outside world and something that participates in the hallucinatory satisfaction Freud speaks about in Chapter VII of *The Interpretation of Dreams*; but it is also halfway between the satisfaction and the eventual dissatisfaction procured by the world. Let us explore the *intermediary* character of the transitional object.[4]

> Winnicott notes, that for things to go well, namely for the child to not be traumatized, the mother needs to always be there at the right moment, and come to place, at the very moment of the child's delirious hallucination, the real object that fulfills him. There is thus, at the outset, in the ideal mother-child relationship, no kind of distinction between the hallucination of the mother's breast... and the encounter with the real object in question.

The objects that appear are therefore transitional in that "we cannot tell on what side they are situated in the reduced and incarnate dialectic of the hallucination and the real object.... There is no point wondering whether they are more subjective or more objective: they are different in nature."[5] Then comes Lacan's maneuver to transcribe things into his own system; had Winnicott been in Lacan's position, he

---

[3] J. Lacan, *Formations of the Unconscious, op. cit.*, seminar of June 18, 1958.

[4] In one of his translations of the term "transitional objects," which he will eventually settle on, like everyone else, Lacan tries to bring out the *metaxu* aspect, μεταξύ, the intermediary aspect of the transitional object, by deliberately mistranslating it as "object transition" or "transitional phenomenon." See the November 28, 1956 lesson.

[5] J. Lacan, *The Object Relation, op. cit.*, seminar of November 28, 1956.

would have called these objects *imaginary*: "Although Mr. Winnicott does not cross the threshold of naming them this, we shall call them quite simply *imaginary*." Exterior and interior, "half real, half unreal," these objects appear to move along a Moebius strip, which can order these objects perfectly according to a rigorous topology, but does not allow deciding which is interior or exterior, and even forbids doing so. Henceforth, it is not only the designation *imaginary* that Winnicott purportedly missed, but also that of the symbolic order underlying it: "It is regrettable that instead of tackling the problem posed by the introduction of this object into the symbolic order, he had to come to it in spite of himself, because one is forced to once one has started down this path."[6] According to Lacan, Winnicott hadn't understood himself, he hadn't understood the theoretical stakes of the conceptual materiel he was bringing. He was missing the strong conceptual structure which is the very one Lacan has had since the beginning of the *Seminar* and that he always triumphantly sets forth: the Real, the Symbolic, and the Imaginary.

Intermediary and metaxic, the object, however, is transitional in another sense: if the child, at the start, has no way of distinguishing between the order of satisfaction based on hallucination and the apprehension of the real that effectively fulfills and satisfies him, "the mother needs to progressively teach the child to experience the frustrations, and at the same time, to perceive, in the shape of a certain inaugural tension, the difference there is between reality and illusion. This difference can only set in via a disillusionment, when, from time to time, the reality does not coincide with the hallucination that emerges from the desire."[7] Therefore, while "it should not be said that it is about the objects of his desires, about which he is frustrated from the outset," that the child constitutes his world, this constitution occurs when "to the extent that, when moving toward something he desires, he can encounter something he knocks into or that burns him." And Lacan uses this opportunity to mark the difference between his own conception of the real and Winnicott's "genetic" conception, which closely follows that found among many English philosophers. No doubt, the object constituted during the shock of the real

---

[6] *Ibid.*, seminar of January 16, 1957.
[7] *Ibid.*, seminar of November 28, 1956.

is not at all an object engendered in some way by the object of desire as it is instituted and organized in infantile development. It is something entirely different. The object, inasmuch as it is engendered by frustration, leads us to admitting the autonomy of imaginary production in its relation to the image of the body. It is an ambiguous object, between the two, about which one can speak neither of reality nor of unreality.[8]

But Lacan makes it clear that that Winnicott's real resembles Klein's: it is an imaginary formation, made compatible, by an interplay of corrections, themselves imaginary, with other imaginary formations or with the imaginary formations of others. The real is the world such as it is constituted by the intersubjectivity of psychotics whose psychosis turned out well. In Winnicott, "the fundamental homogeneity of psychosis with the normal relationship with the world is affirmed as such."[9]

And in a semi-amused, semi-serious way, without antipathy in any case, Lacan notes the similarity of the status of the transitional objects through which we are supposed to gain the world with that which the English authors attribute to abstract objects. About this, Lacan goes so far as to say: "Mr. Winnicott is not mistaken, it is indeed in the midst of this that life happens."[10] He could have added, but the condition seems to ring very loudly here: it is indeed in the midst of this that life happens as long as a political regime does not decide that there exists only one way of life and does not bother you by requiring that you live in this only way that it considers to be the good one, with its lack of imagination. It is clear that Lacan could share with Winnicott this way of conceiving of political and community life. In *Seminar VII*, he cautions against any temptation to "do things in the name of the good, and even more so in the name of the other's good." Under the title of *éthique de la psychanalyse*, he envisions no other ethics than those "that bind us to a particular destiny, which requires with insistence that the debt be paid," the desire that animates it or that sustains it, returning "always to a certain wake, in the wake of what is, strictly speaking, our business."[11] This resemblance is striking, when one

---

[8] *Ibid.*, seminar of January 16, 1957.

[9] J. Lacan, *Formations of the Unconscious, op. cit.*, seminar of February 5, 1958.

[10] *Ibid.*

[11] J. Lacan, *Ethics of Psychoanalysis, op. cit.*, seminar of July 6, 1960.

reads, for example, in Ferguson, the genesis of civil society, the people moving past the barbarian level, still very close to the strict satisfaction of primary needs, to a more civilized level in which the objects that interest us are far from the needs; which does not mean that we don't bring a level of care to them as precise and subtle as we would if our lives depended on it.[12] But in this new world, in this *superstructure*, as Ferguson called it, made of our abstractions and our constructions, we don't ask others to believe, although it constitutes the reality, the armature of what we are living:

> Mr. Winnicott reasons that, after all, this object which is neither real, to which we grant neither full reality, nor a fully illusory character, it's like your philosophical ideas and your religious system, and everything in the midst of which a good English citizen lives, knowing in advance how to behave. About this philosophical or religious doctrine you may possess, no one dreams of saying (of requiring) that you be a firm believer, and no one dreams of taking it away from you. It's a domain between the two, in which things are instituted with a character of semi-existence.[13] This character is well defined by this, that no one normally thinks of imposing upon others, as being an object that must be adhered to, the authenticity or firm reality of what they promulgate in the way of religious or philosophical ideas. In short, the instituted world of the British Isles tells everyone they have a right to be crazy, so long as they are crazy separately. That is where madness would begin, if one wanted to impose his private madness on the subjects as a whole, each constituted in a kind of nomadism of the transitional object.[14]

Madness itself is acceptable as long as long as it is that of a self and that it does not impose upon other selves; the collective is profoundly based upon the preservation by each of his private life and the will not to impede upon the lives of others. Here, Lacan is not content to suggest that the transitional object is radically linked to a conception of the political.

---

[12] Ferguson, *An Essay on the History of Civil Society*, ed. F.Oz-Salzberger (Cambridge: Cambridge UP, 2007), 180.

[13] Locke tried to define this space of tolerance, which, somehow, in many ways has remained our own in the legislation of the States that remain attached to what we call *individual freedom* and, even more perhaps, to what stems from what we call *ethics*.

[14] J. Lacan, *The Object Relation, op. cit.*, seminar of January 16, 1957.

The remark is astute in that it links Winnicott's world to the world of Locke, for example,[15] who simply asks—it is the foundation of his political contract—that each lead his life and tend to his business according to his own values, so long as these don't impede the same project among others; in which case it is necessary to renounce or negotiate. But it is clear that there is no common path to lead one's life and that each must invent one's own; fortunate indeed is one who is able to make common cause with others, and this in any domain. And it may be the closest to Ferguson when we read, a year later, in *Seminar V*, that this doctrine

> has none other than the effect in the rest of [Winnicott's] anthropology than to make him classify, in the same register as the fantastic aspects of thought, almost everything that can be called *free speculation*. He completely assimilates to fantasmatic experience everything that is of a speculative nature, no matter how extraordinarily elaborate, namely everything that can be called *convictions*, whatever they are, political, religious, or other. It's a point of view that fits Anglo-Saxon humor well, and a perspective of mutual respect, of tolerance and also of retreat. There is a series of things that are only spoken of only in quotes or only among people who are well brought up. Yet, they are things that matter somewhat since they are part of the interior monologue we are far from being able to reduce to *wishful thinking.*[16]

We would have liked it if Winnicott had produced the theory of these transitional objects, which seem to relate to a theory of fictions; but, after all, doesn't Lacan produce it more so, even as he clearly shows, here, the British terrain—political liberalism being included where it belongs—of the theory of fictions? It would seem that the true lack suffered by the psychologists and psychoanalysts of our time is that of a theory of fictions not limited to explaining the literary world, and a few aspects of mathematics and perhaps of physics. La-

---

[15] But also George Moore, who insists, although he is utilitarian and in the name of utilitarianism, on the indefinite plurality of the good and not on its unicity.

[16] J. Lacan, *Formations of the Unconscious, op. cit.*, seminar of February 5, 1958. Lacan translates very, and certainly too freely—since he mistranslates—the English expression as "the world of fantasy and the imagination." And yet, there is something to this, for *wishful thinking* is exactly, in Hume and Adam Smith, what derives from the action of the imagination and fantasy.

can, as we have seen, wished for a transcendental aesthetics worthy of our era; isn't there reason to ask for, with the same insistence, a theory of fictions worthy of the name, because the objects it is likely to deal with are precisely the intermediate objects?[17]

If Winnicott had been better initiated to the theory of fictions, he might have escaped from the trap Lacan seeks to set for him on the question of the relationship between the real and the imaginary. Is the real a separate agency, distinct from the play of the imaginary grappling with itself? Or is it what results from this play? But if it is what results from this play, as it does seem to in Winnicott, how could the real emerge from the hallucinatory contentment the psychologist finds at the beginning of the child's life? There is more: how could the real come about other than by way of dissatisfaction? But where does this dissatisfaction come from? And why should the real be necessarily dissatisfying, which seems to imply its imaginary genesis?

The emergence of the reality principle, in other words, of the recognition of reality, from the child's primordial relationship with the maternal object, the object of his satisfaction and also of his dissatisfaction, does not allow seeing how the world of fantasy in its adult form can emerge from it, unless via an artifice of Mr. Winnicott's, which no doubt allows a quite coherent development of the theory, at the expense of a paradox I want to point out to you.

There is a fundamental discordance of the hallucinatory satisfaction of need with what the mother brings to the child. It is in this very discordance that the gap opens allowing the child to obtain a first recognition of the object. This supposes that, despite appearances, the object is found to be disappointing. Then, in order to explain the birth of everything that the world of fantasy and imagination amounts to for the modern psycho-

---

[17] Bentham has shown how, through this theory, one could account for notions like *probability*, which at the same time exists and does not exist. The analysis is done in the *Rationale of Judicial Evidence*. Lacan was unaware of this text, but, when he introduces Bentham's theory of fictions in the *Seminar*, he never fails—as we have tried to show in a 2020 article titled "Le jeu de l'interprétation et de la compréhension chez Freud et chez Lacan" ["The Play of Interpretation and Comprehension in Freud and Lacan"]—to work out, even discreetly, how it could be put to use in psychoanalysis. The attempt seems particularly convincing in the February 26, 1969 lesson. We are certainly very far from a generalization of the notion of "fiction" that would make his "theory" worthy of being called a *method*; but the affirmation that prompted this note needed this nuance.

analyst, namely what he calls in English *wishful thinking*, he points out the following:

Let us suppose the maternal object arrives at just the right time to fill the need. Barely has the child begun to react to have the breast that the mother brings it to him. Here Winnicott pauses, quite rightly, and poses the following problem: what allows the child, under these conditions, to distinguish the hallucinatory satisfaction of his desire from reality? In other words, with that starting point, we strictly end up at the following equation: at the beginning the hallucination is absolutely impossible to distinguish from absolute desire. The paradox of this confusion cannot be anything but striking.

In a perspective that rigorously characterizes the primary processes as having to be naturally satisfied in a hallucinatory way, we end up with this: the more reality is satisfying, the less it constitutes a reality test.[18]

It is clear that Lacan is leading Winnicott into a dialectical precipitate[19] from which none of the actions needed to escape are satisfactory. It is falling into Diodorus Kronos' trap: the probabilities we estimate about a situation, don't they just cover a reality that exists in and of itself, but that is only revealed by our estimates? *Either* the assignments of probability can then be judged by the real when it occurs, *or* the real has broken away from the probabilities emitted in its direction and it is out of the question for the assigned probability to be judged by the real that occurs. In other words: *either* the real is gained by the imaginary act and it is not sufficiently breaking, cutting, sustained, *or* the real is sufficiently sustained, but it is then necessary to discredit the "genetic" perspective, as philosophers call it, referring to deducing it from a play of sensations, imagination, passions, and projection.

So, it is, once again and always, through philosophy that Lacan attacks the psychologies and psychoanalytical conceptions of his era. And when he invokes *experience*, often without adding the details that would allow determining it, characterizing it, if not identifying it, one might wonder if it isn't, for the second time, a question of invoking philosophy, his own, if we dare say; for, can one invoke, in order to refute philosophical theses, something other than experiments entire-

---

[18] J. Lacan, *Ethics of Psychoanalysis, op. cit.*, seminar of March 23, 1960.

[19] Which he elegantly covers with the term *paradox*, implying a far more serious contradiction.

ly woven out of other, philosophical theses that are stronger, if not tru-
er, than those they refute? The question that remains is knowing what
kind of experiment we are dealing with in psychology, in such a way
that it is possible for it to be invoked to refute a thesis. It seems that
when Lacan discovered Popper's theses, he did not have much with
which to oppose them, besides the fact that if Popper wanted to attack
the scientificity of psychoanalysis in that nothing can render its propositions falsifiable, he missed the target, since "psychoanalysis is not at
all a science," which does not mean it must not be taken seriously. Its
status would instead seem to be that of a practical know-how, a kind of
orthodoxa, which one of the first analytic philosophers of action, Eliz-
abeth Anscombe, complained—wrongly, then—had been abandoned
by the Moderns. The most pertinent words of the seminar that are
known concerning this question, those of the November 15, 1977, lesson, say this: "Psychoanalysis should be taken seriously although it is
not a science. It isn't even a science at all. Because the problem is, as
Karl Popper has over-abundantly shown, it isn't a science because it is
irrefutable. It's a practice that will last as long as it will, it's a practice
of chatting. No chat is without risks… analysis has consequences: it
says something." It would be hard to better turn to one's advantage a
critique that sought to be ferocious and decisive....

21
OTTO FENICHEL

November 29, 1967, in a lesson that cites Winnicott and Bentham, Lacan translates a long text by Otto Fenichel, published in 1958, in English,[1] titled "The Genital Character"; he follows it with a commentary that interests us. Here is the text as written by Fenichel, which Lacan translates for, and facing, his audience:

"The Genital Character"

A normal "genital" character is an ideal concept. However, it is certain that the achievement of genital primacy brings a decisive advance in character formation. The ability to attain full satisfaction through genital orgasm makes the physiological regulation of sexuality possible and thus puts an end to the damming up of the instinctual energies, with its unfortunate effects on the person's behavior. It also makes for the full development of love (and hate), that is, the overcoming of ambivalence. Further, the capacity to discharge great quantities of excitement means the end of reaction formations and an increase in the ability to sublimate. The Oedipus complex and the unconscious guilt feelings from infantile sources now can really be overcome. Emotions, then, are not warded-off any more but are used by the ego; they form a harmonious part of the total personality. If there is no longer any necessity to ward off pregenital impulses still operative in the unconscious, their inclusion into the total personality in the form of traits of the sublimation type becomes possible. Whereas in neurotic characters pregenital impulses retain their sexual character and disturb rational relations to objects, in the normal character they partly serve the aims of forepleasure under the primacy of the genital zone; but to a greater extent they are sublimated to the ego and to reasonableness.

---

[1] It is easily found in *The Psychoanalytic Theory of Neurosis* (New York: Tavistock/ Routledge, 1990), 496.

Lacan translates the text as follows:

Un caractère normal "génital" est un concept idéal; cependant il est certain que l'achèvement de la primauté génitale comporte une avance décisive dans la formation du caractère. Le fait d'être capable d'obtenir pleine satisfaction par l'orgasme génital rend la régulation de la sexualité, régulation physiologique, possible et ceci met un terme au dammi-ng up, c'est-à-dire la barrière, l'endiguement des énergies instinctuelles avec leurs effets malheureux sur le comportement de la personne. Il fait aussi quelque chose pour le plein développement du love, de l'amour (et de la haine), c'est-à-dire le surmontent de l'ambivalence. En outre, la capacité de décharger de grandes quantités d'excitation signifie la fin des réactions-formations, des formations réactionnelles et un accroissement de la capacité de sublimer. Le complexe d'Oedipe et les sentiments inconscients de culpabilité de source infantile peut maintenant être réellement dépassé. Quant aux émotions, elles ne sont plus gardées en réserve mais peuvent être mises en valeur par l'ego ; elles forment une part harmonieuse de la personnalité totale. Il n'y a plus aucune nécessité de se garder des impulsions prégénitales encore impératives dans l'inconscient, leur inclusion dans la totale personnalité (je m'exprime comme le texte) et sous la forme de traits ou de poussées de la sublimation devient possible. Cependant, dans les caractères névrotiques, les impulsions prégénitales retiennent leurs caractères sexuels et troublent les relations rationnelles avec les objets, cependant dans le caractère normal elles servent comme partiels les buts de préplaisir ou de plaisir préliminaire, sous la primauté de la zone génitale, mais pour autant qu'elles viennent dans une plus grande proportion, elles sont sublimées et subordonnées à l'ego et the reasonableness, *la raisonnabilité (je ne crois pas que l'on peut traduire autrement).*

The state of this translation, found on the internet, leaves us puzzled. Either Lacan translated, as it is claimed, Fenichel's text—in which case we are then confused by the mediocrity of the outcome, even taking into account the oral nature of the *Seminar* teaching— or the transcription is faulty; but if the transcription is so poor when relating a translation, one wonders how faithful it is to the rest? In either case, the translation is seriously defective. The translation, in the middle of the text, of *then* by *quant à* [as for], makes the hearer completely miss the English conjunction's dimension of consequence. More serious still, the translation of the following sentence completely ignores the main clause's conditional character. The ignorance of the meaning of *whereas* makes him completely miss the last sentence's meaning, which is perfectly clear in English, but which the translation transforms into perfect mumbo-jumbo. With these three or four gross inaccuracies, intentional or not, it is no longer Fenichel's text that is commented upon, but rather a crude text that doesn't even make sense, where the last sentence is concerned, and that Lacan shamelessly attributes to Fenichel with a mind to discrediting its author.

Nevertheless, as defective as the translation is, or the version that has come down to us, our interest stems from Lacan's commentary. He wonders how an author who is among those responsible for the most canonical teachings of psychoanalysis can write such a text. For, says Lacan, "I don't think that anyone—analyst or not, should they have any experience of others and of themselves—can for an instant take this strange *berquinade*[2] seriously. The thing is, strictly speaking, false, completely contrary to reality and to what experience teaches us." So, what is to be understood is why, in psychoanalysis, there is a need for such a disciplinary vulgate, since the author is taken by Lacan, who forces the issue, to be the spokesman and guardian, in a moral sense, of a kind of ideal state of sexuality.

Perhaps Lacan already had Fenichel in mind when, in the June 22, 1955, lesson, he wondered ironically if analysis consisted in encouraging the subject to be nice, to become a true character who has achieved instinctual maturity, having left behind the stages dominated by one orifice or another: "Is it a question, in analysis, of a co-optation to these fundamental images, of a rectification, of a normalization in terms of the imaginary?" Or is it a question, on the contrary, of substituting for the confusion of the imaginary, a veritable access to the symbolic "by returning to discourse its sense of discourse."[3]

And, in his analysis of analysis, which is not unrelated to what Balint was asking, Lacan, who heard him on this point, wonders—if however it isn't simply a question of a gross confusion between the imaginary and the symbolic—about the oversimplification and falsity to which someone expected to deliver a certain kind of teaching is held. If psychoanalysis wants to be vulgarized—and Lacan does not

---

[2] Term that signifies a naïve, simplistic story, meant for children: nursery rhyme?
[3] J. Lacan, Le Séminaire, *The Ego in Freud's Theory*, *op. cit.*, seminar of June 22, 1955.

say that it shouldn't or that it would be contrary to its essence—how should it go about it? How should it project itself into ordinary language.

Treating them as the objects of particular study, in the previous sections we cited the English authors who gave rise, in the *Seminar*, to important developments through the extension they acquired during such and such a lesson, the number of times they were referenced, from week to week over the year, if not from year to year. There are other authors Lacan cites only a few times, sometimes only once in certain cases, for a detail he considers essential. Even if, rhetorically speaking, we are only giving them limited space here, they are no less important if it is true that, as Nietzsche says, and as I believe, we only ever read a book, and perhaps even the works of an author, to retain a few of its details. This latter trait, which characterizes any reading, is obvious in the case of Lacan, who, as we know, follows the *Seminar's* multiple paths with a fundamental structure, which allows discrediting all the authors who do not adopt it, which is to say the quasi-totality, but which at the same time is enriched, on the three axes of the RSI and according to their articulation, precisely by new and prominent *details*.

WILLIAM RONALD FAIRBAIRN

It is thus that Fairbairn finds himself attacked for having tried, in quasi paradigmatic fashion—for the tendency to this type of enterprise was common in psychoanalysis in the 1950s, and Fairbairn is far from being the only one to attempt it, and not without rigor—"to reformulate all analytical theory in terms of object relations";[1] which leads to a radically false point of view on the real of the cure and of the conception, in its totality, of what is involved in psychoanalysis.

---

[1] J. Lacan, *The Ego in Freud's Theory*, *op. cit.*, seminar of June 1, 1955. The article he references is titled "Psychoanalytic Studies of the Personality" and appeared in the *International Journal of Psychoanalysis* 25.

By objectifying what is involved in psychoanalysis,[2] we can no longer consider the play of desire or of desires as an interplay of lacks,[3] but rather as a very thing-driven system of fills that fit together or do not, that allow concatenations or do not, from the point of view of an observer, who is none other than the psychoanalyst, who stands in as the subject of the operation, according to a subject/object axis held to be essentially structuring and as what the analysand could identify with by the end of the analysis. Thus, while "according to Freud," says Fairbairn, "in his language and in his lingo [*langue*] the libido is *pleasure-seeking*," while "it seeks pleasure," Fairbairn claims "to change all that and realizes that the libido is *object-seeking*."[4] We can see, here, Lacan surreptitiously slide into what he describes as a diversion, and that English, through its gerund, is not uninvolved in the intimation of this slide. And, when he speaks, a few lines later, of the "notion of the *object-seeking* libido" in a mixture of Latin and English that is only meant to accentuate the sensitive issue, in order to point out the difficulty of the notion of *object*, that creates the confusion of what, thanks to his *real-imaginary-symbolic* structure, Lacan seeks to untangle.[5]

The problem of the transcription, in terms of objects, towards which the gerund moves, almost unbeknownst to the Anglophone, is that it transforms something on the order of relations, and of relations of relations, which is to say of structure, into characteristics of the object, into properties, in the form of adjectives. Thus, in the Oedipus complex, "the mother and father share the fundamental roles that are inscribed in the primitive division of the object: on one side, exciting desire (the libido being confused here with desire objectified in its conditioning), on the other, rejecting."[6]

Moreover, Lacan wastes no time explaining that the qualifiers only mask the relations, since it is only "too clear that *exciting* and *rejecting* are not on the same level. Indeed, *rejecting* implies a subjec-

---

[2] We know that it is Husserl's error, irreparable in Lacan's eyes, to have conceived of psychic phenomena according to the subject/object model of knowledge.

[3] Which, for example, makes Margaret Little, cited by Lacan in *Seminar X* on anxiety, say, "We only mourn for someone about whom we can say *I was his lack*. We mourn for people we treated well or badly, and for whom we did not know we fulfilled the function of being in the place of their lack."

[4] J. Lacan, *The Ego in Freud's Theory, op. cit.*, seminar of June 1, 1955.

[5] *Ibid.*

[6] *Ibid.*

tivization of the object. On a purely objective level, an object is or is not frustrating. And the notion of *rejection*, it secretly introduces the intersubjective relationship, non-recognition. This tells you the confusion one is perpetually subject to experiencing."[7] Lacan's analysis, then, is that the English gerund encourages objectivization.[8] Not to mention that, when the name of an object is, thanks to the *-ing* form, under the control of an adjective that characterizes it, the object participates in a nominal block, a noun with a set character; and, when the object in question is too distant from this qualification, the moral point of view, of what "must be," takes over for ontology:

> For example, it is supposed that, in her natural function, the mother in no instance is a rejecting object—in the state of nature the mother can only be good—and it is because of the particular conditions in which we live that such an accident can happen. The subject splits from a part of himself, removes Joseph's coat, rather than submitting to the ambivalent incitements. The drama emerges from this ambiguity—the object is at the same time good and bad.[9]

Lacan recognizes that there can be some virtue in this way of thinking, so long as it is only a moment in a dialectic rather than the static figure of "the individual [who] lives in a perfectly defined and stable world, with objects meant for him" and which, in some sense, "are waiting for him."[10] In such a world, "the action of the psychoanalyst cannot be anything else but helping him to recover the path of a normal relationship with his objects,"[11] in an adaptive or re-adaptive view of the subject, based on the psychoanalyst's values and what he believes to be normal: "Any theorization of analysis, organized around object relations, ultimately consists of promoting the recomposition of

---

[7] *Ibid.*

[8] With, as a consequence, the multiplication of characters. "Freud had not confused internal aggressivity with the superego. With Fairbairn, we are dealing with a truly choice idea, because the author does not seem to have found in the English language a term that seems to him to adequately signify the disruptive, if not demonic, function of the superego, and he created one—the *internal saboteur*." The notion appears to be created in order to make up for a deficiency of English, which seems unable to bear the existence of a function without attributing it to an object.

[9] J. Lacan, *The Ego in Freud's Theory, op. cit.*, seminar of June 1, 1955.

[10] *Ibid.*

[11] *Ibid.*

the subject's imaginary world according to the norms of the analyst's ego. The original introjection of the *rejecting object*, which poisoned the *exciting* function of the said object, is corrected by the introjection of a correct ego, the analyst's."[12]

What is striking about these remarks regarding Fairbairn, proceeding via a reflection about English, a language purported to cause the analyst to over-"objectify" his analyses, is the way they contradict another characteristic of English, linked to the same *-ing* form: that of expressing the event, in what is most volatile about it, almost without turning it into a noun (which French, with access to nouns only, is unable to do). This advantage, once granted to English, is now denied it. English is deemed to hide what jumps out at you in French, for instance, as we have seen, that the *exciting object* and the *rejecting object* are not at all on the same level, despite linguistic appearances, since *rejecting* seems to have the same function as *exciting*, which is not logically or psychologically the case. But what position to take in this dialectic? In which cases does English prompt objectivity, leaving French to highlight it and contest it? And in which cases is it English that allows exposing this dialectical illusion? In any case, it is clear that the language in which analytical theory is conducted is not without importance to intimate, more or less clandestinely, its direction.

EDWARD GLOVER, THOMAS SZASZ, HERMAN NUNBERG

Glover, through his October 1931 article, "Therapeutic Effects of the Inexact Interpretation," published in *The International Journal of Psychoanalysis*, allows Lacan to raise another question, which is to know whether it is the knowledge of the truth that cures and if a cure could be effected on false theoretical bases. Lacan is willing to recognize the latter,[13] since he often stresses that psychoanalysts, past and present, are better practitioners than they are theoreticians:

---

[12] *Ibid.*

[13] He recognizes it almost explicitly in the *Écrits*, when, citing the same article, he highlights and explains a kind of placebo effect any spoken intervention can have in analysis: "Any spoken intervention is received by the subject as a result of its structure, but it takes on a structuring function by virtue of its form, and it is precisely the impact of non-analytical psychotherapies, even of the most commonplace medical 'prescriptions,' to be interventions that can be called obsessional systems of suggestion, of hysterical suggestions that are phobic in nature, if not of persecutory support, each deriving its

it is clear that we know more now than at the very beginnings of analysis, and the question is posed as to knowing what our therapies were worth at a time when we did not know the full extent of the fantasy system. Were they incomplete cures, less valuable than the ones we do now? The question is quite interesting, and it leads Glover to draw up a general situation of all the positions taken by whomever is tasked with consulting about a given disorder.[14]

Among these attitudes, there is one that Lacan highlights, less in *Seminar V* than in *Seminar X*, when it is a matter of responding to Thomas Szasz, who defends an intellectual position of analysis; far from Glover, who does not ask the question and for whom it isn't a matter of determining if the analyst's knowledge must become the analysand's. In his article, "On the Theory of Psychoanalytic Treatment," Szasz claims that "the end of any analysis, didactic or not, can only be defined by the initiation of the patient into a scientific point of view regarding his own movements."[15] It is difficult to be more Cartesian, since Descartes assigns the ethical goal, not of abolishing his passions, but of knowing them and thus assuring his mastery over them. Without talking about mastering passions, a doubly or triply illusory idea,[16] Lacan's answer is not long in coming: "If there is something I have often decried, it is the scientific point of view, inasmuch as its aim is always to consider the lack as something to be filled, at the opposite end of the problematics of an experience that includes taking into account the lack as such."[17] And we see here that, while the fate

---

character from the sanction it gives to the subject's ignorance of his own reality." It is not necessary for an intervention to be true for it to be healing.

[14] J. Lacan *Formations of the Unconscious*, *op. cit.*, seminar of June 18, 1958. In *Desire and Its Interpretation*, *op. cit.*, Lacan also salutes Glover's attempt to "locate the perversions somewhere, relative to a chain."

[15] J. Lacan, *Anxiety*, *op. cit.*, seminar of January 30, 1963. The article cited by Lacan is found in *The International Journal of Psycho-Analysis* 38 (1957): 166–182. It seems that Lacan condensed several quotations from Szasz's text, in particular that "the final goal of psycho-analytic treatment is the establishment of a never-ending, ever-deepening scientific attitude in the patient towards those segments of his life which constitute the sphere of psycho-analysis" (176), and that analysis should help the patient in "adopting a progressively more scientific attitude toward himself and his relationships with others" (177).

[16] First, because the passions don't exist and that mastery cannot be exercised over something so imaginary; then, because the goal of ethics is not necessarily one of mastery, be it of oneself, for in this game, who masters whom?

[17] J. Lacan, *Anxiety*, *op. cit.*, seminar of January 30, 1963.

of analysis is, for the analyst, quite inevitably the knowledge of what is going on with the analysand—for the analyst must be able to publicly account for what he is doing, and has no reason to avoid the critique of his technique[18]—on the other hand, the fate of analysis is as much, for the analysand, that of obtaining this knowledge as it is that of attaining supposed autonomy or to identify with the analyst in a kind of narcissistic euphoria.[19] Knowledge tends to assert itself as saturating the void; whereas, if it becomes the analysand's law, the rule of what the analysand must acquire from the analyst, it only contributes a crease to analysis or only consists in having taken the risk of contributing this crease. The analysand is then always at risk of being the one who, in analysis, is in the position of being mistaken, of being mistaken in front of someone who knows more about him than he himself does, or who, at least, is supposed to have this knowledge, if not of being misled by the one charged with reestablishing the balance of knowledge, which risks being the governing principle of an analysis thus conceived: "the *being mistaken* rebounds on the subject. It isn't only that the subject is, in a static manner, lacking, mistaken. It's that, in motion, in his discourse, he is basically in the dimension of the *being mistaken*."[20] So, the question is one of knowing if this narrow dimension must be the only one in which, in psychoanalysis, this governing principle resides ; it can perfectly well be discussed to the extent that, if the psychoanalyst can and must publish his "technique of a handling, an interference, if not, at worst, of a reification of desire," it does not, for all that, transform desire into an object of knowledge and it "leaves entirely open and in suspense the notion of desire."[21]

---

[18] The *Seminar* on anxiety reminds us of it with much solemnity: "Psychoanalysis can only be correctly included among the sciences by submitting its technique to the examination of what it truly supposes and performs." One might find, in the 1950s and 1960s, at least, the same radicalism in Lacan as in Kant, who, in the *Critique of Pure Reason*, measures the scientificity of a theoretical activity by its capacity to appear before the tribunal of reason, without seeking a fraudulent pass. "What this technique truly supposes and performs, such is our point of reference, around which must revolve any disposition, be it structural, of what we have to deploy." J. Lacan, *Anxiety, op. cit.*, seminar of May 22, 1963. The texts from the 1970s say, with a meaning that appears clearly contrary: "The analyst's discourse is not the scientific one." "Avis au lecteur japonais," *Autres écrits, op. cit.*, 499.

[19] See our paragraph on Balint.

[20] J. Lacan, *Four Fundamental Concepts of Psychoanalysis, op. cit.*, seminar of May 6, 1964.

[21] J. Lacan, *Anxiety, op. cit.*, seminar of May 22, 1963.

In an ironic way, by using Nunberg's work, Lacan talks about those patients who use the "truth" of analysis to hear themselves say, or to have confirmed, what they had been seeking: "We find ourselves... in contact with the profound ambiguity of any of the patient's assertions, and the fact that it has, in and of itself, a double face."[22] The demand for analysis and the demand in analysis are extremely ambiguous. Why would the truth have a curative property? And why would the supposed will to get treatment go through the truth "while his symptom is made to bring him certain satisfactions"?[23]

There is, however, a point that may have gone unnoticed for its consequences on our problem of language, the central theme of our work. We have seen Lacan present himself as an adept of the legitimacy of criticism to demand an accounting from whatever is put forth as scientific and as a universally acceptable technique. Very well. But then it becomes difficult to grant a privilege to certain languages for the expression of certain knowledge and certain techniques and to discredit others. By definition, the critical point of view—and it is probably wrong, for that matter, in this[24]—does not bother with language and can express itself in any one of them. But is it really coherent to declare that the language of certain people, because they are those who speak it, renders them unanalyzable, all the while advocating, elsewhere, a universal science and technique? *Either* psychoanalysis is a work of *lalangue* and in *lalangue*, which can only be spoken in a privileged manner in certain languages, and this requires abandoning the critical point of view explicitly advocated in *Seminar X, or* psychoanalysis can justify itself before the tribunal of reason like mathematics and the other sciences, in which case it is the essential obstacle that certain languages are purported to present for psychoanalysis that would no longer be understood, and the remarks concerning English would simply be considered incongruous.

---

[22] J. Lacan, *Four Fundamental Concepts of Psychoanalysis, op. cit.*, seminar of May 6, 1964.

[23] *Ibid.*

[24] We have suggested that dialectics had difficulty resolving issues of language because some of these languages, more easily than others, enter into transcendental illusions. Kant does not take this into account.

THEODOR REIK

In order to hear the patient's deception, Theodor Reik, Freud's pupil and colleague, said that it was necessary to hold steady "listening with the third ear,"[25] as Schumann asked that we listen to an *innere Stimme*, an intermediate voice between the two melodic lines played on the piano. "To tell the truth, I don't approve of the expression," said Lacan, about the *listening* "as if two ears were not enough to be deaf." It is only too clear that the *discourse of the third ear* transforms what must be heard into an object and what hears it into an organ, whereas there exists neither such an object nor such an organ and it isn't even certain that the two other ears are sufficient organs to hear with and that they have actually existing objects to grasp. But Reik "is from the good era, the heroic era, when one knew how to hear what was speaking behind the patient's deception." Is it by chance that, a year before writing the preceding sentences, Lacan had reported Reik's analysis of the shofar, conducted for *Imago*, the instrument that is sounded in the synagogues for a few privileged moments of the year or for ritual events? For "independently of the atmosphere of contemplation, of faith, if not of repentance in which [the sounds of the shofar] are manifested and ring out, an unexpected emotion emerges through the mysterious pathways of a specifically auricular affect, which cannot but touch, to a remarkably unusual extent, all those within range of hearing it."[26] It seems that the signifier of the shofar's strange sonority creates a particular bridge between the human ear, be it physical or virtual, and the voice of God,[27] taken in its absolute alterity,[28] to the point of being able to renew the alliance.

---

[25] J. Lacan, *Four Fundamental Concepts of Psychoanalysis, op. cit.*, seminar of 287.

[26] J. Lacan, *Anxiety, op. cit.*, seminar of May 22, 1963.

[27] Even if it can evoke animal bellowing, "the shofar is indeed," Reik says, "the voice of Yahweh, that of God himself." *Ibid.* The animality is only there to reinforce the idea of God's absolute alterity, the impossibility for it to be assimilated to something human.

[28] The absolute alterity of God's voice is expressed by the shofar, in that the sounds it emits are not such that they can be assimilated, but such that they can intrude and be incorporated. "A voice, then, is not assimilated, but incorporated. This is what can give it a function of filling our void." *Ibid.*, seminar of June 5, 1963. The sound of the shofar fills; one cannot be assimilated by it.

PHYLLIS GREENACRE

The way of discussing Phyllis Greenacre's article "General Problems of Acting Out" is almost a caricature of Lacan's method: "The question is to know how to act with the *acting out*. She says there are three ways. There is the *interpreting*, there is the *forbidding*, there is the *reinforcing the ego*." The *interpreting*? But the *acting out* is specifically made for interpretation. "Only, this, it isn't the meaning, whatever it may be, of whatever you are interpreting that matters, it's the rest," in other words, everything that led to this *acting out*. *Forbidding* it? Who contemplates that? And yet, Lacan recognizes that "many things are done to avoid *acting out* during a session." As for *reinforcing the ego*, we know his opinion on principle. Nevertheless, not without humor, Lacan points out "how minor sicknesses are rare during an analysis that lasts for a while, colds, flus, all that fades away," "and even diseases, if there were more analyses in society, there would be better health. I think health insurance should take into account the proportion of analyses in society to adjust its rates."[29] You heard it here: a hole thought to be deeper than any other has finally been filled, that of the Social Security deficit.

GREGORY BATESON

Lacan reads Bateson because "people kept harping on" this author. Reading him did not prove to be very fruitful: "About the unconscious, Bateson, for lack of knowing that it is structured like a language, only has quite vague ideas. But he creates lovely artifices he calls *metalogues*. Not bad, inasmuch as these metalogues entail, if he is to be believed, some internal, dialectical progress, produced from no more than questioning the evolution of a term's meaning."[30] The critique is typical of the device Lacan uses with authors. The thesis that allows judging and almost gauging the author is unknown to the author himself; on the other hand, it creates an idea that could be useful in that it produces the symbolic, not from objects but through an internal production, as Lacan has shown that signifiers are articulated according to a fictional process.

---

[29] *Ibid.*, seminar of January 23, 1963.
[30] J. Lacan, *Encore, op. cit.*, seminar of June 26, 1973.

LUCIA TOWER

Twice in a row, March 20 and then March 27, 1963, Lacan reads the same Lucia Tower article on counter-transference, which is to say on the way the psychoanalyst manages his/her desire when he/she becomes—which he/she always is in the course of an analysis—the object of a transference on the analysand's part. Lucia Tower spoke, concerning this counter-transference, about "everything the psycho-analyst represses of what he receives in analysis in the way of a signifi-er."[31] Before reading the narrative of this counter-transference, Lacan makes the odd remark that only women have anything sensible to say about counter-transference, if not are the only ones "who have dared speak about the thing." He then cites Alice Balint (who is speaking along with her husband), Ella Sharpe, Barbara Low, and Lucia Tower.[32] He could have noticed that the four people he cites are Anglophones and never need to decide whether the psychoanalyst is *le* or *la*.[33] How, then, can English be disqualified as a language of analysis if Lacan himself draws from it his understanding of ideas as subtle as count-er-transference?

And it is indeed this way of following, by highlighting, here and there, certain English words, that interests us in Lacan's practice of the commentary, in a situation that somewhat resembles that of a didactic analysis. Lacan's text is not without humor: it deals with how a female analyst manages a counter-transference that features "two males that she has been handling,"[34] that she was unable, in Lacan's eyes, to the-orize, but that she was nevertheless able to conduct. The two men had gone into analysis to treat what Tower diagnosed as anxiety neuroses. And Lacan begins to follow the narrative, part French, part English,

---

[31] J. Lacan, *Anxiety, op. cit.*, seminar of February 27, 1963.

[32] *Ibid.* One can read, about this, the very interesting article Michel Plon wrote, titled "Be Not Too Tame," published in the collection *Lacan et le contre-transfert* (Paris: PUF, 2011). He is also struck by Lacan's remark (page 134 of the article).

[33] It is true, on the other hand, that the use of the third person singular personal pronoun (*he, she*) as well as the possessive adjective (*his, her*), which do not reveal the bearer's sex in French, but do so in English, undermine the pertinence of this remark. It is difficult to isolate a trait in a language that allows drawing very general conclusions on the relationship of said language with the unconscious.

[34] *Ibid.*, seminar of March 20, 1963.

I mean like a third voice, without necessarily always translating the English, a little like the way he recounted certain passages of *Hamlet*:

These two men have had some difficulty with their mother and with their *female siblings* [English], which means sisters, but situated as equivalent to their brothers. They now find themselves *accointés*—the term sounds like an Anglicism, but it is true that this Anglicism in the end marks a return to French[35]—with women who really have been chosen to exercise a certain number of aggressive and other tendencies, using it to protect themselves against a certain penchant for the other sex. *With these two men*, she tells us, *I was perfectly aware of what was happening with their wives, namely, she says, that they were too submissive, too lacking in hostility, and in a sense too* devotious [sic], *and that the women were frustrated by this lack of a sufficiently* non-inhibited masculine assertiveness [English], *of a sufficiently uninhibited way of affirming oneself as a man.* In other words, they were not pretending enough.... As for her [the analyst], without knowing what risk she ran of falling into a trap, she feels herself to be *protective*, a little too *protective*, though differently, she tells us.

Keeping *protective* in English allows Lacan to distinguish the analyst's attitude from a maternal conduct that would surely be implied by the French *protectrice*. What is striking, in this narrative, is the analyst's prodigious, really somewhat naïve, honesty, who hides none of the affective attitudes that traverse her; what is singular and funny is the parallelism that occurs in the analyst's head and begins, over time, to play a role in the analyst, who makes a kind of choice between the two men in the transference. It is perfectly clear that, as Lacan had warned one or two weeks earlier, "things are placed on the plane of desire."[36]

"In the first man's case, she protects his wife a little too much. In the case of the second him, a little too much. What reassures her is that she is much more attracted to the second, and this because the

---

[35] Similarly, there are rare terms in French, but which ring so "French" that we do not see how they can be translated into English; yet, we are surprised to see that the same word can be used in English, where it is understood as it is in French. Such is the case with *poignance*, which is easily translated as *poignancy*.

[36] *Ibid.*, seminar of February 27, 1963.

first one has some not very attractive psychosexual problems[37] [English].... But the first manifests himself in a way that is not so different from the other." Simply, the first one is a little more aggressive than the other, through "his tendency to attack her in her analyst's power. For the second, rather than destroying her as frustrating, it's a matter of getting an object from her." Something to which, after all is said and done, she is not inhospitable, for:

> despite the efficaciousness of the transference analysis, there remains nonetheless, of all that, she tells us, something in her that is in no way fundamentally disagreeable, and the counter-transferential answers she perceives as being hers do not at all exceed, she says, the limits of what is reasonable, beyond which any female analyst, who isn't on guard with such characters, risks losing herself. She is [on guard], particularly.

But all it takes is a series of incidents for things to no longer be so simple with the first patient.[38] The first patient's wife suffers a real psychosomatic incident, which triggers the analyst's dream that changes the outlook of the counter-transference. Through the dream, she notices "that it might not be so sure that things are going so badly on the wife's side, that the patient is really trying, in his marriage, to do what is necessary to put his wife at ease, in other words, this man's desire is not subject to drifting as much as all that. Put it this way: he is capable of taking himself for a man, the dignity of which he was being denied until then."

When she made this discovery "she can really accomplish, with him, a revision of everything that until then had deluded her; the transference claims turn out to have been themselves a sham, and from that point on, she tells us, everything changes."

> The analysis becomes particularly hard for her to bear. Everything happens, she says, in the midst of a storm of depressive movements and naked rage, as though he were putting me, the analyst, to the test—I am *scrutinized*—in each of my smallest pieces. If a moment of inattention, she tells us, had made it so each one of these small pieces did not ring

---

[37] The rest of the narrative reveals that sadistic anomalies are involved.

[38] The second one is no longer mentioned in Lacan's narrative from this point on.

true, if there were one that was fake, I had the feeling that my patient would leave entirely in pieces.

"While she does not see everything," comments Lacan, "she nevertheless knows how to name what is involved: it is, she says, phallic sadism cloaked in oral language." The patient notices that he may have the means to *stoop*, to bend his analyst to his desire.[39] Lacan comments: if the analyst provokes a storm like this on the part of her analysand, it's that "she only related in the transference from the moment her own desire became interested in it and in the function where she herself is in a position of third-party rivalry with characters from her own history. She therefore bears the consequences of this desire, to the extent that she experiences what analysts include in the term *carry-over*, which refers to the phenomenon where the effects of the counter-transference are most manifest. It's when you continue to think about a patient when you are with another one."

Lacan fashions a lovely hypothesis concerning what happened in this storm that she did not see coming. She put the character back in his place. She forgot, in passing, "that this place, he was never able to find it. *That*, is his anxiety neurosis."[40]

The epilogue that follows is quite surprising: all the fatigue of this episode that seems to weigh on the analyst's shoulders turns out to be a false fatigue that she sheds in one stroke. "And yet, she says"—Lacan is speaking—"when I was almost completely worn out, it all disappeared in the most amusing and sudden way, amusingly sudden, says the text. Going on an annual vacation, she notices that nothing is left of this episode. This experience is of absolutely no interest to her." How does the desire involved in the counter-transference exist such that it can be gotten rid of so easily, as soon as you have left the theater of operations where this desire found itself implicated? The key that

---

[39] In his translation, Lacan misses the indirect nature of the verb "to stoop" by translating it as "courber" [to bend or curve], whereas it means to bend over, as one might to pick up something. Here, Lacan grants the analysand more power and agency than does Lucia Tower. We have often caught Lacan *in flagrente* of twisting English words into the meaning that best suits his theses; any speaker who incorporates foreign words submits them to a meaning, a value, and an imaginary that are those his own language allows by capturing them in the networks of its own signs.

[40] *Ibid.*, seminar of March 27, 1963.

Lacan gives is the following: it never coincided with the object of the man's desire.

> She knows very well that he can always seek, there was never any question of his finding. That is precisely what is involved: that he realize that there is nothing to find, because what, for male desire, is the object of the search, only concerns him, if I may say so. . . . She knows very well— let me talk and don't get carried away[41]—that he is not missing anything. Or rather, that the mode in which lack plays out in feminine development is not articulated on the level where it is sought by the man's desire, when it specifically involves, for him, this sadistic search. . . that consists of eliciting what must be in the partner in supposed place of the lack.

The interest of this narrative of a narrative, like that of an interpretation of an interpretation,[42] stems from the linguistic fabric that is somewhat intermediate between two languages, that can run in one language and find its peaks in another, in English here. These words, taken as peaks or valleys, give off, to the whole of the fabric, local properties it would not have otherwise. From Joyce, perhaps even more than from Rabelais, Lacan learned that texts did not belong to statutory languages defined by ideally sharp edges.[43] If we wanted to find these languages with sharp edges instead of glazes with vague outlines, we could through an analysis, but we would then create artificial linguistic objects that forget their own movements and treat texts like pure metalanguages, the fate of which is to exist separately. Yet everything can be said in nonexistent languages, in a text that offers them mobile layers.

In a certain sense, Hume wasn't wrong to consider that the plurality of languages could be overcome, but he envisioned it as an imaginary correspondence among languages, which is but a recomposition derived from a symbolic crisscross of an underlying single reality. It isn't a question of making what is said in different languages correspond through a common imagination, but rather of understand-

---

[41] The reader who has followed Lacan in his conception of desire cannot help but be startled when coming across this phrase, which simply prepares that the sadist's lack is not exactly of the same nature as Lucia Tower's, his analyst.

[42] As in the dream reported by Ella Sharpe.

[43] Lacan could have remembered this remark when he discredited English as the language of psychoanalysis.

ing that each term, each expression, each syntactic movement has an effect in a text that is always singular, of which the blurred, glazed structure, could never depend on some mechanical interlocking of the radically heterogeneous and impermeable systems that languages are purported to be. It is intermixing that is authentic and supposed purity that is fake; from this point of view, Bentham and Hume might agree, even if they did not understand the phenomenon in an identical fashion. It may precisely be a reading of Lacan that allows for understanding that what at first might be taken for the most radical inversion is, in the end, less of a stretch than it appears.

This way of constructing texts as layers of symbols derived from diverse languages, but interlaced in such a manner that it is impossible for each one to reappropriate them, does not correspond to a critical philosophy, at least in a classical form, to start with because the latter is not interested in questions of language.[44] It appeared to us that the functioning of these symbols, so layered, was often closer to that found among Anglophone authors than among Continental authors. In particular, one finds in Lacan a deliberate encircling tightening of the concept by words considered limits between which a usage can take place as of right. It is thus that what could be taken upon first reading as translation errors are, in fact, markers of the extension and comprehension of a concept. Let us not forget that, in a system that accentuates the symbolic in its "blind" state, it is out of the question to have recourse to an intuition that would give an exact indication of where something stands; the only thing possible is an apagogic functioning of the ideas put forth. This system is so advanced in what could be called the English-speaking diaspora of Anglo-Saxon origin that it is not limited to affecting language, but also extends to the rationale of judicial and juridical evidence, which only establishes truth in an indirect and negative fashion. It is obvious that we will never know what happened in a case that is being judged, but, in these conditions, it is necessary to confront, from the point of view of a law that presents its own uncertainties and stumbling-blocks, what can be known about

---

[44] While this flaw is inherent to *The Critique of Pure Reason*, it isn't to all critical philosophy, and perhaps not even to Kantianism, since *The Critique of Judgment* manifests, at least in its notes, an interest in the diverse ways concepts are stated. Elsewhere, the Kantian, Ernst Cassirer, in his *Philosophy of Symbolic Forms*, devoted a large part to language.

what happened, based on the necessarily indirect testimony we possess. The rationality is one of tightening and retightening, as it is with measures taken in physics, in evaluations of probability, of degrees of reliability given to eyewitness testimony.

Once again, we have not sought to be any more complete in this chapter than in those preceding. We have only covered an author when he was sufficiently amply cited. Thus, we have said nothing, or very little, about Wilfred Bion,[45] Peter Brown, Karen Horney, Ernst Kris, Rudolph Loewenstein, Sylvia Paine, John Rickmann, Charles Rycroft, Melitta Schmideberg, Robert Stoller, William Gillespie, or even about Erich Fromm or René Spitz. This treatment is obviously unfair because the importance of an influence is not measured by the number of citations and the quantity of lines per citation it occasions. An author does not necessarily cite those to whom he is most indebted; citation even tends to be prompted by opposition, whether it stems from animosity, adversity, even admiration tied to a kind of excess compared to what we would have dared to say ourselves and to the rarity of the expression. We do not cite what we can say ourselves, nor what makes up our own flesh, simply because what constitutes us does not allow itself to be objectified. "No one says Cartesian other than those who aren't"; it's the law of citations, which are better preserved by a hint of hatred than by the dissolving, diluting, and assimilating power of love. And even when it is out of sympathy that we cite, for, after all, it is possible—even though the intellectual act is most often, by nature, more aggressive than conciliatory—it involves getting hold of a position from which we still feel at a distance, or to let ourselves be penetrated by something that is still foreign to us and to which we react with a commentary. The citation signals a withdrawal with regard to discourse cutting something away from itself, at least provisionally. In this sense, it rhetorically resembles the last line of a demonstration, from which it stands out when the latter is successful, on condition of adding that this cut-away product is attributed to the other, who is situated on the other side of a border, either to fence off a dejection or to mark something external and resistant.[46]

---

[45] Who is, nevertheless, mentioned in 1947, when Lacan, who admired the way the English had recently waged the war against the Nazis, wrote "La psychiatrie anglaise et la guerre" in *L'évolution psychiatrique*.

[46] A friable citation is no more than a rhetorical error.

Not seeking, therefore, to engage in the dangerous game of influences,[47] we stuck to Lacan's initiatives involving citations and to his most salient reactions to the texts he read in the *Seminar*. It would, nevertheless, be difficult, after having cited so many names, to say nothing about the importance of the Stracheys in Lacan's intellectual life.

THE STRACHEYS, JAMES AND LYTTON

The names Ernest Jones, Ernst Kris, Otto Fenichel—which are the names of people who, with many others, constantly brought their intellectual support to the dream of an edition of the complete works of Freud in English—compel us to say a few words about James Strachey. The pillar of *The Standard Edition of the Complete Psychological Works of Sigmund Freud*, translated from the German under the General Editorship of James Strachey. In collaboration with Anna Freud. Assisted by Alix Strachey and Alan Tyson. Editorial Assistant Angela Richards. London, The Hogarth Press and the Institute of Psychoanalysis, 1966, 1968, 1971, 1973, 1975, 1978, 1981, 1986, 1991. The general preface found in the first volume (from 1966) is interesting thanks to the autobiographical recounting of the difficulties encountered by Strachey in the work he did rounding up texts, selecting them, and identifying, in German, what was a work of Freud's, according to whether it was reread by the author or not. Strachey shows the difficulties he encountered with the stratifications of certain works like *The Interpretation of Dreams* or the *Three Essays on the Theory of Sexuality*. Without going into the details, Strachey writes of his difficulties stemming from Freud's confusion and oversights regarding copyrights. He also stresses that, for forty years, Freud's English translations were undertaken by Leonard Woolf, Virgina Woolf's husband, at Hogarth Press and that these did not get in the way of the Standard Edition. It is true that James Strachey and Leonard Woolf were bound by an old and solid friendship that went back to the time they were students at Cambridge with John Maynard Keynes.

---

[47] The discourse of influences tends to transform the texts that mattered to an author into causes and the author himself into substance; the author is thereby plunged, like a consistent body, into a context of circumstance. Such a use of cause and substance cannot be justified as part of a work on Lacan's readings of English authors.

Among the elements we learn from the general preface, three seem particularly apt for our concerns. The *first* derives from the double culture of Freud, who was not only a neurologist and physiologist, but also a man whose literary and linguistic culture was immense: "Freud was a striking example of a man equally at home in both of what have been called the 'two cultures'. He was not only an expert neuro-anatomist and physiologist; he was also widely read in the Greek and Latin classics as well as in the literature of his own language and in those of England, France, Italy, and Spain." Strachey doesn't forget the visual arts and even music, even though Freud affected a rather negative attitude toward the latter (xvi).

The *second* derives from the style he adopted in his translation and the kind of reader he targeted: "The imaginary model which I have always kept before me is the writings of some English man of science of wide education born in the middle of the nineteenth century. And I should like, in an explanatory and not patriotic spirit, to emphasize the word 'English'" (xix). It would not be surprising if we found there one of the reasons why Lacan, as though obsessively, assailed the "science" that appeared to us not to exist anywhere but inside his head. Reading the preface, we see that it is indeed the man of science who is the target, even though one might insist on his Anglophone character, as if there existed a privileged link between 'science' and the English language.

But the most precious element of all, the *third*, is where Strachey informs us that he had decisions to make before allowing the first volume to appear, and, among these, decisions concerning the choice of technical terms, even if it meant regretting them later. Strachey stresses that Freud's translation was done by "a few individuals usually engaged in other occupations, and it has been without the background of any established academic machine ready to provide either personnel or accommodation" (xviii). Admittedly, this may be what makes the Standard Edition of interest, but it is also the limit that makes it an "amateur production." On this question of vocabulary, Strachey goes into detail:

> As regards technical vocabulary, I have in general adopted the terms suggested in *A New German-English Psycho-Analytical Vocabulary* by Alix Strachey (1943), which was itself based on the suggestions of a 'Glossary Committee' set up by Ernest Jones twenty years earlier. In only a few

instances have I departed from these authorities. Some individual words which raise controversial points are discussed in a separate note below (xxiii).

It is surprising that translators met to work together to solve problems going from German to English versions.

James Strachey then shares several elements of the method he adopted to respect, in English, the concepts written in German by Freud, in particular, that of "invariably translating a German technical term by the same English one. Thus, '*Unlust*' is always translated 'unpleasure' and '*Schmerz*' is always translated 'pain.'" These two words are not the only ones to have been the result of a choice the translators scrupulously respected. We should neither be surprised nor shocked that '*Abwehr*' is translated by 'defence,' '*Angst*' by "anxiety,' '*Instance*' by 'agency,' '*Phantasie*' by 'phantasy,' '*Unbewusst*' by 'unconscious.' That '*Anlehnungstypus*' is by 'anaclitic (or attachment) type' is more unexpected. The decision that '*Affekt*,' '*Empfidung*,' and '*Gefühl*' would be expressed by 'affect,' 'sensation,' and 'feeling' is understandable given the vague outlines these terms possess in both languages. On the other hand, we know how Lacan hesitated in the face of Strachey's decision to translate '*Trieb*' as 'instinct' and that he refused this translation not least because 'instinct' also refers to the programmed behavior of animals. It is clear that his conception of *the unconscious structured like a language* could only make him go against Strachey's choice, whereas he hardly disputes the treatment of the vocabulary of affectivity because the epistemological stakes do not seem to be very high to him. The reasons Strachey cites for using 'instinct' are interesting; they are those of a translator: to translate '*Trieb*' by 'drive' is not a real translation, in his eyes, but rather a simple imitation by German of English. One might wonder whether Lacan did not find therein his audacious reasons for talking about *dérive* [drift] in French, which in any case, seems better to him than *instinct*.

Strachey recognizes that his technical choices are not always flawless; in particular, they can lead to believing in conceptual distinctions that do not exist in his eyes: he cites the example of the translation of '*psychisch*' by 'psychical' and of '*seelisch*' by 'mental,' whereas there is no distinction between the two terms in German.

What strikes the Francophone reading these pages by an Anglophone talking about his hardships as a translator of German is that they don't compare to what happens when going from a Saxon language—like German or English, which are, from this vantage point, on the same side—to French, where you are forced to use the word *psychisme* to translate *mind*, while keeping *esprit* for *spirit*, where there is no word to translate *Geist*, while *Ghost* poses even greater challenges. With *esprit*, French adds to the spiritualization of *spirit*; or it is compelled to sound scientific when it uses *psychisme* for *mind*, which sounds no more scientific than does *body*.

It is odd that Strachey says nothing, in his preface, about what will create so many problems later on: his translation of *Ich*, *Es*, and *Über-Ich* by *Ego*, *Id*, and *Superego*, instead of *I*, *It*, and *Above-I*, which could be considered more adequate.

Lacan was not unaware that James Strachey was a psychoanalyst and that he had, himself, theorized psychoanalysis; and the two times, from the *Seminar's* beginning, he is mentioned, are two opportunities, for Lacan, to correct an articulation of theory deemed deficient.

The first is precisely a place involving the Ego and Superego, the psychoanalyst needing, according to Strachey, to play the role of the Superego. This is wrong, according to Lacan: an analysis does not work this way. The analyst's position is not that of the analysand's Superego. But what interests Lacan here is the fictions race through which, to escape a fallacy, one has to create another one, and another, as in a race forward that Bentham had already identified among lawyers in particular:

Take, for example, James Strachey's fundamental article, published in *The International Journal of Psycho-Analysis*, on therapeutic efficacy.[48] It is a well thought out text that puts all the accent on the role of the Superego. You will see to what difficulties this conception leads and the number of supplementary hypotheses the aforementioned Strachey has to introduce in order to support it. He proposes that, relative to the subject, the analyst occupy the function of the Superego. But the theory according to which the analyst is purely and solely the support of the Superego's function cannot be sustained, since this function is precisely one of the mainsprings of neurosis. This creates a circle. In order to escape it,

---

[48] James Strachey, "The Nature of the Therapeutic Action of Psycho-Analysis," in *The International Journal of Psycho-Analysis* 15 (1934): 126–159.

the author is forced to introduce the notion of a parasite Superego[49]—a supplementary hypothesis that nothing justifies but that is motivated by the contradictions of his thesis. Moreover, he is forced to go too far. In order to claim the existence of this parasite Superego in analysis, he has to state that between the analyzed subject and the subject analyst a series of exchanges, introjections, and projections occur that lead us to the level of the mechanisms of the constitution of good and bad objects—introduced by Melanie Klein into the practice of the English School. This is not without presenting the danger of tirelessly reproducing them.[50]

What is interesting in the second text, which follows only a few weeks after the first and picks up on the commentary of the same Strachey article, is that it already manifests the characteristic trait of Lacan's critique: the passage of the cited authors through the Procrustean bed of the RSI. Here, the triplicity has not yet been established, but it is already the same mode of criticism at work to highlight a point with which Lacan is incidentally in full agreement: that there is a *kaïros* to grasp for an analysis to have any effect—producing a mutation—on the flow of the analysand's discourse, and that too soon before or after this moment, it would have no effect:

Strachey tried to pin down what he calls the interpretation of the transference and, more specifically, mutative interpretation. See volume XV of *The International Journal of Psycho-Analysis,* for the year 1934, numbers 2 and 3. Indeed, he stresses that it is only at a precise moment in analysis that the interpretation can amount to real progress. The opportunities are infrequent and cannot be seized in an approximate manner. It isn't around, in the whereabouts, nor before, nor after, but at the very moment when what is ready to bloom in the imaginary is at the same time there in the verbal relation to the analyst, that interpretation must be given for its decisive value, its mutative function, to be exercised.

In other words, what?—other than that it is the moment when the imaginary and the real of the analytical situation merge. It's what I am explaining to you. The subject's desire is there, at the same time present and inexpressible. Naming it, to hear Strachey, is what the analyst should

---

[49] Strachey speaks about the psychoanalyst's position as being that of an "auxiliary superego."

[50] J. Lacan, *Freud's Technical Papers, op. cit.,* seminar of 129.

limit himself to doing. It is the only time his speech is added to that which stirs up the patient in the course of his long monologue....

Let us conclude with a short remark. Besides James, there exist multiple Stracheys who have distinguished themselves in all kinds of ways. One of them interested Lacan, who mentioned the name Lytton Strachey in his February 11, 1975, lesson about queen Victoria. The work, *Queen Victoria* (London: Chatto and Windus, 1921),[51] is indeed remarkable thanks to the biographical intelligence it manifests and that psychoanalysis could have garnered. Unfortunately, while the book appears important to the *Seminar's* author, we will never know why.

---

[51] Lytton Strachey is the author of multiple works, including the remarkable *Eminent Victorians* (London: Chatto and Windus, 1918).

23
CONCLUSION

Was Lacan a good reader of the texts he highlighted, or did he only ever engage in raptor-like readings and, like a hawk, swoop down on his prey? We know that Nietzsche sought to distinguish good and bad readers, and even to indicate and inflect how he wanted to be read himself. The question, addressed in Lacan's direction, does not have much more meaning than that of asking what is a good or bad object. And the answer may be found written in the commentary he reserved for Melanie Klein, and so many other psychologists, who made inopportune use of moral categories in their work: any object is at the same time good and bad, and it elicits good and bad actions from those to whom it appeals. Thus, Lacan often behaved like the worst readers Nietzsche speaks of,[1] who resemble plundering soldiers, grabbing here and there what they can use, overturning and soiling the rest. Nevertheless, he was also able to cause others to read authors he does not seem to have read himself, spurring readers who may owe him more than they can imagine. Not to mention that he made a certain number of books better than they were, and as a good adversary, was able to clarify others by sharpening their outlines and revealing their bones.[2] We have pointed it out: Lacan is a fervent partisan of the tableaux that allow situating authors in relation to one another, as Kant had been and as had, in a Fichtean manner, Vuillemin, for example. Thus, one of the results of the work that propels Lacan's theses on a daily basis comes down to creating a topology of the authors he reads: he situates each in relation to the other, according to an extremely effective

---

[1] *Human, All Too Human*, Part. II, *Miscellaneous Maxims and Opinions*, §137, trans. P.V. Cohn (London : George Allen, 1911), 72. "The worst readers are those who act like plundering soldiers. They take out some things that they might use, cover the rest with filth and confusion, and blaspheme about the whole."

[2] *Ibid.*, §153, 79 : "A book is made better by good readers and clearer by good opponents."

interplay of oppositions. Just as it was possible to draw the map of psychoanalytical schools in France from 1926 to 2006,[3] one could—we retreated, faced with the length and complexity of the task—establish that of the psychologists and psychoanalysts cited by Lacan.

But what seemed to us more interesting has precisely to do with this voice, blended with the analyses he cites and relates, whether these analyses come from Freud or another analyst, such as Lucia Tower. In a certain sense, there is no more direct discourse in analysis than that of the citation. Indefinitely, without an initial text, the citation supposes itself; it's through the citation that analysis finds its "object," so to speak. But this leads to a difficulty: how does this reversal of the direct and the indirect, performed so well by Lacan according to the mode of what has been called the *innere Stimme*, not make of Lacan an ally of the English language, which always seems to be citing itself, to know that it is being spoken while it is being used to speak? It is surprising to see Lacan "complete" a Lucia Tower analysis, not by "de-Anglicizing" her remarks, but rather by accomplishing its "Anglicization," for, this action of adding a voice to an already present voice, recalls the way English, by adding some Latin and French to Saxon, developed and continues to be spoken. Our problem, in turn, becomes clearer—for we have a better view of how English functions, which is in no way incompatible with Lacan's speech and language—and becomes more opaque—for isn't the English language, through this interplay of the indirect that is the veritable direct and the direct that always becomes indirect, the language best suited to analysis? Unless, as we have suggested, the saturations of the positions by this language is a handicap to any analysis. We must however recognize that the Lacanian ambiguity is difficult to resolve, since, often, as we have seen, his "outings" concerning English are compromised by his own remarks.

There is another question that remains unresolved, after the preceding investigations, and that we need to address: does it make any sense to talk about *English science* or *German science* or *French science*? Do concepts change from one language to another? And, if the word *science* bothers, where psychoanalysis is concerned, does it make sense to talk about *English, French,* or *German psychoanalysis*?

---

[3] Yann Diener rose to the challenge, with extraordinary courage and persistence, in his article "Schéma des scissions, graphe de la passe et carte de la dispersion," in *Essaim* 28 (2012): 110.

Oddly, Lacan turns enigmatic: we have even seen him side with critical philosophy at decisive times in his research; but how can one remain the adept of a critical conception of the sciences when the notion of *lalangue* comes into play and the expression in a language seems to absolutely determine the concept? Even more odd: whereas he had the opportunity to raise the question in his prefaces to translations, produced while he was alive, into German[4] and Japanese,[5] he only very allusively addresses the problem.

We limited ourselves, in this fourth part, to the English psychologists and psychoanalysts who inspired Lacan in his writings and seminars. It seemed to us that his will to confront all the systems and all the doctrines in this domain to his own Real-Symbolic-Imaginary construct, which takes its measure like a Procrustean bed, was not without ambiguity. Lacan used philosophers to move the frontiers of psychoanalytic and psychological concepts, as well as those of the disciplines themselves. But he soon encounters a problem we came across previously: philosophy seems to establish theses in antinomies, appearing to leave to conviction the choice of adhering to a thesis rather than its antithesis, the reasons for this choice constantly giving rise to similar subdivisions and similar pitfalls. Moreover, the supposed recourse to experience becomes unconvincing as soon as it has been used to read psychologists and psychoanalysts: the philosophical use of their concepts can only render suspect such supposition and such recourse. There remains great attention paid to the way theses are articulated, to the words used to designate them (or to not designate them, for that matter), if not to the words used to make these very theses appear and disappear; this way of proceeding is not the most frequent in philosophy. Lacan showed himself to be very attentive to languages and the difference between doing psychology or psychoanalysis in one language rather than another; one might want to use an idea here that Dorothée Muraro has implemented on the terrain of aesthetics as well as infantile psychiatry, but the frontiers of which we think can be further expanded: language, used as a kind of third voice, the one Schumann spoke of for certain of his compositions, plays an essential role in all the activities of conceptualization of psychic material. It is

---

[4] Introduction to the German edition of a first volume of *Écrits*, dated October 7, 1973.

[5] The "Avis au lecteur japonais," dated January 27, 1972. *Autres écrits, op. cit.*

clear that Lacan constantly had in mind the differences between the modes of expression that languages are, while also being masks. His friendship with Jakobson, who was acting similarly in the neighboring territories of poetics and grammar, may have helped to sustain this interest.

It remains for us to consider that this *innere Stimme* of languages, which appears to us as a kind of solution, most of the time unnoticed by philosophers when they could have recourse to it in order to resolve their antinomies, is not only audible in psychology and psychoanalysis: it can be heard in all the sciences, ignoring the so-called frontiers between the natural sciences and the human sciences, which, once again, exist much less than one might think.

V
ANGLOPHONE SCIENTISTS CITED
FOR EPISTEMOLOGICAL REASONS

We have already widely cited English authors, be they logicians or philosophers, for epistemological reasons; how could we have proceeded differently with an author who does not take a step in analytical practice, technique, or knowledge without reflecting on what he is doing? Kant said that the sciences could advance without doing their philosophy. The remark is rash, even for mathematics or physics, but it is quite simply impossible for psychoanalysis in its Lacanian form. This is what gives psychoanalysis, thus conceived, its very high heuristic value. But, beyond the philosophers we have cited, beyond the logicians, beyond the psychologists and psychoanalysts to whom we have referred, there are other English-speaking authors who practice neither philosophy, nor logic, nor psychology, and to whom Lacan refers to learn from their methods, even though, at first glance, they would seem to have little to do with psychoanalysis. Such as, for example, during the last years of the *Seminar*, the references to the sociologist Rodney Needham, to the works of those who thought they could add to psychoanalysis notions from thermodynamics or information theory, like Siegfried Bernfeld; but also, perhaps because Freud often cited him with admiration, to the works of the biologist Charles Darwin.[1] In addition to these authors is one of the founders of game theory, John Von Neumann.[2] Thanks to his works, we began to see new possibilities emerge through the rewriting of transcendental aesthetics among 1950s philosophers and the notion of logical time. For the theory of knots, Lacan consulted Milnor's work. Finally, there is a major reference in Lacan to Newton and classical physics that he read in Koyré's interpretations, a part of whose work is written in English, and that Lacan read in English. This latter point is most important, for as much

---

[1] To whom Marx dedicated his *Kapital*.

[2] Oddly, Lacan does not cite the name Morgenstern, which is, nevertheless, ordinarily paired with Von Neumann's in the discovery of game theory.

as the references in the preceding part are more or less expected in a work of reflection regarding psychoanalysis, the reference to New-ton scarcely is: isn't physics too removed from psychoanalysis for any methodological profit to be derived from it? As soon as the subject became imaginary and psychoanalysis could no longer claim to be the science of the subject—in order to distinguish itself from a so-called science of matter—as soon as it also cannot call itself a human science, since this term no longer covers anything specific, the two elements through which the natural sciences and psychology were traditionally opposed no longer have a reason to exist and a great number of traits of their respective epistemologies become common or commensura-ble. Pierre Kaufmann, in his work on Kurt Lewin, makes this clear:

> For, on the one hand, psychoanalytic theory targets the determination of singular processes, it seeks to locate them and explain them in their own domain and, consequently, it is descriptive in De Broglie's terms. But, on the other hand, it seems strange to find equivalent to the "de-scription" of physical reality via images the determination of processes that are unconscious.... An analogous problem was posed to physical epistemology from the moment physics itself broke from the demands of spatiotemporal intuition.[3]

What Kaufmann attributes to De Broglie could already be ap-plied to Galileo and Newton, as Kant saw when he shows that the representation of a physical law is not a copy of the phenomenon, but rather an interpretation, a representation of a representation, or, if one

---

[3] Pierre Kaufmann, *Kurt Lewin: une théorie du champ dans les sciences de l'hom-me* (Paris: Vrin, 1968), 7–8. The passage we just cited is followed by a long citation of Louis De Broglie, in which Kaufmann highlights the fact that, while the microphysics that had just made their appearance could in no way copy or represent the processes it treats, it was precisely for this reason that it was criticized by the greatest contemporary physicists, who expected from physics not a blind symbolism, but rather a certain representation of the world, capable of yielding a complete image of reality, one that doesn't stray too far from description: "The success of a mathematical formalism alone is not enough to prove that the interpretation given it is exact." One might maintain that Kaufmann's *Kurt Lewin* is the fulfillment of Lacan's remark in the article already cited on "La psychiatrie anglaise et la guerre," in which Lacan paid tribute to what he termed the nascent "psychology called group" "for having achieved a sufficient elaboration, in the work of Kurt Lewin, to express itself in nothing less than at the mathematical level of vectorial analysis." *Autres écrits, op. cit.*, 106–107.

prefers, a kind of fiction of the first or second degree. We never see a body fall, as it is represented to us, with all necessary precision, by the law of gravity, which presupposes an articulation of the respective symbolizations of time and space, none of which is obvious.[4]

---

[4] Intuition is a historical phenomenon and what appears "obvious" to one era certainly wasn't during the previous era when it appeared.

24
RODNEY NEEDHAM

From Needham, psychoanalysis receives a kind of jolt, in that he seeks to make analysts aware of the fact that the kinship abundantly present in analysis is only one type of kinship among others, and that, henceforth, the range of psychoanalysis, far from being universal, is much more restricted than analysts realize. "I want to call your attention," Lacan tells his audience, April 19, 1977:

> to the fact that there are sociologists who have stated, under the patronage of one Rodney Needham..., that kinship needs to be reexamined, that in fact it features a greater variety, a greater diversity than what—it has to be said, it is to what he refers—analysands have to say about it. But what is really striking is that [even if analysts must put up with the constant harping] by analysands on their relationships with their parents, that it isn't the only thing analysands talk about.

Lacan then explains how the analyst should take this news in such a way that analysis not be trapped by the particularity of a culture and that it be able to gain some universality: *"La parenté en question* [Kinship called into question]—it's a book published by Le Seuil—highlights the primordial fact that it's 'lalangue' that is involved. It doesn't have at all the same consequences that the analysand only talks about that; because his close kin have taught him 'lalangue,' he doesn't differentiate what specifies his own relation with his close kin." The important thing is, for the analysand as for the analyst, the scansion of the former's signifiers through his family narrative, and not dwelling on the relations of a certain type of family (which, to say it in passing, the analyst does not invent). One senses here the slight deviation that a sociological analysis undergoes when it addresses the psychoanalyst and the psychoanalyst returns it to the sender with a new meaning. On the occasion of an accusation of producing a more contingent idea of the family than it thinks, psychoanalysis can demonstrate a new necessity[1] based on the experience it has of the analysand's. The analysand's "familial" discourse does not coincide—or does so only very partially—with the signifiers that structure the family, and that Lévi-Strauss and Needham himself began to establish in their complexity. The problem that is posed, then, is not to teach the psychoanalyst that there are a great many types of families that are not structured the way the analysand imagines; it is rather to ask oneself what the ethnologist structures exactly. Where is the linguistic structuration undertaken by the ethnologist if it differs from that the psychoanalyst can achieve in his confrontations with the analysands? In other words, if Lévi-Straussian ethnology and Lacanian psychoanalysis seem, from afar, to share the same structural discourse, aren't their structurings more disjointed than they seem? What relationship is there between the family the analysand has in his mind and the family the ethnologist structures and categorizes? Care must be taken not to consider the passage from one to the other simple and nearly identical.

---

[1] As Pascal says, "Language is a particular, but universal, science."

25

SIEGFRIED BERNFELD

The remarks we find concerning Bernfeld in *Seminar II*, during the February 9, 1955, lesson, allow us to clarify the affirmation of an analogy between the methods of physics and those of psychoanalysis. An affinity of methods, for example: that it is possible, in both cases, to prefer a non-figurative axiomatization to some supposed description or copy does not mean that it is necessary to blindly apply to psychoanalysis ideas that are valid in physics, as if the two disciplines shared exactly the same notions; psychoanalysis does not become *ipso facto* a physical science. Thus, Lacan bluntly condemns the overextension of analogies, as in a rash identity between the Freudian death instinct and the principle of entropy found in thermodynamics and in information theory.

True, "Bernfeld is a talented analyst, who was able to find a childhood memory of Freud's hidden behind the veil of anonymity the latter had communicated as a *screen memory*." But, ten years later, Bernfeld:

> gives, with Feitelberg, in *The International Journal of Psycho-Analysis* of 1931, the report of God knows what, that doesn't have a name in any language, and that is research, under the title *The Principle of Entropy and the Death Instinct*. They tried to study the paradoxical pulsation of entropy inside a living being, or, more exactly, on the level of the human nervous system, by comparing cerebral temperature and rectal temperature. They thought they were capturing the signs of paradoxical variations, in other words, not conforming to the principle of entropy such as it functions in physics in an inanimate system. It makes for very strange reading, if only because it shows the aberrations to which taking a theoretical metaphor literally can lead.[1]

---

[1] J. Lacan, *The Ego in Freud's Theory*, *op. cit.*, seminar of February 9, 1955.

Indeed, Freud had used this metaphor, but he had not suggested treating it like a concept:

> It's a matter, for Freud, of apprehending human behavior. To this end, he wonders if there isn't a reason to bring into play a category analogous to those used in physics. He then introduces the dimension of entropy inasmuch as it is realized in this original act of communication that is the analytical situation. All these dimensions must be retained in order to understand Freud's remarks, which concern not only the living being, objectifiable on the mental plane, but also the meaning of his behavior, and precisely inasmuch as it is involved in the particular relationship that is the analytical relationship, which can only be understood as a communication. This is the setting that gives its meaning to the comparison of the death instinct to entropy. To take this analogy literally, to translate it into the precise terms that are used in physics, is a misconstruction as absurd as the productions of Borel's typewriting monkeys.[2] This production of typewriting monkeys, we will have to condemn it only too often among analysts.[3]

It remains that the problem posed by Bernfeld's excesses is the question of knowing how to limit the use of a metaphor and if there exist markers that allow distinguishing a concept from a metaphor. This is a problem all the more crucial since all concepts, in whatever science it may be, are indicated by images or metaphors, and that, on a certain pathway, at least, the itineraries of concepts are in step with those of metaphors. This is not all; no one can find fault with the use of concepts by analogy, that is to say, the operation that consists in conveying them from one domain to another. But then we have to

---

[2] The allusion to Borel's famous apologue is the following. It is summarized very well in these terms by Benjamin Matalon: "Borel said that enough Monkeys typing long enough would end up typing all the texts in the Bibliothèque nationale (or, according to other examples, the first sentence of the *Discourse on Method*, or tomorrow's newspaper... the reasoning is the same in each case). Although everyone agrees that seeing a monkey type an intelligible text has zero probability, it is in no way logically impossible. On the other hand, it is absolutely out of the question, by the very nature of things, that a text typed in this manner would be illustrated."

"Épistémologie des probabilités," in *Logique et connaissance scientifique*, Encyclopédie de la Pléiade (Paris: NRF, 1967), 539. Borel wanted to show, in this way, that the logical probability of an event did not coincide with the mathematical probability of this event; an event can be possible, while having zero probability.

[3] J. Lacan, *The Ego in Freud's Theory, op. cit.*, seminar of February 9, 1955.

wonder whether transplantation is possible, and what can validate it or invalidate it. From this point of view, transfers from one language to another that does not necessarily use the same metaphors as the first should be observed, in particular. For not only can conceptualization differ from one language to another, but metaphorization is not segmented in the same way and cannot induce the same illusions.

26

CHARLES DARWIN

With Darwin, we reconnect more closely to English, and even to England. Lacan seems to be of two minds when it comes to him. The first derives from the finesse of an author who did not have access to the linguistic apparatus needed to give his theses their true reach; the second depends on deciphering the famous idea of *the struggle for existence* as the undue, metaphorical generalization, to the whole of the living, of the eristic social state of England in the nineteenth century and, more generally, in the modern era. The difficulty is that the myth of the primitive horde, for example, has been accepted in psychoanalysis, by Freud himself, as if it were a concept. In reality, it is a crude and naturalistic understanding of aggressivity, confused with aggression, the former having nothing to do with the latter.

Let's begin with the question of language, which, as one might suspect, provides Lacan with the best cards of interpretation, including that of rescuing, through them, the theses that, at the outset, seem to be the least acceptable to Darwin.

January 21, 1959, in *Seminar VI*, Lacan stated, in considerations on childhood development, that "even Darwin, who tended toward naturalistic explanations, did not fail to be struck by this: it certainly was funny that, from a child already remarkably clever, allowing him to isolate the quack from the duck—this is how, in Darwin's text, the duck's call, picked up by the child, is rendered phonetically—this quack is, by him, related to a series of objects, from wine to coin," the wine being assimilated to the liquid in which the duck paddles, the coin in that an eagle with wings spread is represented on one of its faces. Darwin is struck by two operations: on the one hand, that of the designation that nominalizes, by isolating through abstraction and then by installing this abstraction; on the other, that of a more adjectival function through which the *duck* function characterizes all kinds of "things" that relate to the duck by eventually transforming them into new nouns through some transfer operation, which struc-

tures the speaker's experience and world. This structuring presents
an autonomy relative to objects, and it would be a mistake to think
that it is under their pressure that language is constituted and modified: "So, you see," concludes Lacan, who finds in the naturalist himself the confirmation of his theses concerning language, "that it is,
in any case, in the register of the signifying chain that we can grasp
what is being founded in the child that is fundamental in his apprehension of the world as being structured by speech." Language is not
structured according to the logic of things or according to that of supposed essences that substitute for them, as in some Platonism; it is
structured like English *nonsense*, in other words, according to its own
logic.[1] In Lacan's eyes, Darwin's interest lies on this side rather than in
his "naturalism," yet, it is this "naturalism," probably stemming from a
free-market ideology in the service of a brutal economy that radically
separates capital and work, that won out among all those who have
used his theories. The *struggle for existence* is the theorized version of
a power relationship in a violently inegalitarian society projected into
all other areas of existence. During the theory report presented at the
11th Congress of French-Language Psychoanalysts on "Aggressivity in
Psychoanalysis," Lacan had suggested the emergence, the treatment,
and the ideological heritage of the Darwinian notion of *the struggle for
existence*, stemming from a primacy granted to space and the struggle
for its occupation, extended to every sphere of existence, as though
the dominant trait of 1850s political economy should be the guiding
principle of being in all its dimensions:

> Wouldn't it be superfluous, the prestige of the idea of the struggle
> for life is sufficiently attested to by the success of a theory that was able
> to make our thought accept a selection based entirely on the conquest
> of space by the animal as a valid explanation of life's developments. As
> well, Darwin's success seems to come from his projecting the predations
> of Victorian society and the economic euphoria that sanctioned the so-
> cial devastation it inaugurated on a planetary scale, from justifying them

---

[1] It is curious that Lacan, who is so attentive to this kind of problem, starting with the
very first *Seminars*, did not notice that the wine and the coin correspond to the categories
identified by Jakobson as metonymy (contiguity of the duck and the liquid) and metaphor
(ressemblance of the duck and the bird). Lacan's citation precedes Jakobson's text by a
few years. This important remark occurred to J. Houis upon reading the text.

through the image of a laisser-faire of the strongest devourers in their competition for their natural prey.[2]

Darwinism is presented as an avatar of Hegelianism, an English and economistic version of the master-slave dialectic.

May 12, 1954, answering a question, Lacan is just as polemical regarding Darwinism. While he does not deny that there exists "between humans a destructive and deadly relation," always under the surface, he nevertheless attacks "the political myth of the *struggle for life* which was useful for inserting many things. If M.[3] Darwin created it, it's that he belonged to a nation of privateers for whom racism was the fundamental industry."[4] It remains perfectly clear that, under the pretext of describing the real, what is being played out is the justification of a way of organizing (or disorganizing) society that could be different.

Lacan then curiously launches into a refutation of Darwinism that is not up to his standards and leads to some kind of preexisting harmony among species, as unconvincing as the thesis he claims to refute: "In fact," he says:

> this thesis of the survival of the fittest species, everything goes against it. It's a myth that is contrary to things. Everything proves that there are points of consistency and balance specific to each species and that species live in a kind of coordination, even of eaters and eaten. It never reach-

---

[2] J. Lacan, "L'agressivité en psychanalyse," *Écrits, op. cit.*, 120.

[3] As soon as one sees, in front of the name of an author, that Lacan has written the M. that stands for Monsieur, one can usually expect a very severe criticism of the person it accompanies.

[4] J. Lacan, *Freud's Technical Papers, op. cit.*, seminar of 276.

It is regrettable that—while using a somewhat handy and facile Marxism—whereas Marx referred intelligently and with admiration to Darwin, Lacan treats Darwin's theory in such an offhand manner, attributing to Darwin ideas later "Darwinians" used to try to justify social, cultural, and economic inequalities through a "struggle for life" applied without limits to all the spheres of existence. This ignores a distinction between Darwin's ideas and what Anglophones refer to as "Social Darwinism" (that of Spencer and Haeckel). Far from justifying racism, colonialism, and social inequality, Darwin, to the contrary, took care to condemn these attitudes that are in no way implied by his doctrine—even though Darwin was an assiduous reader of Malthus, some of whose methods and scientific frameworks inspired him (including the famous opposition between the geometric progression of populations and the relative stability of the lands they can occupy and hence the quantity of available food). (Note shared by the author and the translator.)

es the point of a destructive radicalism, which would simply lead to the eradication of the eater species, which would have nothing left to eat.[5] The close inter-cooperation that exists on the plane of life is not accomplished in a struggle to the death.[6]

The hypothesis—manifestly derived from game theory—is risky and is on the order of those Freud allowed himself in other fields, for example in his discussion of the death instinct.

But the interest of Lacan's work seems to lie still elsewhere to us: specifically, in the distinction he draws between *aggressivity* and *aggression*. Aggressivity is symbolic; this does not mean that it is incapable of turning into real and bloody aggressions, nevertheless, there can be aggressivity without aggression. In his argument, if his evidence is assembled, it seems as if Lacan is trying to play one part of Darwinism against the other; we have seen him note Darwin's very subtle thesis concerning language: Lacan wastes no time adopting this thesis, which conflicts with Darwin's claim to describe the nature of the relationships among living creatures, including humans. Now, language is not fundamentally in the business of describing the real, even if it is, with a certain phenomenal reality, made up of ideas. Where language is fundamental is certainly not in its descriptive function, but rather in that of framing out a world, in its own way, of structuring it. Language may well be able to represent, for the speaker and those who listen to him or read him, the spectacle of destruction, but it plays another role:

> The notion of *aggressivity* that we make brutal use of needs to be broadened. Aggressivity is thought to be aggression. It has nothing to do with it.[7] It's at some furthest point, virtually, that aggressivity turns to aggression. But aggression has nothing to do with the reality of life; it's an

---

[5] We notice here that Lacan does not share the pessimism of the author of *Tristes tropiques*, who feared that humans were unaware they were sacking the planet their lives depended on so directly and who, far from a promethean humanism, advocated that we be conscious of the fact that our actions risked provoking much more destruction than global good. If there is a moral in Lévi-Strauss, it is to be found here: it seems that the balance calculated by game theory is not sufficient, if a certain Rousseauism does not overtake triumphant Prometheanism. (Note shared by the author and the translator.)

[6] *Ibid.*

[7] No more than sexuality has to do with possessing a genital organ. It is also clear that this analysis echoes Lacan's criticisms leveled at Melanie Klein, from the start of the *Seminar*.

existential act bound to an imaginary relationship. That is a key allowing us to rethink many problems, and not only ours, in a completely different register.[8]

Perhaps we should begin with "ours" anyway, which is to say those of the psychoanalysts. In particular, from one end to another of his *Seminar*, Lacan accepts, as a myth only, the hypothesis of the primitive horde, which Freud seems to have picked up from Darwin[9] and which confuses aggressivity and aggression: "The myth's primordial Father is not only the one who conflates all the women in his enjoyment" and who deprives the sons; he is also the father the sons kill, hoping to enjoy the women, something they don't obtain, and only succeed in finding the interdiction reinforced.

More deeply, perhaps, the question is posed of the relationship of language and life. The second part of the twentieth century saw the appearance, through information theories, of a completely different way of viewing biological problems. While, in 1943, *The Normal and the Pathological* could still be unaware of this radical novelty, its 1966 edition could no longer do without an addition that deeply challenges the whole of the work, even though the author seems to hold to his problem and its solutions. This novelty stems essentially from his last chapter, titled "A New Concept in Pathology: Error," where he specifies that "Health is the genetic and enzymatic correction. To be sick is to

---

[8] J. Lacan, *Freud's Technical Papers, op. cit.*, seminar of 277.

[9] Attributing the primal horde thesis to Darwin is risky, and we acquiesce, for our part, to the precautions taken by Richard J. Smith: "Sigmund Freud developed his evolutionary theory for the origin of the Oedipus complex in *Totem and Taboo*, published in 1913. This complex scenario, involving what Freud called 'the primal crime' and its subsequent phylogenetic consequences, incorporated theories from a number of sources, including Charles Darwin. Freud claimed to have found in Darwin a proposal for the structure of early human social organization. Since then, 'Darwin's primal horde' has endured in a variety of literatures that build on Freud's work. In this essay, 'Darwin's primal horde' is reevaluated from the standpoint of Darwin's writing. Darwin's words were taken out of context and exaggerated. The primal horde is a concept that Darwin would not recognize, that he did not propose, and that misrepresents what he wrote. It is Freud's construction, not Darwin's. Modern authors should not cite Darwin when discussing 'Darwin's primal horde.'" R.J. Smith, Abstract of "Darwin, Freud, and the Continuing Misrepresentation of the Primal Horde," in *Current Anthropology* 57.6 (December 2016). On the other hand, it is indisputable that the "primal horde" was utilized by Freud in the way Lacan says.

have been made wrong, to be wrong."[10] Canguilhem then admits to a temptation and shows how he resists it:

> there is a quite strong temptation to denounce a confusion between nature and thought here, to decry attributing to nature the methods of thought, that error is the characteristic of judgment, that nature can be a witness, but never a judge, etc.... But we must not forget that information theory does not divide itself, that it concerns knowledge itself as well as its objects, matter or life. In this sense, to know is to become informed, to learn to decipher or decode. There is therefore no difference between the error of life and the error of thought, between the error of informing information and the error of informed information. It's the first that is the key to the second.[11]

Now, this temptation to denounce the confusion between thought and nature is certainly not Lacan's, who is not burdened with Canguilhem's philosophical baggage; thus, his way of regarding the relationship between language and life is the polar opposite of Canguilhem's.[12] He says so very clearly in *Seminar XXIII*, December 9, 1975:

> The molecular gene is reduced to what made Crick and Watson's renown, namely this *double helix* from whence are supposed to depart those diverse levels that organize the body through a certain number of stages, first cellular division, development, and specialization, then specialization stemming from hormones, which are so many elements that transport so many messages for the direction of organic information. There is therein a whole subtilization of where the real is, by so many messages said.

---

[10] Georges Canguilhem, *Le normal et le pathologique* (Paris: PUF, 1993), 208.

[11] *Ibid.*, 209.

[12] This is probably the reason there is so little mention of Canguilhem in the entire *Seminar*. A single citation is reported by Krutzen on the question we are addressing, that of *Seminar VIII*, in the December 14, 1960 lesson. In this passage, Monsieur Canguilhem's work is judged "excellent"; its pertinence is absolutely recognized, for "What is health? You would be wrong to think that, even for modern medicine, which, compared to all others, believes itself to be scientific, the answer is certain." But, he adds, "[Canguilhem's] influence is obviously quite limited in strictly medical milieus." Canguilhem seems glad to respond to this last remark in his 1966 forward, in which he notes that his thesis "had the good fortune of provoking some interest in the medical community as well as among philosophers."

But, strangely, Lacan, who might be glad to see language thus promoted to the foundation of existence, seems to be on the defensive: the real that is at work in genetics is still only the imaginary organization of phenomena. "This is yet only the veil[13] cast upon the state of language's efficacy, in other words, on this, that language is not in and of itself a message, but that it only takes sustenance from the function of what I have called a hole in the real."[14] The geneses of the years 1960–1970 only view the code's function as one of a transmission, which is only one of the functions of language, not necessarily the most important.

The Lacanian temptation henceforth goes much further, in a direction diametrically opposed to Canguilhem's temptation: "There is, for that, the path of our new *mos geometricus*, in other words, of the substance which results from the efficacy peculiar to language, and that is supported by the function of the hole."[15]

The question of the relationship between language and the real remains the common thread of the multiple Lacanian remarks regarding Newton.

---

[13] Berkeley's "mist and veil of words" is recognizable here.

[14] J. Lacan, Le Séminaire, Livre XXIII (1975-1976). *Le sinthome*, Paris, Le Seuil, 2005, 32.

[15] Lacan's logos is no more a logos of the world than a logos of the subject. The opposition subject/object is only one opposition among others, and a rather clumsy one among those language makes possible. Language served on the object's side does not give any advantage compared to language served on the speaker's side. A more radical conception is needed, which may be that targeted via Spinoza, as the *mos geometricus* indicates, while remaining conscious of the fact that Lacan's mathematics are not Spinoza's.

27
ISAAC NEWTON

Lacan speaks of Newton in two ways: he is the one who found a bit of the real, since the real is only found in bits; but he is also the one who wrote the law of gravitation, which, without explaining the idea of gravity through this writing, substitutes to the imaginary of phenomena an articulation of a few letters. How do these two discourses relate? Does physics tell us, be it only partially, alongside little segments, what the real is? Or does it substitute to phenomenal reality a matheme or an articulation of mathemes? It is clear that this question allows examining a few aspects of the articulation between the real, the symbolic, and the imaginary.

The first thesis, therefore, is that bits of the real can be reached, that physics did it at a certain time, and that it is narrated like a tale:

> There are, of the real, little historical emergings. There was, one day, a certain Newton who found a bit of real. It scared the shit out of those who were thinking, namely of a certain Kant,[1] who, we can say, threw a fit about Newton.[2] As did everyone, all the thinkers of the time, each in their own way. It fell[3] not only on the men, but also on the women. Madame du Châtelet[4] wrote an entire book on the *Newtonian System....*

---

[1] Who wondered how Newtonian science was possible; how, through mathematics, which seem to depend only on the mind, it was possible to give an account of the real, which fundamentally does not depend on it. Lacan is using language here that is not as "select," but perhaps also more colorful than that of Villemin, who delivered his inaugural lecture at the Collège de France, on the same register, by deploring that transcendental idealism had become a new dogmatism with Kant, erasing, under the spell of Newton's dazzling natural philosophy, the difference between the conditions of possibility of experience and the conditions of possibility of the object. *Leçon inaugurale au Collège de France*, December 5, 1962, 11–14.

[2] As Cassirer does about infinitesimal calculus.

[3] Untranslatable Lacanian pun: *ça a plu*, meaning both *it pleased* and *it rained*.

[4] Émilie du Châtelet (1706–1749), important natural philosopher, mathematician,

It is extraordinary, anyway, that it has that effect when you reach a bit of the real. But it's the very sign that you've gotten to the core. That's where you need to start from.[5]

It's the real that puts everyone into a state of delirium or madness. The writing, the very one that entrances, catches some real and entrances because it seems to coincide exactly with what it had almost no chance of encountering: "It's by little bits of writing that, historically, we entered the real, namely, that we stopped imagining. The writing of little mathematical letters is what supports the real."[6] To put an end to the imaginary is to substitute written laws for phenomenal fantasies. Mathematical formulas mark an escape from the imaginary: they inscribe something other than copies, facsimiles, reflections.

But Lacan also happens to play at being a Berkeley, in other words, at being a minute philosopher, those who are not dupes of the infinitesimal calculus that claims to partake of the transcendent, that makes real effects, that dazzles sometimes, but that also causes us to treat as real its own inventions, its own rhetoric. For, right after reminding us that the laws of gravity unify the entire field of classical physics through a single formula that includes three or four letters,[7] Lacan is overtaken by scruples very close to those Berkeley had:

> If you only knew to what extent Newtonian movement is an un-gettable thing when looked at closely! You would see that it isn't the privilege of psychoanalysis to deal with contradictory notions.[8] Newtonian movement utilizes time, but the time of physics; no one worries about it because it doesn't feature anything that concerns the realities, it's just the right language, and the unified field cannot be considered other than as well-wrought usage, like a syntax.[9]

---

physicist, and author, whose annotated translation from the Latin of Newton's *Principia* is still used today. Until recently, she was known mostly as Voltaire's lover and patron.

[5] J. Lacan, *Sinthome, op. cit.*, seminar of March 16, 1976.

[6] *Ibid.*

[7] It obviously refers to Newton's formula, which is not as described, $F = k \cdot m \cdot m' / d^2$; F signifying the force of attraction, m and m' the two masses that attract each other, d the distance that separates them, k, a coefficient.

[8] The argument is based on *The Analyst*, only the theologian has become the psychoanalyst.

[9] J. Lacan, *The Ego in Freud's Theory, op. cit.*, seminar of March 30, 1955.

Newtonian space is no less of an artificial invention than the time that enters into his equations. The mathematicians' straight line or the curve does not exist: "There is a straight line only in writing," Lacan states superbly.[10] It no more inhabits the world than any of the other mathemata (μαθήματα); it only inhabits language. The straight lines of the real, if there are any, have nothing to do with the straight lines of language, which are, themselves, unbelievably numerous. It's obviously the same for curves. Lacan had long before written that there was no phenomenal reality of the cycloid, for instance: "There is no cycloid in the imaginary. The cycloid is a discovery of the symbolic,"[11] a kind of secondary, accompanying curve, obtained by construction from the movement of a point in another curve, the circle, which, if it isn't natural, comes closer to resembling something that might be found in nature. "One should not forget it: our science is only operative thanks to the flow of little letters and graphs combined."[12] The difficulty is that these little letters can reach the real, without it being quite clear what they represent and articulate.[13] The March 10, 1971, lesson speaks of "the formula M. Newton wrote, concerning what is involved under the name of gravitational field, and that is only a pure piece of writing. No one yet has been able to provide any kind of substantial support, a shadow of verisimilitude to what this writing states, which seems until now to be a little hard, because we can't seem to resorb it into a network of other fields where we have more substantial ideas."[14] It is obviously possible to write correct laws with a false imaginary;[15] attraction is a revolting fantasy for any mind that refuses to project itself into matter and see the sympathies and antipathies of

---

[10] J. Lacan, *D'un discours qui ne serait pas du semblant, op. cit.*, seminar of May 12, 1971.

[11] J. Lacan, *The Ego in Freud's Theory, op. cit.*, seminar of June 22, 1955.

[12] J. Lacan, *D'un discours qui ne serait pas du semblant, op. cit.*, seminar of May 12, 1971.

[13] In particular, when one has recourse to coefficients that are said to harmonize the units used to assign quantities to other parameters. In reality, what do they mean? And to what do they refer? But don't think science could do without them.

[14] J. Lacan, *D'un discours qui ne serait pas du semblant, op. cit.*, seminar of March 10, 1971.

[15] This is exactly what happened to Kepler. See J. Lacan, *Transference, op. cit.*, seminar of December 21, 1960.

yesteryear;[16] and it is possible to bring the most refined theoretical attention to phantasmagoria: "Newton, who had other fish to fry, devoted a big book... to a commentary of the apocalypse and Daniel's prophecy. He put as much care into the calculations, the manipulation of numbers—although highly problematical when it comes to situating the reign of Nebuchadnezzar, for example—as in his studies of the laws of gravitation."[17] Thus does Lacan point out that the work of rationalization does not suppose that it is what it targets that is itself rational, including where physics is concerned. Newton's physics is mathematically true for reasons that it does not know any more directly than the Biblical scholar does about what he is discussing or what the results of a trial hinged on. Berkeley's shadow strikes again, since he had asked the mathematicians, crypto-atheists of his era, who saved their blows, in the name of reason, for the theologians, to pay less attention to the speck that was in the other's eye and more to the log in their own.

This is why the rectification Lacan brings to Newton's famous *hypotheses non fingo (I frame no hypotheses)*—to which he replies that, "on the contrary, the famous revolution, which is not at all Copernican, but which is Newtonian,[18] is a hypothesis"—may not be really pertinent. The Newtonian formula is valid as an attempt to distinguish himself from Descartes, who, starting with the *Traité du monde*, suggested that the hypotheses that could be created in physics were so numerous to account for a given situation that the good one could never be certain, and that the bad ones were only gradually recognizable, as their flaws were discovered. This is not the case with Newton; he constructs "the definitive formula everyone was dying to find for a century."[19] He found it and did not seek to justify it through vortices or some other hypothesis: the imaginary that undergirds the formula does not matter. More exactly, this imaginary is henceforth no more than under the dependence of the formula's symbolic. Whereas, with Descartes, there are scarcely formulas, in any case, their equivalents

[16] Pascal, *Pensées*, Sel. 230 (Paris: La Pochothèque, 2004), 949: "Almost all philosophers confuse ideas and things and speak of corporal things mentally and mental things corporally. For they boldly say that bodies... have inclinations, sympathies, antipathies, which are all things that only belong to minds."

[17] J. Lacan, *D'un Autre à l'autre, op. cit.*, seminar of February 12, 1969.

[18] J. Lacan, *Encore, op. cit.*, seminar of 213.

[19] J. Lacan, *The Ego in Freud's Theory, op. cit.*, seminar of May 25, 1955.

are not as powerful as Newton's. But it is precisely the imaginary of the hypotheses that interests him.

The real does not follow any rules, not even its own, if it has any, and could not care less about ours. Pascal said it when speaking about nature[20] and Newton's successors would learn it after the stupor of the initial coincidence passed, for there would soon be a need to furnish an increasingly sophisticated effort to make the law coincide with what it claims to write about things. This task prevents any grasp. The real is what irrupts. But it does not mean that this rupture, this irruption, eludes all writing; it can be grasped in this very irruption, as writing becomes writing of the irruptions and ruptures. Only, one mustn't view writing as reflecting the real; to state the real is in no way to copy it. The little bits of writing may well tie together; however, it is not via this tie that the real is grasped, but rather by themselves, more by their disjunction than by the unity that is supposed to correct their dispersion.

One might wonder why it is so important for psychoanalysis to reflect on Newton, or Pascal, for that matter, or any other physicist who shows what he is doing. The answer is that the meditations of these authors allow learning to distinguish the imaginary from the symbolic. It is easy to attribute to things what we imagine they are; in reality, they never exist as we imagine they do, and if we think about it a little more, we know that they can't even exist: the symbolic must be built that explains the reason for what we think we see or feel. Analysis, psychoanalysis, is very specifically what introduces the rule of the symbolic into the imaginary:

> There is an inertia of the imaginary that we can see intervene in the subject's discourse, that scrambles this discourse, that makes it so that I don't notice that, when I wish someone well, I mean them harm; that when I love them, I love myself; and when I think I love myself, it is exactly at that moment that I love someone else. This imaginary confusion, it is precisely the dialectical exercise of analysis to dissipate it and to restore to discourse its meaning as discourse.

---

[20] *Pensées*, frag. 544 (Sellier): "When we see an effect always happening the same way, we conclude from it a natural necessity, like there will be day tomorrow, etc. But nature often contradicts us and does not obey its own rules."

The only difficulty is "to know if the symbolic exists as such; or if the symbolic is the second-degree fantasy of imaginary cooptions."[21] Lacan speaks, on this point, of a divergence between two orientations of analysis: is it a shaping, representative of something that appears given? Or is it a construction of a reality that has nothing to do with something to be imitated or to conform to (by fancifully seeking some past that is supposed to have happened).

---

[21] J. Lacan, *The Ego in Freud's Theory, op. cit.*, seminar of June 22, 1955.

28

JOHN VON NEUMANN

Lacan's research concerning Von Neumann, one of the founders of game theory, is interesting in that it allows us to situate a very different subject from the one transcendental philosophy thought it could institute in the sciences. Kant's approach, which is also Husserl's, aims to internalize knowledge in a subject:

> It is the possibility of scientific judgments (such as they are read in the texts of the scientists who produced them) and their genesis as moments peculiar to the unfolding of the "subject" that constitute the specific terrain of the critical method and that manifest the transcendental plane where, under the name of critical philosophy, the internalization of knowledge takes place.[1]

The inanity of the process that consists of attributing the reality of texts written as possibly being, or having been, written by a subject has often been decried. Now, while the subject poses a crucial question for psychoanalysis, this is not at all how psychoanalysis deals with it, but rather as a kind of residue necessary to a logic of situations. The way actors act or perform among themselves creates not necessarily stable points of view, whence these situations develop and, eventually, are resolved. The subject does not copy, on the mode of the possible, what is; he is as if expelled by the situation or by the tension in one of its areas. We are not saying that the whole of the situation appears as possible to a subject; the subject's evolving place only acquires its meaning in the topic of a situation. The unconscious is not hidden in the subject who apprehends the situation in general; it is precisely what, in the situation, expels the subject.

---

[1] Jean-Toussaint Desanti, *La philosophie silencieuse* (Paris: Le Seuil, 1975), 21.

"What will we find in the experience of this mathematical logic, if not precisely this residue that marks the subject's presence? This is at least what a mathematician seems to imply, one of the greatest certainly, Von Neumann, to remark, somewhat imprudently, perhaps, that limitations, I mean those that are logically tenable, are only residues of mathematics." The limit is not established on the basis of the subject; rather, the limitations of the subject would be defined on the situation as exactly thought.

Von Neumann is not aiming at any autonomy,[2] none of the classic mind games that consist of figuring, for example, that *obsolete* is an obsolete term,[3] and of speculating, on the basis of that, about the predicates that don't apply to it, with everything that may involve in the way of a paradox. It isn't about that, but about the construction of a limit.

Nothing is discovered in logic that mathematical discourse hasn't already discovered, since it is on a field of discoveries that method is tested.[4] Mathematical discourse is only asked this, which is essential anyway, namely, to what extent can it account for itself. One could say *to the extent it coincides with its own content*, if these terms had any meaning, if this wasn't the domain par excellence where the notion of content comes to be, strictly speaking, emptied. Something appears there that has its necessity, its own *anagké* (ἀνάγκη), its detour necessities, and which Von Neumann tells us in short is very good, it is a sign that, after all, mathematicians are still around for something, it gives them a role to play. In other words, it's because mathematical discourse is lacking something that the mathematician's desire comes into play.[5]

Well, I think, however, that Von Neumann is going a little far here. *First*, the term *residue* is unsuitable. What is revealed here of the func-

---

[2] That takes care of the Kantians.

[3] A recognizable allusion, stated in a quite amusing form, to the type of paradox to which set theory gave rise shortly after its appearance: what status should be granted to the set of sets if it is at the same time the one that assembles them and one of them? Lacan treats as a kind of small talk, which doesn't really get in the way of mathematics, the paradoxes in which their work was attempted to be imprisoned and to which they remained radically indifferent.

[4] Game theory is understood by Lacan as an affirmation of the primacy of mathematics over logic.

[5] This remark is a good expression of the affective play that results from the tension of the situation the mathematician explores and gives form to. We find, in Nash, for example, the diversified designation, in the conflicts that he analyzes, of the structuring of affects that are tied to them. These affects take the privileged form of filling lacks.

tion that I have already evoked from several angles under the title of the impossible is of a different structure than that with which we are dealing in the fall of the *objet a*.[6] *Far more so*, to be no less structural, what is revealed here of lack probably reveals the subject's presence, but of no other subject than the one who has made the cut separating the said metalanguage from a certain mathematical field—which is quite simply its discourse—from another isolated language, from a language of artifice, from formal language.[7]

Game theory obviously isn't the only epistemic area where the subject is expelled from the system in which he participates while remaining immanent, in the absence of which the situation would vanish; the sector of probabilities grants the subject about the same status. The Bayesian subject, the one who calculates degrees of probability with insufficient information for these degrees to not be calculated with a margin of error, is not a transcendental subject in the sense that he would be able to dominate, even ideally, the entirety of a situation; if we care to characterize it as *transcendental*, it is only in the sense that everyone, having to make the same calculations, if they thought about it, could not fail to make them, as Bayes' rule requires them to. The law of gravity is not written, like that of the rotation of planets around the sun, from any point of view; at least, the point of view ends up neutralized by the writing of the law. Bayes' rule is probably as objective, but if it is point of view neutralized, it is as a rule of situations that are constantly variable because of ever changing information that we acquire to act within them.

The question that is raised at this point is the following: is there, in the English language, something that predisposed it to the creation of game theory or to certain types of probability that, for example, we call now, and for some time already, in a very ambiguous way, "sub-

---

[6] Without explaining himself further on this point, Lacan points to a difference between the remainder [*le reste*] that he theorizes in *Seminar X* on anxiety and the remainder that is the subject of game theory. True, the subject cannot lay claim to being the founder of game theory, but neither is he its waste; while he is the result of motor function more than he is motor function, his ejection by the system is not entirely a cut.

[7] The subject of game theory does not belong to some metalanguage, nor is he a basis for metalanguage. He is part, in an immanent way, of conflicting systems, without any overview regarding them, but playing their stakes. J. Lacan, *D'un Autre à l'autre, op. cit.*, seminar of January 8, 1969.

jective probabilities"? In any case, while Bayes identifies the notion of *chance* and that of *probability*, he distinguishes them, as does the English language, according to the Saxon (*kanz*) or Latin (*probabilitas*) origin, referring *chance* to *reasons to believe* and probability to something that appears more objective. We have already stressed that the calculation of probability was done from the point of view of an *I guess* that has no substantiality, but is only there to initiate chances or probabilities that will be gradually corrected: game theory requires no more consistency of its actor, and it gives the *I guess* more *plausibility* and less arbitrariness since it no longer isolates it, but includes it as a feature of a society, which remained allusive with Bayes.

29

CONCLUSION

Reading of readings; writing of writings; indefinite writings; indefinite readings: Lacan's work is a work of interstices, constructing, in the interstices of first series, other series, as did Pascal's "arithmetical triangles" or Leibniz's even more complete ones, which foresaw their inversion. Work in the cuts, without which the symbol does not appear; work in ever finer cuts, for each term, each letter that is introduced in a piece of writing or a formula, is a cut.

Whether one writes or works in English, in French, or in German, language offers a system of cuts and of filling gaps; simply, the targets are not in the same places and the same things are not captured in the filters and the sieves. The sieves of one language can be used to fill, always discretely, however—I mean without continuity—the holes left by another, whether they are holes in the semantics or in the syntax, for, from a turn of syntax in one language to what is supposed to be the same in another language, there is most often a chasm or incommensurability.

These difficulties are well known to translators; the question is to know whether, affecting words, they also affect concepts. It is on this point that perspectives collide. Traditional critics think it is always possible to overcome the difficulties tied to language; they are willing to agree with Hume that some languages furnish terrain that is more propitious than others to the promotion of certain concepts; they can even extend to national values these conditions of first appearance.[1] But they do not go so far as to conclude there exists an English science, a German science, and a French science. The "propitious" character is worthwhile to explain *the birth of an idea*, to account for its momentum; but it seems that it is always possible to recover, more or

---

[1] Which Lacan does in his own way, when he expresses himself in his preface to the German version of a certain number of his works, or in that of his works in Japanese.

less easily, in any language, what is written or said in another. While La-can appeared attached to this critical point of view, he does not seem to have stood still, and he thought that words hewed to concepts and that concepts shared the fate of words. But, an author in his language had a duty of neologism, in other words, of creating. Even though the language of the *Seminars* would become, under Jacques-Alain Miller's impetus, if not creative regeneration, a beautiful classical language,[2] Lacan does not share the classical ideal[3] of saying the most possible with the fewest possible words by simply playing with their order on a scale. It is necessary to invent new words and new syntaxes, and thus stretch the limits of language in every direction. The veil of words be-comes thereby an extremely mobile surface, with very heterogeneous local properties and intimating new properties to words and turns of phrase we thought were well known. Language then becomes a topo-logical phenomenon: "The signifier—as it is promoted by the rites of a linguistic tradition that is not specifically Saussurian, but goes back to the Stoics, before being reflected in Saint Augustine—is structured in topological terms."[4] He had already evoked this theme in *Seminar XIX*, in the March 3, 1972, session: if language must be approached through its grammar, "it has to do with a topology."[5] Not only must the most words possible from other languages be imported into one's own lan-guage—which allows treating foreign words like a kind of metaphor in one's own, since they are no longer used to signify directly—but also what literature teaches that is most precious resides in this possibility of freeing the languages of their boundaries which appear fixed and rigid. Thus, Lacan's project is not to transcend languages as the classic critics claimed, but rather it is, far from any metalinguistic pretentions, to craft and to speak a mobile language that is his, but which can well belong at the same time to others, readers and writers, who follow the same inventive conditions. Each author finds himself obliged to craft the equivalent of a *Finnegan's Wake*, be it in the context of a concep-tual activity, at least, his reading must always be conceived as such.

---

[2] Almost better written than a great number of texts the mannered character of which stops and annoys the reader.

[3] The reference is to seventeenth-century French Neo-classicism.

[4] J. Lacan, *Encore, op. cit.*, seminar of December 19, 1972.

[5] J. Lacan, *... or Worse, op. cit.*, seminar of March 3, 1972.

Which is why, even though, in the preface to *Reading Seminar XI* (xiv), Bruce Fink's humor might make us laugh, we are not able to subscribe to the philosophy that underlies it: "The *Écrits*," he says:

> were not meant to be read. Indeed, they were not written in such a way as to facilitate the reader's task. Rather, they were written to be worked over unabridged dictionaries and an immense library in hand (including all of Lacan's seminars and his other *Écrits*) mulled over, diagrammed, pieced together, dreamt about, and reformulated in non-Lacanian French. Their translation into other languages is obviously impossible, at one level, when not altogether ridiculous.

The humor has to be lauded; not to do so would be ridiculous. But it is precisely this supposed need to retranslate Lacan into French that is a problem, and that is only falsely reasonable, since it does not meet the author's project. With some exceptions. And it could well be that the preface Lacan wrote for the English version of his *Seminar XI* is one. Indeed, those who speak *non-Lacanian French* cannot read it, and its text can even annoy those who are able to read *Lacanian French*, by its useless pedantry that renders it sometimes incomprehensible and, ultimately, badly written; unless the text were mischievously composed to confound the translators, somewhat in the way Mérimée wrote his famous text, full of traps for those who take the *dictée*. But this is not true of *Seminar XI* as a whole, the pedagogical power of which is exceptional. The strange undertaking proposed by Fink, to the extent one takes it seriously, stems from the fact that the one proposing it does not sufficiently take into account the suggestion Lacan was approaching: that there may not exist any languages with clear edges that separate them from each other. Language as such does not exist; it is the more stable whole of its rules, reconstituted, as though by induction, from its mobile, real, written, and oral usages.[6] Rabelais' language and Pascal's do not have much in common. Fink dreams of a common, commensurable language, the better, he believes, to do his work as a translator: if Lacan could be re-translated into French, one could then, he thinks, translate him into

---

[6] "If I said that language is that like which the unconscious is structured, it is indeed because language, first of all, it doesn't exist. Language is what we try to know concerning the function of lalangue." J. Lacan, *Encore, op. cit.*, seminar of June 26, 1973.

English. Direct translation into English seems to him a wager in a game he suggests has been lost. Now, with this method that he dreams of substituting for the one he actually used, Fink does not seem to notice that an entirely different text would be translated.

But in treating things as we have just done, it remains that we might also not take seriously a difficulty pointed out by Fink, and which is perhaps a mirror image of that envisaged in an increasingly obsessive way by Lacan. Fink seems to show us, in reverse, the difficulties Lacan encountered when he reinterpreted the dream reported by Ella Sharpe, stumbling, for instance, on such and such a verb that was simply transitive in English where it was necessarily reflexive in French. The translator of "Position de l'inconscient" notes, on page xv of his preface, that:

> It should be noted that, while many of the papers (including "Position of the Unconscious" by Lacan) presented here refer to the "subject" as he or him, not she or her, this is largely a byproduct of the translation process: in French, the noun "subject" is masculine, and thus all references back to it require masculine pronouns and possessive pronouns.... While we have not changed these references in every case, it should be understood that references to the subject (unless a particular subject is being discussed) always imply a subject of either sex.

It is true that, under these conditions, thinking sexuality, that eminently strategic topos of psychoanalysis, is profoundly changed in ways that the language intimates without our being able to do anything about it. The automatic masculinity of "subject," and, by a shift, of the subject in French, disconcerts the Anglophone reader, who must take into account this linguistic element as an interference that from the outset falsifies conceiving the division of the phallus, for example. Fink could have gone further, because you don't go from a language that sexualizes its nouns, to one that sexualizes almost none, without there being an incredible "remainder" in the translation. But, in this example, the difficulties are too visible to risk being completely submerged and misled by them.

Fink brings other ones that are so enigmatic that the French reader feels, on first reading, like being on his way and leaving them behind. They tend to show that, despite a translation we have no reason to consider bad, the translator gives the impression that he does not entirely understand the text with which he is dealing, that he does not fully know what he is doing by translating it and, consequently, that he only transmits ambiguities to his audience. Here are some samples, in the raw, of the wholesale[7] incomprehension he delivers:

> *Le signifiant, comme tel, a, en barrant le sujet par première intention, fait entrer en lui le sens de la mort. (La lettre tue, mais nous l'apprenons de la lettre elle-même.) C'est ce par quoi toute pulsion est virtuellement pulsion de mort.*[8]
>
> [T]he signifier as such, whose first purpose is to bar the subject, has brought into him the meaning of death. (The letter kills, but we learn this from the letter itself.) That is why every drive is virtually a death drive.

> *Les psychanalystes font partie du concept de l'inconscient.*[9]
>
> Psychoanalysts are part and parcel of the concept of the unconscious.

> *Le sujet, tel que d'abord il s'est produit de l'intimation de l'autre.*[10]
>
> [The subject] was first produced at the other's summoning.

> *Le sujet, le sujet cartésien, est le présupposé de l'inconscient... L'Autre est la dimension exigée de ce que la parole s'affirme en vérité.*[11]
>
> The subject, the Cartesian subject, is the presupposition of the unconscious.... The Other is the dimension required in order for speech to affirm itself as truth.

> *L'effet de langage, c'est la cause introduite dans le sujet. Par cet effet, il n'est pas cause de lui-même, il porte en lui le ver de la cause qui le refend. Car sa cause, c'est le signifiant sans lequel il n'y aurait aucun sujet dans le réel.*
>
> The effect of language is to introduce the cause into the subject. Through this effect, he is not the cause of himself; he bears within himself the worm of the cause that splits him. For his cause is the signifier, without which there would be no subject in the real.

---

[7] They don't even follow one another in the text.
[8] J. Lacan, "Position de l'inconscient," *Écrits, op. cit.,* 848.
[9] *Ibid.,* 834.
[10] *Ibid.,* 844.
[11] *Ibid.,* 839.

What doesn't Fink understand?, we are tempted to ask first. The first reaction of a Francophone reader somewhat familiar with Lacan might be to refer Fink to Lacanian studies, as it happens numerous and often quite well done, that would explain some of the points that he admits cause him to stumble. For example, in the first fragment, there is an obvious mistranslation that could have been avoided with a more rigorous meditation on the signifier and its relation to the subject. Lacan does not say that the signifier has some kind of intention. The expression *"par première intention"* does not necessarily refer to the finality of the signifier's action, whereas the English translation puts that aspect, which is not in the text, in the forefront. We don't mean to incriminate the disjunction of the two languages, but rather a mistranslation tied to a misinterpretation of what is susceptible of having an intention: how could a signifier have an intention? However, Fink is an astute translator, who is not starting out, in 1995, with a work on or by Lacan.[12] If he places these phrases, which appear at first glance well translated to the Francophone who is not ignorant of English, at the head of *Reading Seminar XI*, prefacing a number of contributions by prestigious authors, if he just suggested that it would have been better to translate Lacan into French, before risking an English translation, it's that, without doubt, the difficulties encountered by the English translator are not easy for the French speaker to detect, and that, between English, French, and psychoanalysis (psychoanalyses?), a far more complicated game is being played than one may have figured at the outset. Why be less sure of the meaning when reading "The subject was first produced at the other's summoning" than when reading *"d'abord, le sujet s'est produit de l'intimation de l'autre"*? One might ask the same question about the other brief passages given as examples, with the possible exception of the first.

In truth, translation only substitutes symbols for other symbols, one symbolic system for another. Translation does not help us "better understand" the text; it "doesn't know" what it is doing. The problem that is posed is that of knowing whether one can translate without understanding; now, even though Lacan may have taught us to doubt it, for instance, when he corrected Baudelaire's translation of Poe, he

---

[12] He is not ignorant of the fact that any work on one of Lacan's involves "working it over and over and over." *Reading Seminar XI, op. cit.*, xiv.

nevertheless pushes us in this direction, for symbolic discourse can say what no "conception" can do justice to. But then, if we don't understand, how can we know if the symbols for which others were substituted have been "respected"?

If it were necessary, as it should be, to examine the detail, and especially if there were time to consult, in this manner, some translations Fink proposes to the Anglophone reader of *Reading Seminar XI*, one would see how difficult it is to render in sufficient detail the author of the *Seminar's* intentions, inasmuch as they are knowable. How can English mark the difference between *L'effet de langage* and *L'effet du langage* using "the effect of language"? Wouldn't *the language effect* be better? Why does Fink's English require saying "part and parcel" where French simply says *faire partie*? Why doesn't the translator have recourse to "to be a member of" or "to belong"? Why does Fink settle for "to split" for *refendre* (which implies a second split)? Etc.

We shall limit ourselves to more general remarks. To begin with, the impression left by "the signifier" in English, seems much stranger than *le signifiant* does in French, to the extent that the Francophone, almost naturally Saussurian, distinguishes, as we have already noted, *langue* and *parole*, a distinction English does not favor. This distortion between the two languages makes it so that, for the Francophone, language being made up of signs, he will easily believe that each sign can be differentiated into signifier and signified, whereas the distinctions that result from a difference that is not spontaneously made in English, like that of *langue* and *parole*, lack pertinence for an English speaker. As little of a Saussurian as Lacan is in his use of the term *signifiant*, the French he uses is for him, in his stead, and requires paying tribute to the Saussurian distinction; such a requirement would be absolutely out of place and artificial in English.

As we know, Lacan claimed that an analysis could not take place under the same conditions in English as in French or German; and that psychoanalysis—if it makes any sense to speak of it in the singular—could not be exposed the same way in each of these languages. "L'étourdit" finds him on familiar terrain: "Speech [the analyst's] only proceeds from the fact that the unconscious, from being 'structured *like* a language,' which is to say *lalangue* it inhabits, is subject to the ambiguity that distinguishes each one."

Which does not go without posing singular problems, including within Lacan's affirmations. For, if each speaker uses his own language, in what way could what remains of statutory languages, those that one imagines possessing relatively impermeable (to each other) identities, become an obstacle to psychoanalysis, as Lacan contends concerning English? Wouldn't languages need to exist as such for them to be able to constitute obstacles to psychoanalysis? As soon as they no longer exist as such, how could they bar the way for psychoanalysis? Or, are we to understand that the boundaries between languages are only blurred by the speaker, but that they continue to exist, intimating to the latter, whether he wants them or not, ways of thinking and feeling that belong to them? This alternative can scarcely be adopted based solely on reading Lacan, who was not explicit about his claims and left things open to suppositions.

We have also seen that English, if we accept treating it like a distinct entity, maybe more than other languages, has a tendency to split in two and to maintain this split. Paradoxically, while English does not distinguish between *langue* and *parole*, the gap between spoken and written may be greater than in other languages: Rousseau perceives its structural character. Far from *langue* being all structure and *parole* being all subjectivity, it's the very distinction between *langue* and *parole* that is structural;[13] the double Saxon and Latin origin, moreover, means that English features encircling, appropriating gestures, which can thus leave the impression of lack, indispensable to the expression of desire, tantamount to saying of its being.[14] The greater consciousness, required by English itself, on the part of the one speaking it, that he is in the process of speaking it, and that he is located in (or by) the circumstances in which he is found, may make the work of the unconscious more difficult to find. We have had two things to say about the *-ing* forms, since, on the one hand, English blurs the cate-

---

[13] "To know English, you need to learn it twice, once to read it and the other to speak it. If an Englishman reads aloud and a foreigner looks at the book, the foreigner will see no relationship between what he sees and what he hears. Why is this? Because England having been successively conquered by diverse peoples, the words have always been written the same, whereas the way of pronouncing them has often changed. There is quite a difference between the signs that determine the meaning of the writing and those that rule pronunciation." J.J. Rousseau, "Essai sur l'origine des langues," *Oeuvres complètes* Vol. V (Paris: Gallimard, 1995), 393.

[14] Lacan did not stint—as we have seen—on this caliper function to measure and frame objects between two languages, so that holding on tightly is always easy, although it is less so in less "diplopic" languages.

gories of grammatical units (nouns, verbs, adjectives) that are usually impermeable in other languages, and establishes a kind of circulation among these functions, but it also leads to objectifying. It is then that the language of events becomes the one that objectifies them. That each of the traits we have stated has an effect on the enunciation of the unconscious and its formations, no one will contest: we have seen them influence the law (and the conduct of a trial), the way of setting probabilities, thus scientific discourse and practical knowledge. But who will weigh its traits and calibrate the advantages and disadvantages of using English during an analysis or when doing theory.[15]

Put thus, the problem of the reciprocal advantages of languages to express psychoanalysis risks being as delicate a question as the famous eighteenth- and nineteenth-century quarrels to know which language was the most philosophical, the most scientific, the most juridical, the most diplomatic, the most commercial, etc. Indeed, we have just seen that Lacan used "foreign" languages, and English in particular, as metaphors inside his own language, if it can still be deemed to be French. But the functioning of metaphors, in the scientific use of a language, is that of segments that only serve, from time to time, for rather brief periods, the concept's launch, before hindering it in multiple ways. No language lends another, or its concepts, the play of its segments in the same fashion. This activity is so complex, so tangled, so singular, and it abandons you so suddenly, that it would be foolhardy to qualify it in the form of some generalizable outcome, valid for one language or another (granted that these languages exist with a modicum of identity).[16]

Does the translation of psychoanalytic texts—Lacan's being at the fore—pose greater challenges than the translation of other scientific texts, in areas like mathematics or physics? If such is the case, it's that gestures, acts, attitudes come into play to restrict or encourage the functioning of expression in psychoanalysis, and do not in other disciplines. These gestures, acts, and attitudes are even more active in the analysand's work than in the theoretician's. Everyone understands well enough, in a general way, that what someone is talking

---

[15] Two actions that may tend to coincide if the analysand tries to be his own analyst, but that cannot be treated in exactly the same way, if only for the reason that a psychoanalysis is a time of apprenticeship.

[16] On this point, see *Chrestomathia's* singular Appendix VIII.

about, what authorizes him to speak his language, is not without importance or effect on the relation of a speaker to his language (one is almost tempted to write *salangue* [*hislanguage* or *herlanguage*] to manifest the impossibility of distinguishing the speaker from his language and the impossibility for him of instrumentalizing it). The particular difficulty of the problem we are posing stems from the fact that no one—today, in particular, and for several decades, if not several centuries—would claim that English is more of an obstacle than other languages to scientific discourse, since English is tending to become, increasingly, the language of the production and communication of knowledge, a form of "globalization" that, although it began well before the one we currently know in the economy, is not without presenting certain difficulties, since every language intimates ways of thinking that have, no more than others, but also no less, the right to claim universality. Now, it is English that Lacan seems to tell us is an obstacle, without sufficiently distinguishing whether it is an obstacle to the analysand's discourse and/or to the analyst's, in his very act of theorizing. Why would a language in which the sciences are most likely to express themselves become an obstacle where psychoanalysis is concerned? Unless it is precisely because English has become the language of science, in what it represents as most dominating, that it has become consequently the most inappropriate for analysis? In other words, isn't it its great facility for objectification and especially for encouraging the speaker to objectify, rather than having him experiment, and represent lacks, deficiencies, voids that particularly qualifies English for the scientific task and concurrently disqualifies it for that of psychoanalysis? Can what is extremely qualifying in one function become, as a result, extremely disqualifying in another? This argument is at best debatable, since English provides both the framework for a critique of the subject—in particular when the latter claims substantiality—and that of "subjective" probabilities, which only treats the object through the detour of the *reasons to believe* what it is.

But, some will say, in order to progress a bit on a terrain where distinctions have remained fleeting, what is the relationship between the researcher who uses English to report, demonstrate, explain results and the analysand who has no other language at his disposal to express his pain or simply his life and what troubles him ? The fact of speaking English does not stop certain Anglophones from being sick or feeling psychic pain ; and it isn't clear why psychoanalysis would be unable to help them in their own language. The problem Lacan poses when he says that an English person cannot be psychoanalyzed (as it is not possible to analyze a Japanese or a Catholic either), if, however, these aren't jokes that we are taking too seriously,[17] is obviously that of the boundaries, more imaginary than real, of the individual, who is alone, at least in appearance, reclining on the sofa, monologuing in the psychoanalyst's presence, eventually dialoguing with him. The question is to know whether it's a language that makes up the fundamental relationship of the psyche's constitution, in such a way that the one being psychoanalyzed is always more fundamentally taken in his function of speaker than in any of the other functions in which is engaged he whom we believe to be an individual. It would then be enough for the analysand to speak a language that favors "objective" facility, masks and fills gaps and lacks, for his analysis to be impossible: but how would he be able to ask to be analyzed? For, after all, it isn't because you are an English speaker that you are immune from any psychic difficulty and any mental suffering.

I don't know whether and with what success Lacan ever had any Anglophone analysands. In any case, he himself did not do without the theoretical possibilities offered by English. His texts gladly play on the two axes we spoke about: that of the opposition between Saxon and Latin; that of the opposition between spoken and written.

Concerning the *first axis*, there is probably a difference between the speaker's action, which is essentially situated in a language and conveys the words of another, to make it act and signify otherwise, and that of a language which, of itself, saturates the positions and compels the speaker to hold fast to what he wants to say, as does English, which seems to settle in as a third language, as an intermediate language between two others. If it is the speaker himself who creates and articulates this third language, there is no difficulty. It even happens that Lacan conjures an Anglicism from a Greek word reworked by him, but which leaves a crack through which it was not expected: thus, the word *lathouse*, or *lathousie*, which seems to combine the verbs λανθάνω (λαθών, without having been seen) to the aorist and οὐσία, substance, can also sound the word *house* and even delivers the har-

---

[17] We all know he would never turn down a witticism. But we also know that only a lack of finesse leads to not taking jokes seriously, thanks to another twist.

monics of the declensions of some slang expression. But if the reader finds it finished, perfected, like a requirement imposed on him, the saturation of the positions, stops him from speaking the void, from saying the lack which has been too well filled. A language that is too filled, too rich, does not really advantage speaking lacks, voids, splits, tears.[18] We find ourselves then facing a contradiction of the kind we noted regarding forms ending in *-ing*, alternately an instrument of objectivization and its obstacle. For we were saying that English forces the speaker to become conscious of a situation, of his situation as a speaker in particular, all the while denying him the possibility of taking the initiative of this situation, since the language seems to take it too well in his place.

The *second axis* poses yet another problem. We are not going over Rousseau's comments, which we find generally justified, but we consider English an intermediary language in yet another way. One could say, as before, that there is some difference between setting in a language a third path between written and oral, even if it does not take on the look of a phenomenon, and leaving it to the speaker to trace it. Lacan himself played a lot on this axis, and, in a certain sense, continues to do so through the intermediary of those who attend to his work today,[19] and through the attention of those who will care for it in the future.[20] It is remarkable that Lacan's written style, in the texts that he published himself, is not the written style of the transcriptions supposed to be those of the oral *Seminar*. The written and the oral are not states that are identifiable as things, but only as functions. The words of the *Seminar* haven't flown away and Lacan wasn't talking to the walls as much as he feared, since he has become the classic author of a text that has preserved his voice. A text can stand in for speech; speech can shelter a text that does not necessarily call itself that, and

---

[18] With this theme of the third intermediate path (or just of the third path), we find ourselves in the position that Robert Schumann thematized and put forward as *innere Stimme* or *voce intima*, for example in a work like *Humoreske des Klavierwerke* IV. This intimate voice is not meant to be performed by the pianist, but only given to the audience to "hear" between the two parts played by his two hands. In her thesis *L'art du signifiant* (Paris X – Nanterre, July 2012), Dorothée Muraro has commented remarkably on this.

[19] By "establishing" what has been said.

[20] For example, by referencing what was provided beforehand in the way of explanatory notes, the absence of which is a painful experience for the reader, who is not familiar with the period during which the *Seminars* took place.

that a kind of accounting allows delivering. We must not forget that what we have in our hands when we read a *Seminar* is not a simple transcription that doesn't change anything of what was said and is content to preserve it; the account radically alters what is supposed to be communicated. We are not saying that the account is less worthy than direct publication, for, particularly in Lacan's case, a text can be so mannered that it is only worth as much as an oral version, which would have been preferable, especially if its written essence had given rise to an oral account. The intertwinings are multiple and we have not traced all of them here. It sufficed that we show the great relativity of written and spoken and that these functions must not be taken in too realist a fashion, even if primacy is always granted to the written over the spoken: "the language only being effective when it turns written."[21]

But how are Lacan's choices made if they are between theses or between a thesis and an antithesis, as is typical of the antinomies of philosophers? How to untie what resembles a game of hide and go seek or loser's chess? Why do we need to think that language founds psychology rather than the reverse? Why wouldn't English be, by virtue of its double origin and its double functioning, the best instrument of analysis? But also, since it is the analysand's work that is the key work, why wouldn't his impediments via the English language not be hindrances transmitted to psychoanalytical theory? Between obstacle and means, in turn one and the other, the English language offers the elements of an intimation to the hinge of the experience of the analysand, who speaks his pain, his tear, and the concept that theorizes it. What allows Lacan to gain some certainty that he surpasses the game of antinomies, which, among Kantian philosophers, is only resolved by treating thesis and antithesis as two concurrent but equivalent methods, or by positing one as needing to be acquired for its practical advantage? This is where we must remember a point that Lacan gained on the very terrain that was Hintikka's, without knowing he was making this discovery, which is a claim, at about the same time as him: we remember that, understanding that space and time could have a logical and not only intuitive meaning—as the reading of *The Purloined Letter* had established—Lacan asked for an effort on the part of philosophers, that of replacing transcendental aesthetics with an interplay of space

---

[21] Opening of the Rencontres de Caracas, July 12, 1980.

and time that game theory would allow formalizing and systematizing. But this effort has no reason to be limited to transcendental aesthetics; why shouldn't it also apply to dialectics? The different aspects of the entire antithetic, opened up by "the unconscious is structured like a language," are resolved by a contest that stems from game theory rather than the contradiction, of an Aristotelian type, susceptible of existing between a thesis and an antithesis. The Lacanian contest gives rise less to a choice than to a weighing: "language determines psychology more than psychology explains it," he says in his speech at the first World Congress of Psychiatry.[22] The game of theses is not decided by a subject in the name of his own interests or with the help of a division that would allow him to situate himself, like those of phenomena or of things as such; theses do not become dominant through a voluntary choice, but through dynamic action that a calculation can formalize. We understand, then, that a thesis which settles for affirming intuitions or certainties is a weak thesis compared to a thesis that works more "blindly" though its symbols. Here, we are touching upon the reason Lacan ultimately entrusted mathematics with the formalization of analysis, even though it yielded ambiguous results.

The weaving along two axes that entail quite diverse intertwining strands, which themselves are of a great variety, and the calculations to which they give rise belong to a theory of fictions. Lacan, who held this to be a live theory and not just some Benthamian archaism, only cultivated it piecemeal. This does not make it seem less constantly present in his work, through the interplay it entails between real entities and fictional entities. To speak, to write, involves, for each discourse, knowing how to allocate: to hold as *real* a certain number of entities, while a certain number of others are held to be *fictional*. It is clear that the writing woven from the outset by the triple orientation and articulation of the real, the symbolic, and the imaginary entailed a mastery of this general method of fictions. When we say that this work was "woven from the outset," we do not mean to say that it is a closed system that only defends and confirms itself, without reinventing itself or changing over the weeks. It is precisely the point on which the flexibility of the theory of fictions seems to us to account for the relativity

---

[22] J. Lacan, "Intervention au Ier Congrès mondial de psychiatrie," *Autres écrits, op. cit.*, 128.

of points of view, for there are no inherently real entities or fictional entities; the entities can, in turn, become one or the other according to the practical or theoretical need of the speaker, who is always confronted with other speakers' strange and practical needs.

That this theory was born in the English language does not seem fortuitous to us; we are speaking of the theory exclusively, for as far as the usage of fiction is concerned, it appears in Greek ($\pi\lambda\acute{\alpha}\sigma\mu\alpha$) and Latin (*fictio*) Antiquity and, with growing precision, until the present, in all European languages. For fiction to be theorized, a split language was needed, like English, that could say things twice and make them ring true once, and another time, almost simultaneously, with another word or another expression, fictionally and according to all kinds of resonances. What English seems to leave to the speaker's initiative, namely the choice of real entities and fictional entities, is distributed, in reality, syntactically inside of itself. A crucial analysis would consist of discovering what the English language considers real in itself and what it considers fictional, if, at least, there exist rules for this division that would not be the fruit of a pure spoken invention.

In any case, Lacan used the theory of fictions at strategic points of his doctrine, not only toward the end of his investigation, where everything that involves *psy* means *fiction*,[23] but as early as *Seminar II*. Even before he cites Bentham in a fundamental way, as he does at the very end of the fifties, in the *Seminar* on *L'éthique de la psychanalyse*, that is to say after Jakobson introduces him to the Benthamian theory of fictions in Ogden's version,[24] he asks a crucial question in the very terms of this theory: "It's a question of knowing whether the symbolic exists as such, or if the symbolic is only the fantasm to the second degree of imaginary cooptions. This is where the choice is made between two orientations of analysis."[25] Must the symbolic be presented as a mimetic and similar figuration of the real, as if it were copying it? Should it be endowed, on the contrary, with independence? Does it diverge from the *real* like it does from the *fictional* and the *fictional of fictional*? Or is it more real than what is imagined as such? We know that Lacan granted a kind of independence to the symbolic that al-

---

[23] As he says in the preface to the English edition of *Seminar XI*. See "Préface à l'édition anglaise du Séminaire XI," *Autres écrits, op. cit.*, 571.

[24] C.K. Ogden, *Bentham's Theory of Fictions* (London: Routledge and Kegan, 1932).

[25] J. Lacan, *The Ego in Freud's Theory, op. cit.*, seminar of June 22, 1955.

lowed it to be distinguished from the imaginary and to transport this imaginary by depriving it of its pretention to be the depository of the real. For it would be wrong indeed to consider essentially imaginary entities to be real entities, even though the former tend to claim to be the latter. Fictional entities can have a lot more reality than entities we would spontaneously consider more real, and that, indeed, is what the symbolic signifies.

There is more. We might wonder whether Lacan does not owe part of his theory of the four discourses to his reflection on Bentham's theory of fictions. Certainly, this would not happen directly, for Bentham does not mention anything that resembles the theory of the four discourses (of science or the university, of the master, of the hysteric, of the psychoanalyst) in his *Ontology*, the text in which the theory of fictions is exposed with the maximum of theoretical rigor. But this theory never stops being at work for Bentham and it could have been exposed even more subtly if he had addressed questions of religion early enough.[26] For it is at their level, when he explores the catechism of *The Book of Common Prayer*, that it becomes visible as a theory of discourses, in other words, of entities that don't know the distinction between *langue* and *parole* but that are structured by it nevertheless. We are not saying that Lacan read the work because nothing allows us to make this claim, but it is surprising to see these two so close in the determination of types of discourse—a determination that seems so rough at first glance—without having consulted each other, but through the same internal comprehension, through the autodevelopment, of the theory of fictions. Being interested in the work of Paul, the self-proclaimed apostle, and that of diverse Christian churches, including the Anglican church, Bentham shows how a quadruple historical narrative, constituting the New Testament, ends up becoming the fixed elements of a cult, of a liturgy, which, through the will to master and subjugate of those who use them, say something completely different from the narrative that was their starting point, giving to such and such a fragment of history a universal range it cannot possibly have and transforming this hypertrophy into an enslavement machine. It is clear that Bentham's religious critique locates the progressive drift of a scientific-sounding discourse, of a narration, at least, into a hys-

---

[26] Or, at least, if he had published about them early enough.

teric discourse,[27] and then into a discourse of mastery, at the absolute polar opposite of Jesus Christ's. Bentham then produces the inverse discourse of this mastery, of this hysteria, of this knowledge, and seeks to tell its truth in his *Church-of-Englandism and its Catechism Examined* (London, 1817), or at least to take the point of view that would allow telling it.

This business is therefore unbelievably complicated if Lacan makes use, in a lively and inventive way, of a doctrine eminently tied to the English language; for, while fiction existed in Greek, Latin, and French, as well as in all sorts of languages, before it was theorized, it was nevertheless in English that it was theorized and used as such for the first time. And it is very probable that this is not fortuitous. But to what extent does this remark invalidate the Lacanian critique of the English language's ability to theorize psychoanalysis?

One last observation before concluding: we have not asked the question of what an "international of psychoanalysis" means, whether conference, association, or journal; we haven't raised the obvious power tensions this question raises. Behind the diversity of languages, more or less propitious to psychoanalysis, it could be that power struggles are (or were) happening, despite the almost universally accepted opposition of the master's discourse and the psychoanalyst's discourse. Doesn't the treatment of languages by the analyst function according to a kind of return of the repressed? And what if the opposition we are discussing contained a share of denial that reemerges on the occasion of the strange and contradictory treatment Lacan imposes on languages in their relation to analysis, whether it be that of the analyst or that of the analysand? But that is another story; or rather, it's the same, since, if the unconscious is politics, the question of language is the question of power(s). It's in this area that, going forward, we will need to seek the solution to our enigmas. Rarely has a movement been divided among so many different acronyms: "European," "Worldwide," "International" (which often means "English"! And what if that were the answer?), "French," if not just "Parisian," as the psychoanalytic movement, if, however, the singular[28] can even be used. This

---

[27] Which ascribes to almost banal facts a scope they could not have.
[28] While Michel Plon speaks of "new life" being breathed into psychoanalysis, he also speaks of a "French withdrawal," which he calls "painful... in the eyes of the Anglophone world." To this point, he provides some evidence when he cites, for example, the "Acte

question is particularly enigmatic, given the extreme, truly aporetic difficulties to which we have been led by the question of the relationship between languages and the unconscious. To be addressed, this question would entail being able to retrace the history of the splits and regroupings of the movement. We would not be capable of this work and—to our knowledge—very few historians are interested, if not would even be interested, in writing the history of this movement, which, however, sinks its roots deep in the social and political. Moreover, there are few psychoanalysts[29] sufficiently experienced with historical methods capable of writing a work that would nevertheless be so precious to the knowledge of what we call the *unconscious*.

Let us admit to harboring the secret hope that this book on the English language amounts to but one panel of a tryptic of which the other two deserve essentially the same treatment as the first; the other two being devoted, on the one hand, to the recourse to ancient languages (Hebrew, Greek, Latin) and, on the other, to German (and to a few other European languages rarely cited: Italian, Spanish, Russian). The remarks on other languages (Japanese and Chinese, in particular) could find their place in a separate chapter. We would see more clearly, even in the use of English and English citations, if we had confronted this language to the use of other languages. This work having been completed, the essay we are offering here would perhaps become a veritable book rather than a simple investigation.

---

de fondation" in *Autres écrits*, which reads: "The school [EFP] affirms that it is first of all Freudian in that... the radical nature of the Freudian message goes well beyond the use practitioners of Anglophone obedience make of it." Not just practitioners of institutional obedience, nor practitioners of American or British obedience, but obedience in regard to a language. However, blaming English does seem to be the mask of the bitterness of not having been able to participate in the IPA's executive committee; for, until 1962, at least, as it can be seen in *Seminar X* on *Anxiety*, he remains admiring of English, so that all the elements appeared gathered for a theory that could have been balanced of languages in their relations with the unconscious.

[29] We have cited a happy exception in the person of Yann Diener, to which we should add the team of *Essaim* contributors, the first issue of which, as it happens, addressed the question of "the dispersion and gatherings of analysts," which was the title of Eric Porge's article in this Spring 1998 issue, titled "On the Community Born of Lacan's Teaching." Michel Plon devoted a very interesting communication to what he called "Institutional Worries" to the symposium "Psychanalyser avec l'adolescence" of the Société de Psychanalyse freudienne, November 25, 2012.

FROM AFTERWARDNESS TO AFTERWORD

"To be off to a good start is not to have done nothing, but it's not to have done much."
Denis Diderot, *Principes de la philosophie morale de Socrate, art socratique, philosophie*

"Each idiom establishes between those who speak it correctly and those who hear it, a communication of ideas equally prompt, clear, and easy.... Any just thought belongs to all idioms, they all have the clear means to express it.... There is no one who can... assign to the harmony of speech universal and constant principles. Each language has its own."
Paul Guy de Chabanon, cited by Claude Lévi-Strauss in *Regarder, Écouter, Lire*

"The only mastery is that of the language."
Attributed to Jacques Lacan in Charles Melman, *Lacan aux Antilles: Entretiens psychanalytiques à Fort-de-France*

There are different ways of taking a step back from a work and transforming it. One is to submit it to the critique of conferences and round table discussions. This is what happened to the present book, which, soon after its publication in French, in January 2017, was immediately submitted to appraisals which deeply changed its perspective, first on the occasion of a round table at the Institut Protestant de Théologie de Paris, in June 2017; then at the September 23, 2017, London conference, which resulted in a superb *Lacan's English*; finally, in June 2019, in the same Parisian Institute, at the round table occasioned by the publication of the same *Lacan's English*, which, thanks to the perspicacity of the critical remarks of its contributors regarding our work, resulted in a change in focus. This allows, if not a solution to the problem, which is a long way off, at least an opportunity for psychoanalysts and philosophers to do a lot of work in concert. The present afterword is the effect of a second or third "afterwordness" of the writing of the first work, which was meant to be a simple commentary on Lacan's extremely diverse attitudes regarding English; with, however, from the outset, a point, a detail at first, that became increasingly insistent, related to his casting doubt on, if not discrediting, English as a language able to express psychoanalysis or even the unconscious. Prevarication or real beginning of a solution?

But there is perhaps no better way for an author to take the step back in question than to be lucky enough to be translated by a sensitive, intelligent, cultivated, and creative person. This experience of translation by Jacques Houis has allowed me, through the constant New York to Paris back and forth that it provoked between the translator and myself, to take a very direct measure of what Lacan knew of English, the mistranslations he committed, the overestimation of the mastery of the language he thought he possessed when reading and translating it. It allowed me to sift through the version published by Éditions Érès and expunge the mistakes it still contained; but, more radically, it happened that the English version of a text initially written in French identified as lacking in meaning places we had counted as among the most essential of our discussion, and sometimes, as well, a meaning would appear as worthy of being developed that we had not directly noticed as such in French. Translation is the best experience of "afterwardness" we can have, on condition of having the humility to not attribute to the language in which we usually write our own weaknesses as a writer, and of having the discernment to not attribute the merits of the translation to the language in which it is delivered alone, rather than to the scrupulous work and the intelligence of the translator.

Let us start by posing the problem such as it appears now, and we shall see, later, if it is possible to propose the outline of an answer.

The problem is easy to pose, though admittedly long to expose, but it is, by all appearances, very difficult to solve, even by people whose job is being psychoanalysts, in other words, professional decipherers of enigmas. Let us try to pose the problem, as it is the easiest part. One of Lacan's most repeated theses, from the beginning to the end of his work, is "The unconscious is structured like a language." From that point, two options are possible. Either: understand the *like* in the phrase as an analogy with the diversity of languages, which would not prevent the unconscious from having its own or specific structure(s); or: understand it in a much less analogical sense, in such a way as Lacan would specify in the lecture he gave in the United States (in Baltimore in February 1966), "language" should be understood as something like English, French, German, and each of the other languages. This would mean this strange[1] but to a certain extent admissible thing: that the unconscious is structured differently according to the diverse languages in which it is expressed through a subject or through the object of theoretical research. There would be a resemblance, perhaps an identity, between the structuring of a language and the structuring of the unconscious. This would mean that the functioning of the unconscious is radically influenced by the functioning of each language; that the diversity of the functioning is to be narrowly related to the diversity of the functioning of languages; and that therefore there is no reason to make a distinction between the linguistic unconscious and the psychic or psychological unconscious, as is done from time to time.

We could stop there, defend this thesis, often challenged by linguists, that the style of the functioning of the unconscious and the limits of the functioning of the unconscious coincide with the limits of languages. The objection that arises immediately comes from the difficulty of considering bilinguals (something Lacan rarely addressed, but to which Charles Melman, Jalil Bennani, Lorena Escuerdo, and others have devoted considerable time).[2] For it is one more of the difficulties of this thesis which, owing to its terse formulation, scarcely makes any distinction between the functioning of the unconscious and the functioning of the language in which analysis takes place and is reflected: does it refer to what is going on with the analysands? Or does it concern the analysts who theorize the functioning of the unconscious? Maybe both, but then how are things articulated?

Besides this objection, the weirdness of the statement stems from the fact that the unconscious would thus scan in its structure and its functioning like the languages the borders of which it would depend on. No one denies that there is a linguistic unconscious, but why should this unconscious coincide with the unconscious psychoanalysts deal with, or that Freud dealt with? It is certainly likely that "the subject who tried to consciously apply to his discourse phono-

---

[1] Strange even from Lacan's point of view, whom we have seen little inclined to identify the language that weaves the unconscious with the language that encodes the DNA of the living, while he could have seen, during the 1950s, a kind of confirmation of his thesis by genetics itself. He was perfectly capable of conceiving a language the "reality" of which was not that of English, French, or German. See the end of Chapter 26 on Darwin.

[2] Psychoanalysts are often bilingual, if not polyglot.

logical and grammatical laws, supposing he possessed the necessary knowledge and virtuosity, would almost immediately lose his train of thought."[3] There is, indeed, an unconscious in this sense; but is the unconscious the psychoanalyst encounters always exactly of this nature? Doesn't the answer to this question deserve a somewhat lengthy detour, longer in any case than a simple epiphany, be it a striking one? The diversity of the ways of analyzing or being an analysand would depend on the language in which one is analyzed or in which the unconscious is expressed. The proposition is risky: the risk is measured by the difference between the way Lacan sees the unconscious in his American lecture in Baltimore and how Levi-Strauss more skillfully treats a parallel problem in a lecture given thirteen years later, on the other coast of the United States, in Berkeley in 1979: "What does 'to mean' mean? It seems to me that the only answer we can give is that 'to mean' means the ability of any kind of data to be translated in a different language. I do not mean a different language like French or German, but different words on a different level."[4] Lévi-Strauss takes care not to make what he calls *language* coincide with the diversity of particular languages; it is translation that he puts forward more than any particular language.

But Lacan goes further, and he wasn't forced to interpret this modal or qualitative diversity as degrees susceptible of qualifying a language for analysis and of disqualifying another; rather radically, from the same vantage point, he affirms that we aren't only differently analyzed or analysand according to whether we express ourselves in one language or another, but that there are languages that lend themselves better or worse than others to analytical work; there are even languages that would block this work or render it impossible. Must this proposition be recognized and treated as a fact (which would entail that it be soundly based on evidence in order to move beyond the stage of its reception as a pleasantry)? If this recognition were plausible, why would English be a language that does not permit this expression of the unconscious without it being really possible to know whether Lacan is talking about the analysand's expression or that of the theoretician of psychoanalysis who is very often, even most often,

---

[3] C. Lévi-Strauss, *Mythologiques: le cru et le cuit* (Paris: Plon, 1964), 19.

[4] *Myth and Meaning: Cracking the Code of Culture* (New York: Schocken Books, 1995), 12.

the psychoanalyst? Leaving aside the fate of the Japanese, which poses the same type of problem, and that of the Catholics, which is different still, since, speaking very different languages, they can, through their religion, create difficulties for psychoanalysis, but without posing any particular linguistic problem, except perhaps if they are English or Japanese, thus compounding the difficulties.

The problem can be posed differently. What characterizes a language is being translatable: "If not," as Lévi-Strauss says, "it would not be a language because it would not be a system of signs able, by means of a transformation,"[5] to become another system of signs. This does not mean that translation does not leave, each time, a remainder. No language divides another in a translation without leaving a remainder. However, why should this remainder, when it occurs between French and English or German and English, constitute an obstacle to psychoanalysis, not only as that particular act between analysand and psychoanalyst, but also as the discourse with which it accounts for the unconscious theoretically? And only in one direction, to the detriment of English alone.

Lacan is so reserved on the question that we do not need to admit as a fact that English does not lend itself well to the expression of the unconscious; let us admit it however by way of hypothesis—reserving the right to withdraw it—and let us see what problems are posed under these conditions.

There is one that revives the most obscurantist prejudices: the idea that there are languages better suited to a given use (French for law; English for science). Absent any explanation, we might fear that Lacan's judgment of English is in the same vein, if he wasn't just joking around. I tend to agree with Lévi-Strauss when he cautions "to refrain from attributing the strengths and weaknesses of works to the languages in which they were written."[6] What is true of books has some chance of also being true of the other acts of discourse.

Let us disregard the suspicion that it was just a joke and try to consider what, among the characteristics of English, would create an obstacle to the expression of the unconscious in the psychoanalytic

---

[5] C. Lévi-Strauss, *Entretiens avec Claude Lévi-Strauss*, ed. G. Charbonnier (Paris: Les Belles Lettres, 2010), 146.

[6] C. Lévi-Strauss, *Regarder, Écouter, Lire, op. cit.*, 104.

act and in the theory of the unconscious. We shall then try to extract some general remarks from our investigation.

The best question is to wonder what, in English, could create an obstacle for the unconscious, or what, in any language, either favors or impedes analytical work, be it that of the analysand or that of the psychoanalyst who practices analysis or theorizes about it. It is the best because it poses the inverse problem[7] of the one that yielded the, somewhat dreary, generality of the affirmation "The unconscious is structured like a language": what could create an obstacle to this generality?

Any attempt at explaining the reverse problem must consist of two distinct moments to be acceptable.

The *first* must seek the distinctive traits of English compared to other languages, since this exclusion of English—once again if it means anything and isn't just nonsense—can only be done on the basis of these differences.

The *second* moment of the explication consists in searching for the way in which the distinctive features that singularize English are obstacles to the expression of the unconscious, be it with the analysand in the context of a cure or with the theoretician of psychoanalysis. It is more difficult to acquit ourselves of the latter task, because it entails much greater invention, therefore greater effort.

---

[7] We use the expression "inverse problem" here as it is understood in mathematics and logic. Thus, Bayes' problem is the inverse of Bernoulli's. I can, indeed, wonder, if I can do as many experiments as I wish, how many must I do, to be sure to a high degree of probability, that the relationship of the number of events (or phenomena) that present a certain characteristic to the number of those that do not is such—this is what happens in opinion polls. It is the problem that leads to the law of large numbers. The inverse problem, which is Bayes', consists—when we don't have the ability to make many experiments, and when we find ourselves faced with events or phenomena that present certain characteristics others do not—of wondering with what chance of being right (or wrong) we can assign, to an event of the same type that is going to happen, such and such a degree of probability of presenting the expected characteristic. Thus, by analogy, we can say that the question "Is the unconscious structured like a language?" is a direct problem. But the question "Are there languages that allow better than others (or that impede more than others) expressing the unconscious or making our knowledge of it possible?" is the inverse of the preceding problem. The second problem is subtler than the first. By posing the first, I don't risk meeting many objections to the thesis I am defending; on the contrary, in the second I am searching for objections. The direct problem and the inverse problem are indeed two distinct problems that are not resolved in the same way.

As we are unable to directly designate the characteristic or characteristics of English that it does not share with other languages and which render the expression of the unconscious impossible or very difficult, we are forced to test several options.

Let us take a few of these options as examples to show where the passage is difficult and to begin to indicate where the areas of research are the most promising. Noticing that English humor may not only be a speech effect, but an effect more deeply rooted in the language, is probably a good suggestion; but the real difficulty lies in questioning how the structure that allows humor in this language also allows constituting an obstacle rather than an advantage in expressing the unconscious.

They tell us English is dizzying by virtue of the freedom this language supposedly gives the speaker; it matters little here whether the proposition is true or false, but the delicate point is knowing how this dizzying freedom is a handicap for the expression of the unconscious.

They tell us as well that certain words are difficult to translate into English. How can anyone who has done a little translation deny this? For example, the word *drive* has a hard time translating the word *pulsion* in French and the word *Trieb* in German, but why not simply reverse things by saying that *drive* is difficult to translate into French, which only has *pulsion* to do so, and in German, which only offers *Trieb*?[8] We need to be careful of what, for languages, is the equivalent of ethnocentrism for sociology. We should be able to speak of linguicentrism or linguisticentrism to designate centering on one's own native language and wonder whether Lacan's "*sortie*" concerning English doesn't constitute a typical example. How could a language fail to have a relationship with the unconscious? That this relationship differs from one language to another is certain. We must, however, avoid the almost inevitable temptation of transforming our own language—our native or usual language—into a measuring stick used to measure all the others, as if English were only missing being French! "Would Anglophone readers be coming to Lacan with certain preexisting shortcomings that bring about his difficulties?," ask Denis Echard and Diana Caine, two authors from the September 23, 2017, London conference, with an impertinence that is nothing other than an exquisite pertinence. I like

---

[8] Setting aside *Instinkt*, which poses a different set of problems.

this conditional that suggests the possibility of reversing the question and asking whether Lacan's language, or rather the way he has of using the language, does not present shortcomings that make him able, only with difficulty, to capture what is at play in English in the relationship this language has with the unconscious?

It is tempting to invoke—in order to explain English's supposed difficulty expressing the unconscious—the greater profusion of its words, which the Francophone immediately experiences through the fact that a large number of French words are doubled up in English, each time taking on different meanings that are untranslatable into French, such as *liberty/freedom*; *value/worth*; *force/strength*, etc. But, here again, why would the fact of disposing of a great number of words be a disadvantage for dealing with the unconscious? How does the advantage of finesse in the determination of terms—a structural finesse, since English can, through its extraordinary suppleness, invent words and expressions where the Francophone can feel bound—end up as a disadvantage in the expression of the unconscious? Anyone who translates English knows to what extent English is a fluid language that offers its services to all kinds of analyses. Does this mean that the Anglophone is better situated to see what the speakers of other languages fail to see, of which they may not even be conscious? Hence, is it because of this "consciousness excess," which the English language supposedly brings to its speakers, that it ought to be discredited in all the tasks related to psychoanalysis? The excess of ease English shows, compared to other languages, allegedly allows its speakers to avoid the traps other speakers fall into because they do not have the same escape routes. In other words, is it because "with two (or several) words for everything, it is difficult for the subject to come face to face with his desire"?[9] But the statement remains enigmatic and seems to vanish just when we would want to have the greatest amount of detail on the consequences of English's bifidity (or multifidity), especially since bifidity should not be considered the prerogative of English alone (we should not find French to be exempt of a double origin: the Latin of the church and the judiciary had little in common with the dialects of

---

[9] This amounts to what Jones says when Lacan cites him in November 1975 at Yale. *Scilicet* 6/7 (1975): 32–37.

serfs and commoners, not to mention the extremely diverse contributions from which it benefitted).

I think this problem of bifidity must be examined much more closely because it typically encourages Francophone psychoanalysts to go in a direction that seems very dangerous to me when the theory of the unconscious is involved. We know that French allows, perhaps more than English,[10] two or three readings of the same word, not only through the act of semantic interpretation, but also through a homonymic or rebus phenomenon. Thus *raisonne* sounds the same as *résonne*, *mer* as *mère*, *père* as *paire*, etc. The proximity of other words may also be exploited—such as *tour* and *trou*, *dérive* and *rive*, *tâche* and *tache*, *littéralise* and *littoralise*—and this plays a role in theoretical texts themselves where Lacan did not hesitate to deliberately bring into play this kind of ambivalence, which happens in one language and cannot be reproduced in others. Lacanian psychoanalysts still take great delight in them. It isn't that these plays on words are unpleasant, although the less they are repeated, the more opportunity they have to be amusing; it's the fact that they are sometimes overrated in their role as evidence that is puzzling. We are then no longer facing, as in the preceding cases, insufficient explanations; we are facing the will to add a supplemental meaning to the word that risks muddling the concept's precision. What seems very dangerous to me in the immoderate use of wordplay, of puns—in the effectiveness of theory itself, and not in its objects—is that, thanks to them, ambiguity is introduced into an area where, not only must it not be involved, but where it must be constantly and radically tracked down and excluded. That wordplay should strike our fancy, very well; that it plays the role of

---

[10] And yet, as early as 1962, it is in English that he discovers a superb pun around the idea of comprehension: "My God, it's taken me a while to get around to it, but how beautiful the English language is! Who here knows that, already since the fifteenth century, slang found this marvel of sometimes replacing *I understand you perfectly* with *I understumble you perfectly*? I'm writing it because the phonetization may have allowed you to miss the nuance. This *understumble*, untranslatable into French, incorporates to the *understand*, which means *je comprends*, the *stumble*, which means, as it happens, *trébuchement*. To understand is always to stumble along into misunderstanding." *Anxiety, op. cit.*, seminar of December 19, 1962. We take note of the fact that English is celebrated here as a beautiful language and that the untranslatability is, in this phrase, less owing to English than to French, whereas, soon, his entire strategy would consist of rendering the French he uses untranslatable. There were thus, in 1962, all the elements needed for a balanced theory of languages in their relationship with the unconscious.

evidence is much more debatable. Lacan only fooled around with it, but he sometimes fooled others who fell into the trap. For, if theoretical work has any meaning, it is—whether mathematics, philosophy, or psychoanalysis are involved—to constantly lessen ambiguities, not to introduce new ones. Why does wordplay, which would be absurd in mathematics, in physics, and in the human sciences, have more of a place in psychoanalysis without running the risk of discrediting itself in the eyes of those who, to some extent or other, must use evidence, explanations, and demonstrations in their work. Why add confusion to the inevitable confusion that results from the need to designate and express concepts using words?

We know the principle of a dodge that could be put forward, as it was in its time, in particular at the time of the second generation of sociologists in France, the one that followed Durkheim, in particular in ethnology. It involves replying that psychoanalysis is not a science like any other, even though it theorizes its practices with the same rigor as others, that the analysand's language and speech create rebuses on their own. And we gladly agree with this. But the question is one of knowing why this distribution in rebuses of the analysand's productions should invade the very knowledge of this distribution? The science of rebuses is not necessarily itself a rebus, no more than the science of masses is itself a mass or the science of triangles a triangle. Is the aim of the theoretician the same as the analysand's aim in the same language? We cannot confuse the analysand's ordinary use of words—which, at best, is gently shaped in psychoanalysis, as though by Moebius strip—with that of the theoretician, who has another aim, which is on the order of the truth. Now, the analysand's aim is not truth, but to feel better, to be less sad, to bear life more lightly, to fail less often at love, to be more creative at work, less lazy, less futile, etc. It is very strange to include under the same heading the project of commonly using the language with that of using it in order to theorize. Ethnology, then, experienced this kind of ambiguity when, wanting to account for the attitudes of human groups, of ethnicities distant from our own, Marcel Mauss advocated that the researcher retain the notions held by these human groups without translating them, claiming to better stick in this way to the social realities that interest the ethnologist. It is thus that he speaks of the Melanisian's *hau* without seeking to translate the notion. Mauss has been heavily criticized for this, and not without reason. It seems to me that psychoanalysis does not have anything of interest, either, in this area: I mean in directly mimicking in its work the language of the person whose behaviors and usages it analyzes.

This point can be further developed to challenge an attitude that consists of refusing to translate certain terms and integrate with no change—or with the pretense of no change, as though the introduction of a foreign term in a language did not change the balance of the other terms—a term used in one language, French, for example, into another language, say, English. Let's take the case of *jouissance*, which, it seems, is not translated by *enjoyment*. For my part, I think it is better for Anglophones to translate the term rather than leave it as *jouissance*. The argument of those who reject the translation is well known: the term *jouissance* allows inserting a certain number of parameters in the concept that are not in *enjoyment*. But, in this case, it would be better to translate nothing at all, because what is true of *jouissance* and *enjoyment* is true without exception of all notions designated by words: we would even need to stop translating *un*, *deux*, *trois*, *quatre*, *cinq*, and the following numbers, because the way they are said in French is not the way they are said in English, although in both cases the decimal concept is respected. *Seventy*, for example, which follows *twenty*, *thirty*, *forty*, *etc.*, does not derive from the same logic as *soixante-dix*, which entails adding ten to sixty. *Septante* is better and more coherent; *eighty* does not follow the same logic as *quatre-vingt*; etc. Isn't the problem exactly the same for *jouissance* and *enjoyment*? The real is there: the relationship of the word (and of its imaginaries) with the concept it expresses and designates in one language cannot be made to coincide with the relationship of the word and the concept in another language. We must accept a trade-off of relative gains and losses as soon as we translate and seek the best ratio of gains to losses, based on what we want to obtain in the translation; isn't the word *jouissance*, moreover, particularly polysemous in French?

There is—in the obstinacy of some to want the polysemousness of *jouissance* in French to coincide with that of some word in the English language and the enjoyment of not being able to do so, as if to show who knows what superiority of the French language or inferiority of the English language in psychoanalysis—a simple fetishism of the noun. We want a noun to contain the same thing in both languages, which is not possible and is even an error regarding the functioning of languages, because English is no more made up of an accumulation of nouns than French, and the meaning of a noun in a sentence depends on the integrality of the sentence's syntax in one language as in another. Is it so serious that *étrenel* cannot be translated by a single word? It is, at best, a joke in French and, at worst, gibberish. Does it matter that equivalent gibberish cannot be found in English? Why this dogmatism of the noun, or of the word become noun, as any word does when it is isolated? Doesn't this dogmatism derive from an error regarding the functioning of languages or from the imperialism of a language (or rather of the speaker who hides behind this language) over other languages (or rather over those who speak these other languages)?

It seems to me that any language, each language, involves a precarious and evolving balance, even if it has its style, with a set of other functions or other authorities: those of the speaker who is speaking, those of its other speakers, those of the world, those—perhaps more generally—of what is. To get to know the meaning of a word, it's this balance that needs to be observed or consulted, which represents a fantastically elevated set of rules. For I do not think, as it has sometimes been suggested, that there are languages that are freer than others (which, according to Xavier Fortou,[11] is the case for English) whereas there are others that allegedly have more rules (like French or German). English has just as many rules as French; and, if it appears to the Francophone to have fewer than French, it is simply because they are different from the French ones and not in the same places. The simplest proof there is that English has rules is that mistakes can be made in English and perceived as mistakes by an Anglophone, for whom not only can a sentence be incorrect, but, even while being grammatically correct, can sound like it isn't English. The Francophone is often baffled when it comes to knowing, in English, whether or not to use an article in front of a noun, if he should use *should* or *would*, if a comma should go here rather than there, whereas the Anglophone makes this choice infallibly according to his intentions, regardless of the circumstances. The rules of grammar may be subtler in English than in French or German, where it seems they can be spelled out

---

[11] As author of the incidentally very evocative article "Dispositif vs. policy" in *Lacan's English*. He did tell us that he was much less certain about the chapter.

more easily, but they are still present. And this does not only extend to pronunciation!

It becomes apparent that the initial problem—the problem we called "inverse," which was promising and likely to yield important discoveries—hardly keeps its promises and that Lacan's remarks concerning English and Japanese scarcely point the way to posing it, let alone resolving it correctly. It does not seem possible to me to decisively discredit English from the point of view of its incompetence in psychoanalysis, be it clinical or theoretical. The Lacanian remarks have, however, allowed displacing the problem and calling attention to bilingualism and transference, as well as helping us to understand that these two points of view are probably key to resolving the problem by avoiding the naiveties that consist in believing that its solution is found in the characteristics inherent in a given language.

The time has come to generalize our preceding remarks, and to do so in the most positive way: in the particularly open way Lorena Escuredo concluded the texts that make up *Lacan's English* or the way Charles Melman and Jalil Bennani made progress over challenging terrain in the areas of bilingualism and transference (and without much direct help—as we shall see—from Lacan's texts, which, incidentally, may be an advantage for the researchers who, under these conditions, do not risk being simple spokesmen for their teacher).

1. I think, first of all, that bilingual people should be given an opportunity to speak on this subject: those who were born into more than one language and those who were born into one and spent a great part of their life using another. How do they experience their English-French bilingualism, or any other, the possible combinations yielding greater numbers than the languages themselves? How do bilingual analysands allocate their languages during analysis, even, when the opportunity arises, during the same session? In the case of countries that experienced a colonial past, this interplay of the native language and the other's language is doubled by that of the former colonizer and the former colonized. Jalil Bennani, Charles Melman, and Jean Bernabé have begun to describe this very important aspect of the question.

Overall, the work remains to be done. I have spotted, from Lacan himself, only two references, more descriptive and phenomenological than strictly analytical; they were spoken one week apart in November 1957. The *first*, during the November 13, 1957, lesson:

It isn't exactly the same thing, for a German speaker, to say *Signor* or to say *Herr*. I would even add: it is not unimportant that our bilingual patients, or simply those who know a foreign language, having something to tell us at some point, tell us in another language. This change of register is always, rest assured, much more convenient for them, and is never without reason. If the patient is really multilingual, it has a meaning; if he only knows the language he is using imperfectly, it naturally has another; if he is bilingual from birth, it has yet another. But, in every case, it has one.

The *second* occurs a week later, November 20, 1957:

It is striking—you will easily notice this if you have any experience of a foreign language—that you much more easily discern the components of the signifier in another language than in your own. When you begin to learn a language, you notice compositional relations between words that you omit in your own language. In your own language you don't think about words by breaking them down into stem and suffix, whereas you do it in the most spontaneous way when you are learning a foreign language.[12] It is for this reason that a foreign word is more easily fragmented and used in its signifying elements than any word in your own language. It is only an auxiliary element of this process, but if Freud began with the forgetting of a foreign name, it is because the example was particularly accessible and demonstrative (*Herr Signorelli*).

2. But, in some sense, even when they are not bilingual, people are, in great numbers, confronted with other languages. What language, moreover, can claim to be pure and to not be an inextricable mixture of other languages? Umberto Eco once said—I do not recall where—the Europeans (he could have added: and other citizens of the world), had, as a language, translation, which is to say that they are in their language, in its heart but also on its fringes, on the in-between it forms with the other languages, or rather with a certain number of them, even if, in fact, languages form impermeable and, in a way, substantial entities. This is how I interpret the excellent program-idea, which remains to be researched, of our relation to transference where languages are concerned. "It would be interesting to be able to put in

---

[12] Any language well known to its speaker appears to vanish, leaving room only for what it signifies and for the effect it produces on the situation and whatever the speaker retains of it.

perspective the possible links between the uses of language and the transference," Lorena Escuredo says in the conclusion of *Lacan's English*. How can one not subscribe to such a program? And isn't it one of the most original ways, for psychoanalysis, to exist next to linguistics— or to the diverse forms of linguistics—in order to study how languages structure the unconscious?

The weak point of what Lacan says about English or Japanese, in order to reject them as languages unsuited to expressing the unconscious, stems from the narrowness of the outlook such a position presupposes on the nature of languages. Lacan acts like he knows how English is limited. True, languages are codes, if not codes of codes; but these codes are open, at the same time, to the space of other languages—which represents a number of relations even greater than the number of existing languages in the world—and to time, in such way that their confines are indefinite. It is impossible to erect barriers around any language. Lacan is well aware of it;[13] yet, it is what his remark about English entails. Or, it would need to be shown that English so modifies the languages it assimilates that it renders them unsuited to the expression of the unconscious, but this could only remain allusive and it would need to be shown. To claim that English—even as an entity produced by induction—does not allow expressing the unconscious, either in analysis or in its theory, is a lost cause from the start in that English is, like all languages, a set of open codes that only has meaning through its contact with other languages, mobile contact that allows translation. For the equivalent of transference resides, for languages, in translation.

We need to dig into what, for now, counts for little more than a simple analogy between transference and translation and try to reach the point, which, until now, has remained extremely obscure, where it appears that certain languages are obstacles to psychoanalysis.

Transference is not an avatar of the cure, a contingent phenomenon that comes to impede it or, somewhat randomly, to favor it; it is the very essence of the unconscious, its mode of being. The unconscious is only in the transition from one situation to another, of a mode of structuration to another. Transference is the governing principle of the unconscious; it is the reason for which topology is the language of

---

[13] We cited the text of *Encore* in our conclusion.

the unconscious, the language that allows detecting that, from one situation to another, there is sameness—certainly not substantial—even when this resemblance or identity is immediately unrecognizable.

Transference can happen from analysand to analyst; there can be a counter-transference on the analyst's part. But transference is not limited to the passage from individual to individual and its concept can account quite well for what happens. What we are most capable of saying in one language—in our native language—can be said in other languages, but as though through a filter that disarms us somewhat by taking on a status that is more that of a representation than of an insentient engagement.

When we operate a transference, it obviously does not mean that we really take the person for a kind of equivalent of our father, our mother, our brother, etc. We are in no way dupes of these roles and we are, on the contrary, perfectly conscious of the exchanges we are engaged in; what we are not conscious of, on the other hand, is the choice to invest such and such a person and not another with such and such a role. We invest, without being taken in by, but also without having deliberately chosen, someone with one or several roles.

When we wish to express ourselves in another language, we project, without wanting to, the intentions we form within one language into another. It is thus that Locke points out that Saint Paul, who is Jewish, speaks Greek like a Jew or a Syriac,[14] which means, not that his language is incorrect, but that it doesn't ring true, that it says something else in Greek than what could have been said if one had not begun by learning Hebrew or Syriac. Transference affects us a little like when we want to speak in a language that is not our native language. What emerges from it is a curious objectivity that is less engaged than a native language, allowing for less empathy, more detachment. The unconscious may well be structured like a language: it is ignorant of linguistic frontiers, it crosses them and scrambles them at will.

---

[14] "The terms [used by Paul] are Greek, but the idiom or turn of phrase may be truly said to be Hebrew or Syriac. The custom and familiarity of which tongues do sometimes so far influence the expressions in these epistles that one may observe the force of the Hebrew conjugations, particularly that of Hiphil, given to Greek verbs, in a way unknown to the Grecians themselves." J. Locke, *An Essay for the Understanding of St. Paul's Epistles, by consulting St. Paul himself, The Works of John Locke* Vol. VIII (Aalen: Scientia Verlag, 1963), 5.

Lacan's remarks on transference invite the analogy between what happens for individuals and what happens for languages. He insists so much on language, in his analysis of transference, that we may wonder whether transference is not fundamentally a relationship of languages. An analysis transfers—Francophones admire the English word "convey" to say it—something from one language into another. It is in this transference that something changes and works itself out. But to transfer into another language is also to make this other language work. The idea has been known for a long time (I quoted Locke); it is beautifully expressed by Jalil Bennani when he highlights, in his *Entretiens avec Ahmed El Amraoui,* that the unconscious does not contend with the plurality in the sense that "in the unconscious, all languages are articulated through the words of each one, as if this plural formed a single language. Unconsciously, one language shapes another. It is apparent for Francophone writers of Maghrebian origin: their writings are shot through with the Arabic language."

What would it mean to say that there are languages that act like a brake to the expression of the unconscious, if the unconscious is fundamentally transference? It would mean that certain languages function as communication black holes, that they absorb without remainder, without exchange, without restitution to the other languages in a decisive capture that does not allow itself to be traversed and returns nothing. The English language purportedly functions this way vis à vis other languages, which would explain its amazing propensity to dominate other languages and put them in its service. Is it by essence that it does so, supposing languages have an essence? Or is it because it is the language of economically and politically dominant countries? What is surprising, from the outset, about this discussion of English is that Lacan learned a lot about transference and counter-transference from English psychoanalysts: Lucia Tower, Ella Sharpe, Alice Balint, Barbara Low.

What explains this *overridingness* [*sic*] of English relative to other languages? What creates its dominant character relative to other languages? Is it through its very structure that the dominant character of the English language can be explained, made visible by the dominance of Anglophones in all the international power structures? Is it because it is itself composite and that it contains at least two languages? Through its singular composition of Romance and Saxon, it may annihilate strangeness effects relative to itself, like those of French or

German, for example. This very great faculty of absorption of languages and of distancing of the latter has often been remarked, either to complain about it or to admire it (which is the case of Deleuze, who, while being a man of the left, cannot help but admire the extraordinary ability of English to absorb other languages).[15] Romance on one side, the English language absorbs French; but it also keeps it at a distance, because it is Saxon on the other. This mixture that is English, which verges on emulsion, accounts for its great power. Without ceasing to be one, this language coheres a multitude of languages.

Might we say, through this status of emulsion, that English captures transference and makes it as though it were turning in place, without ensuring transition or by avoiding transmitting to other languages? This would explain why English speakers effectively capture international positions in medicine and psychoanalysis. True, Lacan is particularly disqualified from comparing the case of psychoanalysis with that of medicine, since he has constantly opposed them to each other during his entire career; at the very least, he is in no position to immediately invoke the comparison. But we can affirm that the fate of psychoanalysis closely followed the fate of psychiatry and that, only a few years later, the same scenario was reproduced with the same del-

---

[15] The two chapters Deleuze devotes to English, to Anglo-American in particular, in his *Dialogues* with Claire Parnet, are worthy of contemplation. In particular, pages 72–73 of the book published under this title in the collection Champs essais, Paris, 1996, pages in which the author shows that "the American language only bases its official despotic pretention, its majority pretention, on its amazing aptitude for twisting, for breaking, and for secretly putting itself in the service of minorities that shape it from the inside, involuntarily, informally, gnawing away at this hegemony as it spreads: the reverse of power. English has always been shaped by all these minority languages, Anglo-Gaelic, Anglo-Irish, etc. that are as many war machines against English: Synge's AND, who takes on all the conjunctions, all the relations, and "the way," the highway, to mark the line of language that uncoils. American is shaped by black English, but also by a yellow, a red, a broken English that are each time like a language shot out of a color pistol: the very different use of the verb *To Be*, the different uses of conjunctions, the AND's continuous line... and if the slaves need to have a knowledge of standard English, it's to flee and make the language itself flee. Oh no, it's not a matter of creating a patois or restoring dialects... it's a matter of making the language move, with increasingly sober words and an increasingly refined syntax. It isn't a matter of speaking a language as if one were a foreigner, it's a matter of being a foreigner in one's own language, in the sense that American is indeed the language of the Blacks. Anglo-American has a vocation for that."

eterious effects.[16] The capture of power positions may be as though inscribed in the language. The English language has no need of an other; it has its other within itself. It needs less than others to reflect and become like a transmission belt toward other languages. It is self-sufficient; it is not in a position to give back; it does not have the obligation to exchange; it is as if it captures exchanges.

This last point helps explain Lacan's parry: to transform his language, the French language, into a blind alley by blocking the system of absorption. To *render* it untranslatable without settling for its own untranslatability. To *render* it opaque and elusive to the Anglophone by placing the crux of psychoanalysis on the side of this untranslatability. He succeeded only too well, in a kind of Pyrrhic victory, by creating sycophants who imitated the worst of his aspects, who infinitely repeat the same witticisms without realizing their reasons; but it comes at the cost of confining French psychoanalysis within narrow borders and to have it be almost completely ignored by other psychoanalysts: it's a dangerous game that threatens its rationality. The just argument that underpins this attitude is that there is no knowledge that is not rooted in vernacular languages; basing himself on Husserl's text, *The Origin of Geometry*, Lacan suggests that even when reason is at work in a sector where its universality and necessity are least contested—as is the case with mathematics—it is no less of the essence of a particular language; thus "mathematics are Greek in essence and its entire history cannot deny that it carries its original trace."[17] The danger is believing that it is by cultivating the particularities of a vernacular language, by forcing them with puns, by turning to them in what is most particular about them, that we obtain, as if as a bonus, the universality and necessity which remain the characteristics of a rational discourse, even though, to explain itself, this discourse needs to have recourse to everyday language.[18]

---

[16] We have outlined an analysis of the problem of the psychiatric lexicon's Anglicization in an article entitled "Ethics and the Increasingly English Speaking Psychiatric Tower of Babel," published in *Annals of the University of Bucharest* 65.2 (2018): 1–20.

[17] He says it in the admirable March 10, 1965, lesson that can be found at the address: ecole-lacanienne.net/wp-content/ 16 uploads/2016/04/1965.0310.pdf.

[18] Lacan rightly says, in the lesson referenced above, speaking of the development of mathematics, that "there is always a discourse that must accompany it, this development, at certain of its turning points, and that this discourse is the same as the one I am using

Thus, after having posed the inverse problem and having tried to evaluate the famous remark about English, which we still have not determined whether it is a provocation, a joke, or a probe—at first with a lot of enthusiasm for having inverted the problem and having extricated it from a rather drab analogy, then with more modest expectations—we discovered other readings. This constitutes evidence that the problem, while not resolved—but could it be in these terms?—has progressed by opening up the two fronts of bilingualism and applying the notion of transference to languages.

It is time to conclude this afterword.

1. The remark concerning Anglophones, whether true or false, at least has the merit, if it is not interpreted as a practical maxim that would prompt us to act as if there were languages that are superior to others for expressing the unconscious and psychoanalysis, of opening up an extremely diversified field of research. For it is clear that the joke—if it is one—allows reversing the status of the general thesis on *the unconscious is structured like a language. Language* is henceforth perceived without ambiguity as English, German, French, etc. Even though psychoanalysis would not be of interest to the whole of the speakers of the world's thousands of languages, there exist at least a few hundred the singular relation to the unconscious of which could be studied, while asking oneself if the linguistic unconscious always exactly covers the extension of the psychoanalysts' unconscious, inasmuch as it is possible to set identity boundaries for these types of unconscious. Rather than considering the question in terms of a very small number of languages—around ten at most for Lacan: French; English; German; Italian; Latin; Greek; Hebrew; a little Russian; a little Chinese; and a little Japanese, enough, in any case, to disqualify these languages, along with English, from expressing the unconscious—we could extend the question to a much larger and more diverse sample. I am thinking in particular—and here there has been an opening for several decades—of the countries of the Maghreb where psychoanalysis exists and functions in Arabic: what does it mean to conduct an analysis in Arabic? To my knowledge, if Lacan said a few words in this direction, it was by referring to Islam rather than Arabic; he did not

with you right now, namely, a common discourse in everyday language," going so far as to specify that this language is "that of uneducated people and children." *Op. cit.*, 9–10.

have much to say about the relationship of psychoanalysis with Islam, nor with the Arabic language.

2. The idea entailed by the remarks concerning English—which upend the general and direct thesis—is, on several levels, quite revolting. If Lacan were right, it would suppose or involve a whole series of things as unbelievable as they are unacceptable: first, that all the speakers of a language—the English for example—share the same relationship with their language and that this relationship presents the same defect in each of them; that the language is so formative of our ways of thinking that we can overlook the particularity of the relationship each speaker has with his language, a neglect which could only stem, if not from a complete fallacy, at least from a prejudice, from a sectarian and ideological structuralism. How could a language behave the same way in each and every one? A language would not be able to exist as an instance that is the same for all those who speak it. Just as there is a societal illusion that makes people believe they belong to the same society, there is a linguistic illusion that makes the speakers of a language believe they speak the same language. To treat all those who speak a language according to the same template stems from a clumsy error as to the way people take on a language; within the same language, it is not possible to say that it is the same for everyone, nor to guarantee that each speaks it like the other, while the foreigner is detected instantly. The philosopher John Locke presents a good defense against this narrow linguisticism.[19] To the contrary, Lacan is so imbued with his structures and their stability that he does not for a moment weigh the existence of a multitude of different ways to refer to them and depend on them. He imagines a structural impossibility of the English to be analyzed by virtue of their language, falling into the same illusion condemned by Locke.

I would like to highlight, in this regard, a clever idea of Charles Melman's, who gives us a break from the "objectivism" of language by pointing out that you can make yourself foreign in a language, that you can, by a gesture that is neither completely conscious nor unconscious, want to break the rules by intentionally making mistakes in order to be recognized as a non-native speaker.[20]

---

[19] *An Essay Concerning Human Understanding* B III, X, §18, §20.

[20] "When I speak a foreign language, I risk, if I speak it correctly, to experience a depersonalization effect. This is why I have a tendency to cultivate a difference that will

However, while Lacan's idea concerning the English language is in some sense abhorrent, it does allow taking up anew the question of the speaking subject, that of the effect of the language on the speaker, and to conceive these questions from a different angle.

3. Finally, I would like to end on a little refinement brought to the Lacanian thesis. It is true that, in theoretical work, there are languages that do not allow the emergence of certain theses, but that, once emerged, these languages render their development absolutely possible, the process of which does not require the same dispositions as their genesis. It could be that, as in other practices and bodies of knowledge, a certain number of notions can only optimally emerge in certain languages; on the other hand, nothing prevents—with gains, losses, and displacements—these notions, born of and expressed in a particular language, from being able to be expressed in all sorts of other languages, which profit from this discovery by following very different routes, very different means and techniques.

4. Lastly, while we need to acknowledge Lacan's rancor toward the English language as the language of those in power and probably as the language of power, it is up to us, who do not necessarily share this partiality and this rancor, to take on the Lacanian perspectives and project before us an immense and inspiring horizon of work, for several generations, and without having to repeat what Lacan says in the partial terms that were often his.

---

recall my importation into this language. It will sometimes be on the order of the mistake, a grammatical mistake meant to communicate to my interlocutor that, in this language, I am only there in passing and not as a native. This easily communicable remark constitutes a first reference to what concerns us in the problems of bilingualism." Charles Melman, *Lacan aux Antilles: Entretiens psychanalytiques à Fort-de-France* (Toulouse: Érès, 2014), 17.

ABRIDGED BIBLIOGRAPHY

Works of Lacan

In French:

De la psychose paranoïaque dans ses rapports avec la personnalité, 1932, followed by *Premiers écrits sur la paranoïa*, Paris, éd. du Seuil, 1975.

La psychiatrie anglaise et la guerre (1947), in: *L'évolution psychiatrique*, Desclées de Brouwer.

Écrits, Paris, éd. du Seuil, 1966, 1995. (Abr.: *Écrits*, followed by the page number).

Autres écrits, Paris, éd. du Seuil, avril 2001. This text includes in particular "Lituraterre."

Le Séminaire de Jacques Lacan (Abr.: S, followed in Roman numerals by the volume number, when it is published, and by the page number in Arabic numerals):

Livre I: *Les écrits techniques de Freud*, Paris, 1953–1954, éd. du Seuil, 1975, 1991, 1998.

Livre II: *Le Moi dans la théorie de Freud et dans la technique de la psychanalyse*, 1954–1955, Paris, éd. du Seuil, 1978, 1992.

Livre III: *Les psychoses*, 1955–1956, Paris, éd. du Seuil, 1981.

Livre IV: *La relation d'objet*, 1956–1957, Paris, éd. du Seuil, 1994.

Livre V: *Les formations de l'inconscient*, 1957–1958, Paris, éd. du Seuil, 1998.

Livre VII : *L'éthique de la psychanalyse*, 1959–1960, Paris, éd. du Seuil, 1986.

Livre VIII: *Le transfert*, 1960–1961, Paris, éd. du Seuil, 1991, 2001.

Séminaire, 1961–1962, *L'identification*, unpublished, available at the Bibliothèque nationale as n°L1.9 M3 34 et le n°4-R-16853 (1961–1962, 1, 2).

Livre X: *L'angoisse*, 1962–1963, Paris, éd. du Seuil, May 2004.

Des noms-du-père, 20 novembre 1963, Paris, Le Seuil, 2005.

Livre XI: *Les quatre concepts fondamentaux de la psychanalyse*, 1964, Paris, éd. du Seuil, 1973.

La logique du fantasme, 1966–1967, Paris, Association lacanienne internationale, 2004.

Livre XVI: *D'un Autre à l'autre*, 1969, Paris, éd. du Seuil, 2006.

Livre XVII: *L'envers de la psychanalyse*, 1969–1970, Paris, éd. du Seuil, 1991.

Livre XVIII: *D'un discours qui ne ferait pas semblant*, 1971, Paris, éd. du Seuil, 2007.

Livre XIX: *... ou pire*, 1971–1972, Paris, éd du Seuil, 2011.

Le savoir du psychanalyste, 1971–1972, Association freudienne internationale, 2001.

Livre XX: *Encore*, 1972–1973, Paris, éd. du Seuil, 1999.

Les non dupes errent, 1973–1974, Paris, 1981. Lisible à la Bibliothèque Nationale de France sous le numéro 4- D1 MON- 3214.

R.S.I., 1974–1975. Available at the Bibliothèque Nationale de France as 1999-31172.

R.S.I., Paris, Association freudienne internationale, 2002.

Livre XXIII: *Le Sinthome*, 1975–1976, Paris, Le Seuil, 2005.

Le moment de conclure, 1977–1978, Association lacanienne internationale, 2004.

A stenograph of the works not yet published by les éditions du Seuil of Lacan's *Seminar* (*Le désir et ses interprétations* [VI], *L'identification* [IX], *Problèmes cruciaux pour la psychanalyse* [XII], *L'objet de la psychanalyse* [XIII], *La logique du fantasme* [XIV], *L'acte psychanalytique* [XV], *Le savoir du psychanalyste* [XIX*], *Les non-dupes errent* [XXI], *Réel et symbolique et imaginaire* [XXII], *L'insu que sait de l'une-bévue s'aile à mourre* [XXIV], *Le moment de conclure* [XXV], *La topologie et le temps* [XXVI], Leçons de 1980 & Séminaire de Caracas [XXVII]) with the Opening of the Rencontres de Caracas, July 12, 1980, as well as those that have been published, is available on the internet at: www.ecole-lacanienne.net

Conférences de Bruxelles, 1960. The typed text—from pages 1 to 23—is available at the Bibliothèque Nationale as PIECE 4-D1 MON-561. (Abr.: CB, followed by the number of the page).

Le triomphe de la religion, Paris, éd. du Seuil, 2005.

Exposé chez Daumézon (1970) Typed text at Bibliothèque Nationale de France as Pièce 4 - D1 MON - 562.

Conference de Genève sur « Le symptôme », October 5, 1975.

Mon enseignement, Paris, éd. du Seuil, 2005.

543 impromptus de Jacques Lacan, Paris, Mille et une nuits, 2009.

In English:

Of Structure as an Inmixing of Otherness Prerequisite to Any Subject Whatever, conference given at Johns Hopkins University in 1966, translated from French by A. Wilden, published in 1970 in *The Structuralist Controversy* (Baltimore: Johns Hopkins UP, 1979).

The Instance of the Letter in the Unconscious, translated by J. Miel, in *Yale French Studies* 36/37 (1966): 112–147.

The Function and Field of Speech and Language in Psychoanalysis, in *The Language of the Self* (Baltimore: Johns Hopkins UP, 1975).

Position of the Unconscious, translated by B. Fink, in *Reading Seminar XI: Lacan's Four Fundamental Concepts of Psychoanalysis*, edited by R. Feldstein, B. Fink, and M. Jaanus (Albany: SUNY Press, 1995).

Reading Seminars I & II: Lacan's Return to Freud, edited by R. Feldstein, B. Fink, and M. Jaanus (Albany: SUNY Press, 1996).

Reading Seminar XI: Lacan's Four Fundamental Concepts of Psychoanalysis, edited by R. Feldstein, B. Fink, and M. Jaanus (Albany: SUNY Press, 1995).

Returning to Freud, edited and translated by Stuart Schneidermann (New Haven, CT: Yale UP, 1980).

Écrits, translated by B. Fink (New York: W. W. Norton, 2006).

Fink, B., *Lacan to the Letter: Reading* Écrits *Closely* (Minneapolis: University of Minnesota Press, 2004).

Weber, S., *Return to Freud: Jacques Lacan's Dissociation of Psychoanalysis* (Cambridge: Cambridge UP, 1991).

Works of Freud

Gesammelte Werke, en 18 vol., Frankfurt am Main, ed. Fischer, 1981.

The Standard Edition of the Complete Psychological Works of Sigmund Freud, translated from the German under the General Editorship of James Strachey, in collaboration with Anna Freud; assisted by Alix Strachey and Alan Tyson; editorial assistant Angela Richards (London: Hogarth Press and the Institute of Psycho-analysis, 1953–1964, 1966, 1968, 1971, 1973, 1975, 1978, 1981, 1986, 1991.

Oeuvres complètes, Paris, PUF, 1994–2010, 20 vol.

Dictionaries in English and in French
that Take into Account the Lacanian Vocabulary

Chemama, R. (under the direction of), *Dictionnaire de psychanalyse*, Paris, Larousse, 1993.

Cléro, J.-P., *Le vocabulaire de Lacan*, Paris, Ellipses, 2002. 2^d ed. in : *Le Vocabulaire des philosophes*, T. IV, Philosophie contemporaine (XXème siècle) (p.555–619). 3rd ed. in August 2006.

Cléro, J.-P., *Dictionnaire Lacan*, Paris, Ellipses, november 2008.

Evans, D., *An Introductory Dictionary of Lacanian Psychoanalysis* (New York: Routledge, 1996).

Kaufmann, P. (under the direction of), *L'apport freudien: Éléments pour une encyclopédie de la psychanalyse*, Paris, Larousse, 1998.

Kreutzen, H., *Jacques Lacan, Séminaire 1952 à 1980, Index référentiel*, 3ème édition augmentée, Paris, Economica, Anthropos, 2009.

Some Texts, Cited or Referred to, Concerning Lacan's Relationship
with the English Language (Among Other Languages)

Andrès, M., *Lacan et la question du métalangage*, Paris, Point hors ligne, 1987.

Apollon, W. and R. Feldstein, *Lacan, Politics, Aesthetics* (Albany, NY: SUNY Press, 1996).

Boothby, R., *Death and Desire: Psychoanalytic Theory in Lacan's Return to Freud* (New York: Routledge, 1991).

Borch-Jacobsen, M., *Lacan: The Absolute Master* (Stanford, CA: Stanford UP, 1991).

Bowie, M., *Freud, Proust, and Lacan: Theory as Fiction* (Cambridge: Cambridge UP, 1990).

Cléro, J.-P., *Lacan et la langue anglaise*, Paris, Essaim, 2012. Une partie du propos coïncide avec ce qui a été dit au Colloque sur « Penser avec Lacan ; nouvelles lectures », dir. Guy-Félix Duportail, Paris, 30 et 31 mars 2012.

Cléro, J.-P., "Ethics and the Increasingly English Speaking Psychiatric Tower of Babel," published in *Annals of the University of Bucharest, Analele Uniniversatiii Bucaresti*, Philosophy series, Vol. LXVII, n° 2, 2018, 1–20.

Copjec, J., *Read My Desire: Lacan Against the Historicists* (Cambridge, MA: MIT Press, 1994).

Dean, C. J., *The Self and Its Pleasures: Bataille, Lacan, and the History of the Decentered Subject* (Ithaca, NY: Cornell UP, 1992).

Forrester, J., *The Seductions of Psychoanalysis: Freud, Lacan, and Derrida* (Cambridge: Cambridge UP, 1992).

Gallop, J., *Reading Lacan* (Ithaca, NY: Cornell UP, 1985).

Grigg, R., *Lacan, Language, and Philosophy* (Albany, NY: SUNY Press, 2008).

Grimberg, H., *Remarques sur le concept de l'énonciation dans l'oeuvre de Jakobson et dans le discours de Lacan*, Saint-Mandé, 1995.

Groupe franco-japonais du Champ freudien, *Lacan et la chose japonaise*, Paris, Navarin, 1988.

Jakobson, R., *Language in Literature* (Cambridge, MA: Harvard UP, 1987).

Lacan, J., *Conférences aux USA, Scilicet* 6/7, Paris, Le Seuil, 1976.

Millot, C., P. Pachet, et E. Marty, *Lacan & la littérature*, Houilles, Le marteau sans maître, 2006.

Rabaté, J.-M., *Lacan in America* (New York: Other Press, 2000).

Stewart, E., M. Jaanus, and R. Feldstein, *Lacan in the German-Speaking World* (Albany, NY: SUNY Press, 2004).

Strachey, A., *A New German-English Psychoanalytic Vocabulary*, 1943.

Strachey, J., "The Nature of the Therapeutic Action of Psychoanalysis," *The International Journal of Psychoanalysis* XV (1934). Reproduced and printed photo-litho offset for London: Wm. Dawson & Sons, 1953: 126–159.

Strachey, L., *Eminent Victorians* (London: Chatto and Windus, 1918).

Žižek, S., *Lacan in Hollywood* (Vienna: Turia und Kant, 2000).

Some Texts, Cited or Referred to,
Concerning Lacan's Relationship with Philosophy

Baas, B., *De la chose à l'objet: Jacques Lacan et la traversée de la phénoménologie*, Paris, Louvain, Vrin, Peeters, 1998.

Balmès, F., *Ce que Lacan dit de l'être: 1953–1960*, Paris, PUF, 1999.

Bibliothèque du Collège international de philosophie, *Lacan avec les philosophes*, (Acts of the colloquium held in August 1990 at Collège international de philosophie), Paris, Albin Michel, 1991.

Book of Common Prayer (The), The New Testament, authorized King James Version, The Gedeons International.

Cathelineau, P.C., *Lacan, lecteur d'Aristote*, Paris, Ed. de l'Association freudienne internationale, 1998.

Cités n°16, *Jacques Lacan, Psychanalyse et politique*, Paris, PUF, 2003.

Cléro, J.-P., *Lacan et les philosophes*, Acts of the Rouen colloquium, tenu sous le titre *Lacan et la philosophie*, en nov. 2001, Presses de l'Université de Rouen, à paraître en 2005.

Cléro, J.-P., *Lacan, lecteur de Bentham. La vérité a structure de fiction*, Paris, Unebévue, revue de psychanalyse, École lacanienne de psychanalyse, 1999.

Cléro, J.-P., *'Dessaisissement', 'brillance' et 'catégories d'expression' dans la philosophie de P. Kaufmann*, in the special edition of the journal *Noesis*, Centre de recherche et d'histoire des idées, Université Sophia-Antipolis, Nice, 1999.

Cléro, J.-P., *'Il faut réécrire l'Esthétique transcendantale'; deux interprétations de Kant par Lacan et Hintikka*. In: *Kant, les Lumières et nous* (p. 367-389), texts collected by A. Labib et J. Ferrari, Maison arabe du livre, (UR Lumières et modernité, ISSH de Tunis, Société des études kantiennes de langue française), 2009.

Cléro, J.-P., « Le jeu de l'interprétation et de la compréhension chez Freud et Lacan », in *Essaim*, n° 44, 2020.

Derrida, J., *La carte postale*, Paris, Flammarion, 1980.

Granon-Fafont, J., *La topologie ordinaire de Jacques Lacan*, Paris, Point Hors Ligne, 1986.

Guyomard, P., M. Aisenstein, et D. Widlöcher, *Lacan et le contre-transfert*, Paris, PUF, 2011.

Haddad, G., *Lacan et le judaïsme*, Biblio-Essais, Le livre de poche, Desclées de Brouwer, 1996.

Juranville A., *Lacan et la philosophie*, Paris, PUF, 1988.

Kaufmann, P., *L'expérience émotionnelle de l'espace*, Vrin, Paris, 1968.

Kaufmann, P., Kurt Lewin, *une théorie du champ dans les sciences de l'homme*, Paris, Vrin, 1968.

Kremer-Marietti, A., *Lacan et la rhétorique de l'inconscient*, Paris, Aubier-Montaigne, 1978.

Lacoue-Labarthe, P., *Le titre de la lettre: une lecture de Lacan*, Paris, éd. Galilée, 1973, 1990.

Lang, H., *Language and the Unconscious: Lacan's Hermeneutics of Psychoanalysis* (Atlantic Highlands, NJ: Humanities Press, 1997).

Le moment cartésien de la psychanalyse: Lacan, Descartes, le sujet, under the direction of E. Porge and A. Soulez, Arcanes, Les Cahiers des Arcanes, 1996.

Leupin, A. (editor of the colloquium *Lacan and the Human Sciences* held in 1986 at Louisiana State University), *Lacan & the Human Sciences* (Lincoln, NE: University of Nebraska Press, 1991).

Milner, J.-C., *L'oeuvre claire: Lacan, la science, la philosophie*, Paris, éd. du Seuil, 1995.

Moulinier, D., *De la psychanalyse à la non-philosophie. Lacan et Laruelle*, Paris, éd. Kimé, 1999.

Ogilvie, B., *Lacan. Le sujet*, Paris, PUF, 1987.

Porge, E, *Les noms du père chez Jacques Lacan: ponctuations et problématiques*, Paris, érès, 1997.

Porge, E., *Transmettre la clinique psychanalytique: Freud, Lacan, aujourd'hui*, Paris, érès, 2005.

Porge, E., *Des fondements de la clinique psychanalytique*, Paris, érès, 2005.

Rajchman, J., *Erotique de la vérité: Foucault, Lacan et la question de l'éthique*, Paris, PUF, 1994.

Ragland-Sullivan, E., *Jacques Lacan and the Philosophy of Psychoanalysis* (Champaign, IL: University of Illinois Press, 1985).

Ragland-Sullivan, E., and M. Bracher (editors of the colloquium held in May 1988 at Kent State University), *Lacan and the Subject of Language* (New York: Routledge, 1991).

Recanati, F., *Intervention au Séminaire du Dr. Lacan*, *Scilicet* n° 4.

Regnault, F., *Conférences d'esthétique lacanienne*, Agalma, Paris, dif. Seuil, 1997.

Roustang, F., *Lacan. De l'équivoque à l'impasse*, Paris, Les éditions de Minuit, 1986.

Sipos, J., *Lacan et Descartes. La tentation métaphysique*, Paris, PUF, 1994.

Samuels, R., *Between Philosophy and Psychoanalysis* (New York: Routledge, 1993).

Stavrakakis, Y., *Lacan and the Political* (New York: Routledge, 1999).

Turkle, S., *Psychoanalytic Politics*, second edition (London: Free Association Books, 1992).

Žižek, S., *Looking Awry: An Introduction to Jacques Lacan Through Popular Culture* (Cambridge, MA: MIT Press, 1991).

Zupancic, A., *Ethics of the Real: Kant, Lacan* (New York: Verso, 2000).

Some Texts Concerning Lacan's Relationship with Mathematics

Cléro, J.-P., *Les raisons de la fiction. Les philosophes et les mathématiques*, Paris, A. Colin, 2004.

Cléro, J.-P., *Lacan et les mathématiques*, Revue de Synthèse, T. 129, n° 2, Springer, avril 2008.

Cléro, J.-P., *Lacan and Probability, Electronic Journ@l for History of Probability and Statistics* 4.2 (Décembre 2008). www.jehps.net

Cochet, A., *Lacan géomètre*, Paris, Anthropos, Dif. Economica, 1998.

Porge, E., *De l'écriture nodale*, *Littoral* n° 5, Paris, Epel, 1982.

Porge, E., *Lettres du symptôme, versions de l'identification*, érès, Toulouse, 2010.

Porge, E., *Pourquoi les mathématiques comptent pour la psychanalyse*, *Essaim* n° 28, Paris, Ed. érès, 2012.

Viltard, M., *Le nœud borroméen généralisé: une présentation de la coupure*, *Littoral* n° 1, Paris, Epel, 1981.

Other Books and Articles Quoted or Referenced

Adam, R., *Surface and Symbol: The Consistency of James Joyce's* Ulysses (New York: Oxford UP, 1987).

Alexander, F., "Logic of Emotions," *International Journal of Psycho-Analysis* 16 (1935).

Aristotle, *Organon*, in *Complete Works of Aristotle* (Princeton, NJ: Princeton, Princeton UP, 1984).

Balint, M., *Primary Love and Psychoanalytic Technique* (London: Hogarth Press, 1952).

Bayes, T., *An Essay Towards Solving a Problem of the Doctrine of Chances*, *Philosophical Transactions of the Royal Society of London for 1764* 53: 370–418. [E.S. Pearson and M. Kendall, *Studies in the History of Statistics and Probability* Volume I (London: Griffin, 1970), 134–153].

Bennani, J., *Un psy dans la cité. Entretiens avec Ahmed El Amroui*, éd. de la Croisée des chemins, Casablanca, 2013.

Bentham, J., *Church-of-Englandism and its Catechism Examined*, London, 1817.

Bentham, J., *The Theory of Fictions*. See below: Ogden C.K.

Bentham, J., *Deontology Together With a Table of the Springs of Action and Article on Utilitarianism*, ed. Amnon Goldworth (Oxford: Clarendon Press, 1983).

Bentham, J., *De l'Ontologie et autres essais sur les fictions*, Paris, Le Seuil, 1997.

Bentham, J., *The Rationale of Judicial Evidence Specially Applied to English Pratice*, 5 vols. (London: Hart & Clarke, 1827).

Bentham, J., *Chrestomathia* (Andesite Press, 2017).

Bentham, J., *Chrestomathia*, ed. M.J. Smith & W.H. Burston (Oxford: Clarendon Press, 1993).

Bentham, J., *Universal Grammar* Vol. 8 (Edinburgh: Bowring, 1943).

Bergson, H., *Essai sur les données immédiates de la conscience*, in *Oeuvres*, Paris, PUF, 1970.

Berkeley, G., *Alciphron: Or the Minute Philosopher*, in *The Works of George Berkeley* vol. 2 (London: George Bell and Sons, 1898).

Berkeley, G., *The Analyst*, in *The Works of George Berkeley* Vol. IV, ed. A.A. Luce and T.E. Jessop (London and Edinburgh, 1951).

Berkeley, G., *The Defence of Free-Thinking in Mathematics*, in *The Works of George Berkeley*, ed. by A.A. Luce and T.E. Jessop (London and Edinburgh, 1948–1957).

Berkeley, G., *Dialogues between Hylas and Philonous*, in *The Works of George Berkeley* Vol. II, ed. by A.A. Luce and T.E. Jessop (London and Edinburgh, 1949).

Berkeley, G., *An Essay Toward a New Theory of Vision*, *The Works of George Berkeley* Vol. I, ed. by A.A. Luce and T.E. Jessop (London and Edinburgh, 1948–1957): 1–139.

Bernoulli, J., *Ars conjectandi*, opus posthumum, Thurnisiorum Fratrum, 1743, Pars Quarta, tradens usum & applicazione praecedentis Doctrinae in Civilibus, Moralibus Oeconomicus, in: die Werke von Jakob Bernoulli, Birkhäuser, Basel, 1975, vol. III, 239–259.

Boyle, R., *A Free Enquiry into the Vulgarly Received Notion of Nature* (1686) (Cambridge: Cambridge UP, 1996).

Brykman, G., *Berkeley, philosophie et apologétique*, 2 vols, Paris, Vrin, 1984.

Brykman, G., *Berkeley et le voile des mots*, Paris, Vrin, 1993.

Canguilhem, G., *The Normal and the Pathological*, Dordrecht, Springer Netherlands, 1978. [*Le Normal et le Pathologique*, Paris, PUF, 1993].

Cassirer, E., *Philosophy of Symbolic Forms* (New York: Routledge, 2019).

Châtelet, E., Mme du, *Newton I.*, *Philosophiae Naturalis Principia Mathematica*, *The Mathematical Principles of Natural Philosophy*, Paris, Blanchard, 1966.

Cléro, J.-P., *Réflexions sur la critique de Kant des paralogismes du point de vue d'une théorie des fictions*, Montréal, 2017.

Cléro, J.-P., « Les philosophes et la différence des sexes », *Letterina*, Bulletin de l'Association de la Cause freudienne en Normandie, n° 59, April 2012.

Coleridge, S.T., *Shakespeare and the Elizabethan Dramatists* (Edinburgh: J. Grant, 1905).

Coleridge, S.T., *Characters of Shakespeare's Plays* (Cambridge: Cambridge UP, 1908).

Deleuze, G., *Logique du sens*, Les Éditions de Minuit, Paris, 1969.

Deleuze, G., *Empirisme et subjectivité*, Paris, PUF, 1953.

Derrida, J., *La carte postale*, Flammarion, Paris, 1985.

Descartes, R., *Oeuvres*, Bruges, La Pléiade, 1953.

Desanti, J.T., *La philosophie silencieuse*, Paris, Le Seuil, 1975.

Desanti, J.T., *Le philosophe et les pouvoirs*, Paris, Calmann-Lévy, 1976.

Diderot, D., *Letter on the Blind for the Use of Those Who See* (Chicago: Open Court, 1916).

Diderot, D., *The Nun [La Religieuse]* (Oxford: Oxford UP, 2005).

Diener, Y., "Schéma des scissions, graphe de la passe et carte de la dispersion," *Essaim* n°28, 2012.

Fairbairn, W.R., *Psychoanalytic Studies of the Personality*, in *International Journal of Psycho-Analysis* XXV (1953).

Ferguson, A., *An Essay on the History of Civil Society*, ed. F.Oz-Salzberger (Cambridge: Cambridge UP, 2007).

Field, H.H., *Science Without Numbers* (Princeton, NJ: Princeton UP, 1980).

Fontenelle, B., *Éléments de la géométrie de l'infini*, Paris, Fayard, 2000.

Frege, G., *Foundations of Arithmetic* (London: J. Wiiley & Sons, 1980).

Glover, E., "Therapeutic Effects of the Inexact Interpretation," in *The International Journal of Psycho-Analysis* XII (October 1931).

Goethe, J.W., *Elective Affinities*, trans. by H.M. Waidson (London: Oneworld Classics, 2008).

Greenacre, P., "General Problems of Acting Out," in *The Psychoanalytic Quarterly* 19.4 (1950).

Hazlitt, W.C., *Shakespeare* (London: B. Quaritch, 1902).

Hazlitt, W.C., *Characters of Shakespeare's Plays* (London: Templeman, 1838).

Hegel, F.W., *The Phenomenology of Spirit* (Cambridge: Cambridge UP, 2018).

Hintikka, J., *Models for Modalities* (Springer, 1969).

Hintikka, J., *Time and Necessity* (Oxford: Clarendon Press, 1975).

Hobbes, T., *The Elements of Law, Natural and Politic*, ed. by F. Tönnies (London: Frank Cass & Co. and Cambridge UP, 1984).

Hume, D., *A Treatise of Human Nature*, ed. Selby-Bigge (Oxford: Clarendon Press, 1978).

Husserl, E., *Phenomenology of Internal Time-Consciousness* (Bloomington, IN: Indiana UP, 2019).

Husserl, E., *Origin of Geometry, with An Introduction by J. Derrida* (Lincoln, NE: University of Nebraska Press, 1989).

Jones, E., *The Phallic Phase* (Institute of Psychoanalysis, 1933).

Kant, I., *Critique of Pure Reason* (London: Everyman, 1998).

Kant, I., *Critique of Pure Reason* (Cambridge: Cambridge UP, 2000).

Kant, I., *Critique of Judgment*, trans. P. Guyer (Cambridge: Cambridge UP, 2006).

Kant, I., *Anthropology*, ed. by R.B. Louden (Cambridge: Cambridge UP, 2006).

Kaufmann, P., *Kurt Lewin, une théorie du champ dans les sciences de l'homme*, Paris, Vrin, 1968.

Lantham, R.A., *Tristram Shandy: The Games of Pleasure* (Berkeley, CA: University of California Press, 1973).

Leibniz, G.W., *Meditations on Knowledge, Truth and Ideas*, in *Philosophical Essays*, trans. R. Ariew and D. Garber (Indianapolis, IN: Hackett, 1989).

Leibniz, G.W., *Correspondance Leibniz-Clarke*, presented according to the original manuscripts of the Hanover and London libraries, by Robinet, Paris, PUF, 1957.

Lessay, F., *Le débat Locke-Filmer*, Paris, PUF, 1978.

Lévi-Strauss, C., *The Structural Study of Myths*, in *The Journal of American Folklore* 68.270 (October–December 1955): 428–444.

Lévi-Strauss, C., *Anthropologie structurale*, I, Paris, Plon, 1958.

Lévi-Strauss, C., Anthropologie *structurale*, II, Paris, Plon, 1973.

Lévi-Strauss, C., *Mythologiques, le cru et le cuit,* Plon, Paris, 1964.

Lévi-Strauss, C., *Myth and Meaning: Cracking the Code of Culture* (New York: Schocken Books, 1995).

Lévi-Strauss, C., *Entretiens avec Claude Lévi-Strauss,* G. Charbonnier, Paris, Les Belles Lettres, 2010.

Lévi-Strauss, C., *Regarder, Écouter, Lire*, Paris, Plon, 1973.

Locke, J., *An Essay Concerning Human Understanding* (ebooks@Adelaide, University of Adelaide Library).

Locke, J., *An Essay Concerning Human Understanding*, ed. by P.H. Nidditch (Oxford: Clarendon Press, 1987).

Locke, J., *An Essay for the Understanding of St. Paul's Epistles, by consulting St. Paul himself*, in *The Works of John Locke* Vol. VIII (reprinted by Scientia Verlan Aalen, 1963).

Mac Clay, E., D. Caine, D. Echard, et X. Fourtou, *L'anglais de Lacan. Lacan's English*, Encore, Paris, 2019.

Mandeville, B., *The Fable of the Bees*, in *Collected Works of Bernard Mandeville* Vol. 3, (Hildesheim, NY: G. Olms, 2017).

Matalon, B., "Épistémologie des probabilités" in *Logique et connaissance scientifique*, Encyclopédie de la Pléiade, NRF, 1967.

Mill, John Stuart, *System of Logic, Ratiocinative and Inductive*, in *Collected Works of John Stuart Mill* Vol. VII–VIII (London: Routledge and Kegan Paul, 1973).

Moore, G., *Ethics* (New York: H. Holt and Company, 1912).

More, T., *Utopia* (New Haven: Yale UP, 1964).

Needham, R., *Rethinking Kinship and Marriage* (Tavistock, 1971).

Needham, J.T.M., *Science and Civilization in China* (Cambridge: Cambridge UP, 1954–2008).

Nietzsche, F., *Human, All Too Human*, Part II, *Miscellaneous Maxims and Opinions*, trans. P.V. Cohn (London: George Allen, 1911 and 1934).

Ogden, C.K., *Bentham's Theory of Fictions* (London: Routledge and Kegan Paul, 1932).

Pascal, B., *Les Provinciales et Pensées*, Paris, La Pochothèque, 2004.

Peirce, C.S., *The Essential Peirce: Selected Philosophical Writings* Vol. I, ed. by Houser and C. Kloesel (Bloomington, IN: Indiana UP, 1992).

Peirce, C.S., *Semiotics and Significs: The Correspondence Between Charles S. Peirce and Victoria Lady Wilby*, (Elsah, IL: The Press of Arishe Associates, 2001).

Peirce, C.S., *Reasoning and the Logic of Things*, ed. K.L. Ketner (Cambridge, MA: Harvard UP, 1992).

Peirce, C.S., *Collected Papers of Charles Sanders Peirce* Vol. 1, *Principles of Philosophy*, ed. C. Hartshorne & P. Weiss (Cambridge, MA: Harvard UP, 1931).

Peirce, C.S., *Collected Papers of Charles Sanders Peirce* Vol. 6, *Scientific Metaphysics*, ed. C. Hartshorne & P. Weiss (Cambridge, MA: Harvard UP, 1935).

Peirce, C.S., *Collected Papers of Charles Sanders Peirce* Vol. 8, ed. C. Hartshorne & P. Weiss, (Cambridge, MA: Harvard UP).

Pellion F.: « Quelques remarques sur 'lalangue' et sur le cas particulier de la surdité préliguale », *Essaim*, n° 29, 02/2012.

Plato, *Republic*, trans. C.D.C. Reeve (Indianapolis, IN: Hackett, 2004).

Plon, M., « Be not too tame », in: *Lacan et le contre-transfert*, Paris, PUF, 2011.

Plon, M., « *Institutional Worries* », Symposium « *Psychanalyser avec l'adolescence* » of the Société de Psychanalyse freudienne, November 25, 2012.

Roget, *Thesaurus of English Words and Phrases* (London: Longham, Brown, Green, and Longmans, 1853).

Rousseau, J.-J., *Discourse on the Origins of Inequality Among Men* (Hanover, NH: University Press of New England, 1992).

Rousseau, J.-J., *Emile or Education*, trans. B. Foxley (London: J.M. Dent & Sons, 1925).

Rousseau, J.-J., "Essai sur l'origine des langues", in *Oeuvres completes*, vol. V, Paris, NRF, Gallimard, 1995.

Russell, B., "Recent Work on the Principles of Mathematics," in *The Collective Papers of Bertrand Russell* Vol. III, *Toward the Principles of Mathematics* (London: Routledge, 1993).

Russell, B., *The Analysis of Matter* (London: G. Allen and Unwin, 1954).

Russell, B., *An Inquiry into Meaning and Truth* (London: Routledge, 1992).

Sartre, J.-P., *Being and Nothingness: An Essay in Phenomenological Ontology*, trans. S. Richmond (London: Routledge, 2018).

Saussure, F. de, *Cours de linguistique générale*, Bibliothèque scientifique Payot, 1989.

Smith, A., *Theory of Moral Sentiments*, ed. by Knud Haakonsen (Cambridge: Cambridge UP, 2002).

Smith, R.J., Abstract of "Darwin, Freud, and the Continuing Misrepresentation of the Primal Horde." https://www.journals.uchicago.edu/doi/abs/10.1086/688885?-mobileUi=0&journalCode=ca).

Spitz, R., *Yes and No: On the Genesis of Human Communication* (New York: International Universities Press, 1979).

Swift, J., *Gulliver's Travels* (Paris: A.-A. Renouard, 1823).

Szasz, T., *On the Theory of Psychoanalytic Treatment*, in *International Journal of Pycho-Analysis* (1957): 166–182.

Toole, J.K., *A Confederacy of Dunces* (Baton Rouge, LA: Louisiana State University Press, 1980).

Van Fraassen, B.C., *The Scientific Image* (Oxford: Oxford UP, 1980).

Vuillemin, J., *Leçon inaugurale au Collège de France*, December 5, 1962.

Wilkins, J., *An Essay Toward a Real Character and a Philosophical Language* (London, 1668).

Woods, J., *The Logic of Fictions: A Philosophical Sounding of Deviant Logic* (Paris: Mouton, 1974).

INDEX

absence: 44, 88, 119, 121, 134, 137, 163, 172, 266, 267, 279; presence: 280

abstraction: 57, 58, 106, 110, 127, 203, 251

acting out: 28, 30, 76, 182, 221, 324

actor: 79, 89, 134, 135, 137, 143, 150, 265, 268

Adams R.: 127

aesthetic(s): 84, 117, 237, 316; transcendental aesthetics: 81, 84, 205, 241, 281, 282

affectivity: 41, 96, 99, 100, 230; affect: 18, 23, 26, 29, 42, 44, 53, 68, 84, 96, 125, 141, 142, 166, 187, 189, 220, 227, 230, 231, 266, 269, 304; emotion, emotive: 41; affective: 32, 41, 44, 46, 72, 77, 90, 104, 113, 136, 143, 223, 266; affection: 176

aggressivity: 185, 215, 251, 252, 254, 255; aggressive: 184, 223, 224, 228; aggression: 251, 254, 255

Alexander F.: 44, 321

algebra: 55, 112, 183; algebraist: 54; algebraical: 55; algebraic: 55

American: 24, 25, 26, 66, 71, 95, 163, 286, 292, 306, 325; American people: 13; America: 162, 163, 317; American way of life: 162

analysis, analytical: 12, 16, 19, 24, 25, 26, 27, 30, 33, 39, 48, 64, 72, 75, 84, 89, 95, 96, 105, 112, 118, 122, 129, 131, 133, 134, 136, 141, 142, 143, 156, 173, 174–180, 190, 193, 196, 205, 207, 211, 213–225, 232, 233, 236, 241, 242, 245, 248, 254, 263, 264, 275, 277–283, 285, 291, 292, 294, 296, 301, 303, 305, 307, 308; psychoanalysis, psychoanalytic(al): 11, 13–16, 25–28, 31, 32, 42, 44–48, 53, 55, 59, 67, 71, 72, 79, 89, 90, 96, 105, 109, 111–113, 118–122, 129, 130, 142, 143, 154, 156, 159, 160, 162, 165, 168, 169–238, 241, 242, 245–247, 251–253, 260, 263, 265, 272–278, 281, 283, 285, 289, 290, 293, 294, 296, 298, 299, 301, 303, 306–310; analysand: 24, 26, 27, 88, 89, 104, 138, 143, 176, 178, 179, 199, 214, 217, 218, 226, 232, 233, 245, 246, 277–279, 281, 285, 291–294, 298, 301, 304; analyst, analytician: 24, 30, 58, 59, 88, 130, 138, 161, 168, 174, 175, 177, 178, 179, 206, 211, 216–218, 232, 233, 236, 245, 247, 248, 260, 275, 277, 278, 285, 286, 291, 304; psychoanalyst: 12, 24, 27, 32, 33, 37, 42, 59, 96, 100, 102, 104, 105, 125, 154, 158, 168–238, 247, 252, 255, 263, 277, 279, 284–286, 289–294, 297, 305, 307, 308; unanalyzable: 24, 25, 219; analysis situs: 58; to analyze: 23, 24, 39, 59, 81, 104, 126, 127, 129, 130, 133, 173, 174, 181, 233, 266, 279, 292, 299, 309; to psychoanalyze: 25, 57, 113, 129, 279, 286

Titles Published by The Sea Horse Imprint:

Betty Bernardo Fuks — *Freud and the Invention of Jewishness* (2008)

Gérard Haddad — *Eating the Book: Dietary Rites and Paternal Function* (2013)

Erik Porge — *Truth and Knowledge in the Clinic: Working with Freud and Lacan* (2016)

Paola Mieli — *Figures of Space: Subject, Body, Place* (2017)

Alain Didier-Weill — *The Three Times of the Law* (2017)

Marie-Magdeleine Lessana — *Marilyn: Portrait of a Shooting Star* (2019)

Jean-Pierre Cléro — *Lacan and the English Language* (2020)

www.ingramcontent.com/pod-product-compliance
Lightning Source LLC
Chambersburg PA
CBHW032049020426
42335CB00011B/246